WHY AM I HERE?

BLESSINGS)

WHY AM I HERE?
A NEAR-DEATH EXPERIENCE
with The ANCIENT of DAYS

SARAZEN BROOKS

THE
VENUSIAN
PRESS

TheVenusianPress.com

Why Am I Here?: A Near-Death Experience with The Ancient of Days

©2018 Sarazen Brooks. All rights reserved.

ISBN 978-1-9995202-0-5

Printed in the United States of America, November 2018

Cover design and illustration by Robert Grey.

Back cover portrait ©2018 Patrick Parenteau / DVPix

The persons, places and events described in this book are based on the author's personal experience. Some names have been changed to protect the identities of certain people involved.

"Mind creates the abyss, the heart crosses it."

~ *Sri Nisargadatta Maharaj*

Acknowledgements

THANK YOU

To my guides for revealing to me the magic and mystery that is existence.
To my higher self for creating the most marvellously complicated plan.
To all my teachers who have crossed my path.
I am eternally grateful for it all.

Preface

THIS BOOK IS a recapitulation of an experience I had in 2009 which shook my whole concept of reality to the core. It involved the first of two near-death experiences to come within the next eight years, summarized here as clearly and accurately as possible.

I recorded the majority of this book only days afterwards, which translated to roughly one hundred pages of written material. I was still in a very surreal, ungrounded state. I called my uncle, who at the time was the most spiritual person I knew and the only one I felt would not judge me. I had a tremendous amount of information I needed to share. My uncle, whom you will read more of in this book, encouraged me to buy a voice recorder so that I could vocalize the whole experience, which he could then transcribe. He believed the preservation of this experience was very important and wanted to retain as much of the initial clarity as possible.

None of the dialogue that took place between me and my spirit guides has been altered or exaggerated for dramatic effect.

I had very little previous conscious spiritual knowledge or background, so everything I was shown took me by tremendous surprise, although if I had been asked I would have said I was very spiritual. There is a vast difference between believing you are fundamentally spiritual and being taken on a tour across the universe with your guide, which then confirms certain esoteric beliefs as fact.

At the time, I had recently dropped out of college, where I had been studying kinesiology. After three-and-a-half years, I found myself at a juncture where I was excelling academically but couldn't have been more unsatisfied spiritually and emotionally.

On a whim I took to painting, and after completing my first piece knew unequivocally that art was what I was supposed to be doing with my life. I began mentoring with the famous Canadian artist James Picard over the next year after having recently quit my restaurant job as a fine-dining server, due to a car accident. I remember thinking how mundane my life seemed, and that if I was ever to become an interesting artist my life would surely require some adversity.

I was also in a long-term relationship with someone I loved deeply, but we had broken up and come back together several times. Subconsciously, I knew that he didn't fully accept me. These events combined had created a gridlock of feelings, nearly paralyzing my ability to make decisions for fear of making a wrong one.

On the fateful night of the experience, I had driven to a print shop to pick up my first set of business cards for my new art enterprise, then on the way home stopped by my former workplace, The Washington Avenue Grill, to say hello to some former colleagues. The day itself was haunted by foreboding and a thick mental fog. I was feeling very sombre, reflective and depressed, believing I was stuck in a rut. While I did start on the right path with art, there was a persistent feeling lurking in the shadows that there was something more I was supposed to be doing.

Enough time has passed that I'm able to revisit my story and put the finishing touches on it that it deserves, even if it is ten years later. In the effort, many obstacles arose – the inner critic's attempts to discredit the experience and my interpretation of it, for example – yet it remains the most profound event of my life to date. Not a day goes by that is not filled with deep gratitude for it. Nothing quite that mysterious has so far happened again, but I can die happily fulfilled, knowing that there is so much more to the "other side" of life. I will say that the experiences have continued, albeit less dramatically, and life continues to be more magical than I ever thought possible.

This story reveals my personal search for truth, but I suggest strongly that the reader go within to discover it and make it their own.

~ Sarazen Brooks

Contents

1.

Transitioning between Realities

AFTER WHAT SEEMED a long wait, Mikey slipped into the driver's seat of my car. We drove into the night. That was when things began to get confusing. It has taken me the better part of ten years to order the events in the sequence in which they seemed to occur. The major issue in recounting this story is that in numerous cases there is more than one set of what I call "Active Memory Streams." I define this term as a sequence of memories that seemingly retains all the normal sensations of "real-life" events in the waking state, what most people assume is reality. In one stream of memory, but not my predominant one, I made it home safely with no problems.

In another, more vividly clear version of the experience, or in the "Active Now," Mikey jumped into my car and fumbled with the shifter. He was not familiar with operating a manual transmission, so I had to give him some coaching. We had driven no more than five minutes when he stalled the car in the middle of an intersection. The time had to be approaching at least midnight, so there were not many cars on the road. All was quiet. Neither of us were worried about any imminent danger, a completely incorrect assumption.

I looked up at him from my prone position. We both laughed. I instructed him to step on the clutch and put the shifter back into first gear, then start the ignition. Just as he began to follow my instructions, something in my peripheral vision made me look over my right shoulder through the passenger window. The sight took my breath away. My heart stopped. *We were out of time!*

I was facing a red semi-trailer truck bearing full speed down on us with no obvious intention of stopping or even ability to stop in the seconds we needed to avoid a collision. The intersection traffic light clicked over to amber for our lane. Soon it would turn red, giving the truck the right of way.

Everything happened in super slow motion. There was no sound, nor was there time for any thoughts or fears. Looking back now, that was a blessing. I'm not even sure if I managed a full exhalation. Everything I'd been holding onto a moment before in the outside world fell into blackness. My soul remained there for some indeterminate period.

In both versions of memory, the story continues, otherwise I wouldn't be here to tell it! In the main Active Memory, there was only dense darkness, numbing pain, recoil and shock. After some doubt, I began to realize I was still conscious. Perhaps what I had just witnessed was a phantom memory or... I had no real explanation. I paused and took a deep – was it an actual – breath?

Everything about this night had been unusual, from the unexplained simultaneously heightened and impaired sensory experiences to the formation of a "double memory." I chose to ground myself in the present. My attention shifted from the darkness of that terror back to Mikey driving my car safely. We soon arrived at my home – in one piece.

Now parked in a visitor's spot outside my mother's townhouse, we sat tight and waited for Jordan. I was now sitting in the driver's seat. That was extremely incongruous. I didn't remember getting out and switching places with Mikey. The strange symptoms of being impaired were returning. But I'm getting ahead of myself. Let me explain.

2.

Life Prior *to* Time Travel

IN THE WEEKS preceding the strangest night of my life, I had become aware of an increasing anxiety and slight depression for no apparent reason. The moods came on so gradually I barely noticed them at first. They showed up in small ways to begin with, such as not enjoying my coffee in the morning. It was like the flavour of life, both good and bad, had abandoned me. Life just seemed tasteless. There was neither pleasure nor rest in sleep. I had become prone to crying fits when driving alone.

After a couple of weeks, the symptoms disappeared, so I passed them off as minor mood swings. After all, until a little more than a year earlier I had been studying sports medicine at college, but it had become too prosaic and I lacked the will to continue. After more than three years there imagination had atrophied. It had been almost four years since I had done anything creative and, belonging to a family of artists, I considered that almost a lifetime. I had assumed happiness would return instantly upon dropping out, but it didn't. I could think of nothing else to blame than the college for depleting my energy. Later I blamed myself for following parental advice to go to school for "*something*" instead of following my intuition. I had not trusted myself to make my own decisions, and the $40,000 in student loan debt was now an additional burden as a result of that choice – or lack thereof.

I had also just recently been in a car accident, apparently a relatively minor one according to the insurance agency. The other vehicle had hit me from behind, travelling close to 80 kilometres per hour, and was totalled. My vehicle was a sturdy Jeep, so well-built there was almost no damage to it. My body, however, absorbed the majority of the impact, making it impossible to work, properly walk or even sleep. I had extreme soft-tissue damage, that much was clear, but was not responding well to any ongoing standard medical treatment. My condition slowly and steadily declined.

Because I was confined to spending the majority of each day lying in bed, I decided I should at least start reading again to learn something new. One day while in a relatively relaxed state, I passed my mother's bookshelves and felt a very strong attraction to a particular selection. One of a series of books caught my eye, *Tales of Power* by Carlos Castaneda, that rapidly became a great source of joy in the following days. It invoked a deep state of reflection in which I began to question everything I believed, including the decisions that had led to my stagnant and unhealed state.

I instantly recognized that nothing could be taken for granted. A spark of magic had returned, accompanied by the strangest physical sensations while reading, ranging from a euphoric tingling starting at the top of my crown – sometimes travelling down my arms, sometimes all the way into my legs – to heat, especially in my solar plexus when reading a particularly important passage. There were also moments of déjà vu when reading certain chapters. But to call it déjà vu isn't really accurate. It was visionary, more like reliving something similar to the events described. In the previous four years, perhaps more, all I had read were textbooks, and this kind of compelling reading experience was unprecedented. Until that day I had felt little connection to "soul" and had not been able to access anything like guidance on command, never mind interpret such bizarre physical phenomena. Nevertheless, my body seemed to know something important was being revealed. What was even stranger, it seemed to suggest that I too may be capable of performing the wildly unbelievable acts of sorcery reported by Castaneda.

The term "sorcery" as he used it had a connotation very different to a dark art that manipulates disembodied entities to do the sorcerer's bidding, black magic. What he described was almost sacred. It was about becoming wholly in tune with oneself and one's environment, to walk the path of "knowledge," a complete and beautiful understanding of existence, the meaning of life. Once achieved, feats that seemed to defy the laws of nature were possible, the sorcerer able to bend the environment to their will, having become one with the will of the totality, one could say. While the first three books in the series (*The Teachings of Don Juan: A Yaqui Way of Knowledge; A Separate Reality: Further Conversations with Don Juan;* and *Journey to Ixtlan: The Lessons of Don Juan*) were published as non-fiction after first forming the basis of his bachelor's and doctoral degrees in anthropology, science gave me no grounds for believing I could experience any of the fantastic worlds he described.

A shift began. I would often catch myself slipping into spells of daydreaming about the Divine. This, however, was not enough to quench the fire that had been ignited within that now burned intensely for something greater than my little self and her little life.

After realizing that *Tales of Power* was in fact Castaneda's fourth volume in an ongoing story, I took to reading books one to nine in sequence. Then I started from the beginning once more, and later gravitated to *Tales of Power* a fourth time. I attempted to apply as many of the exercises that I could, such as adopting more of a fearless warrior lifestyle, one in which the warrior has such a zest for life that she samples one of everything, yet lusts for nothing, and one that puts great emphasis on every decision because every choice could very well be her last. This is what gives her actions meaning. These teachings encouraged me to commit to being the best possible version of myself every day. I acquired the desire to change my character dramatically for the better to a much more intentional version.

One night, when I felt I had absorbed enough of the teachings, I began to command similar experiences to occur. I had learned that the power of the spoken word combined with a strong enough will had the power to forge the reality one desired. For a moment, I truly believed the experiences I had read about could and should happen to me. The moment passed. Then it was gone.

The night before my initiation into non-ordinary realms, I found myself rereading the chapter that claimed an ordinary person could accomplish extraordinary acts of power with the proper application of intent. In retrospect, it was an extremely significant moment. I became charged with a pure, focused purpose and total clarity. All I can remember is thinking that I had nothing to lose and went into a deep state of concentration, then commanded with force that I be taken out of my body.

I included imagination as an aid, thinking it might increase my new-found paranormal superpower. I fully believed that people had performed those stupendous acts many times in order to enter other realms. But I was still not absolutely sure yet whether I could be one of them. After fervent effort, I opened my eyes. I felt a little pang in my heart, since nothing had happened, embarrassed to think that I could make it happen on the first try. Arrogance had been replaced by doubt.

That night, however, as I lay in bed drifting into sleep, I saw seven translucent beings floating above my bed. They seemed to be discussing something. I instantly discredited what I thought I was seeing and tried never to think of it again.

3.

Prelude

IT WAS A LATE January afternoon. I opened my eyes to a bright patch of sky piercing the gap between the panels of my bedroom window curtains, forming a dagger of penetrating light. Sleepily, I remembered I had quite a bit of running around to do, errands which required driving long distances and a lunch date with one of my girlfriends. My boyfriend Alexander would be working that evening in his studio, recording music he'd written. I wouldn't see him until after midnight.

As the day wore on, I felt a bit pressured. That heavy, morose feeling had returned. As I completed my errands the stress only increased.

"Ashley, I have to cancel lunch today," I said over the phone. "I'm sorry, the printer charged me twice what I expected. I didn't bother asking in advance. I know, I know, I should have asked for an estimate. Why not meet me later at The Washington Avenue Grill? Let's meet for a drink. I've already blown my budget, and then I'll head home for dinner."

I wanted to feel as I did when younger, when it seemed so easy to brush things off, bounding from activity to activity, so free to enjoy myself, sometimes in a state of blissful unawareness. I had to remind myself that I was only twenty-two. Something had become very apparent: I was seeking fulfilment of something unknown because nothing known was doing it for me.

Ashley agreed: "Okay, call me again when you get there."

I arrived at the restaurant around eight in the evening, then called her. She said she would be another half-hour or so, which was fine. I was quite the night owl anyway, so to me it was more like mid-day. It was no problem waiting for Ashley, because I knew so many people at the Wag, as we often called it. I'd only recently quit working there as a server after the car accident and subsequent whiplash, although I had tried to return to work several times over the course of months as I underwent physiotherapy, as well as many other treatments. What should have been only days off work became weeks, then months. It became clear greater healing was required to get back to normal. What I did not know at the time was that I was going to remain close to unable to walk for two years, and close to dysfunctional mentally for the next four. I was able to walk up stairs, but that activity would be

6

preceded by a long break due to painful widespread muscle spasms. Leaving the house on errands or for treatments required planning in order to pace myself and minimize flare-ups.

At the bar I ordered a glass of a Cabernet Sauvignon I liked. The day had been particularly stressful. My body was not holding up well after the errands I'd run. If I was going to ask it to stay out a few hours longer than it wanted to, it seemed wise to give it something to help it relax. I was afraid of the repercussions if it didn't, which would essentially immobilize me for days or weeks afterwards if not properly checked. None of the recommended treatments had worked so far. A glass of wine seemed to accomplish what the gym, physiotherapists, chiropractors, acupuncturists and orthopedic surgeons could not. I had also made some significant dietary changes, cutting down on foods shown to cause inflammation, such as sugar, dairy and processed foods, as well as limiting alcohol, meat and caffeine, and incorporating supplements like turmeric. While I felt I was doing everything in my power to help the healing, it seemed to have only a very subtle noticeable effect.

Each day included a great deal of pain, something I was struggling with for the most part in silence. This added a lot of strain on all my relationships, as now they consumed so much energy to maintain, especially the one with Alexander. This tenuous state was becoming the new normal, however, but I was not ready to accept it. Nevertheless, the fairy tale land of Carlos Castaneda's writings provided an appealing escape from my body's pain. Eventually, an intriguing idea arose from my subconscious, that I might heal and transform the body by applying universal laws.

Meanwhile, although none of my former workmates had much free time to spend with me yet, my favourite local band started playing near the bar where I sat. The restaurant was packed. I was glad to have come on such a good night. The full moon illumined the grounds adjacent to the beach, a charming scene beyond the old windowpanes of the nineteenth-century wood frame building. I noticed the music getting very loud as I took the first sip of wine, nothing unusual considering the band was so close to the bar. A couple unknown to me, but who seemed to know my friends, sat down beside me.

"Hi. I'm Alana. Do you mind if we sit here? This is Jack," said the woman as she indicated the young man beside her. "I just got hired. I'm starting tomorrow. Jack's an artist – and an electrician – in his spare time." She smiled at her boyfriend.

"I'm Sarazen. I'm an artist too. I paint. I used to work here – in my spare time – but had to quit recently when I got some bad whiplash in a rear-ender."

"Oh, I'm so sorry to hear that," Alana said.

"It's okay, it was just too painful to be on my feet all night and I couldn't lift anything, so I wasn't really that helpful." I smiled. "I just stopped by to say hello and tell everyone about my new exhibition."

"Cool. Listen, Sarazen, do you want to step out for a toke?" Alana grinned.

I made a dismissive gesture with my hand.

"No? Okay then, we'll see you in five."

While they were out, a couple of other people I knew sat down. We talked casually, but I started to notice I was becoming unusually detached. It couldn't be the wine. I'd barely started in on it. Following what anyone was saying was becoming increasingly difficult. I kept asking them to repeat themselves. It was only made worse by the seemingly escalating volume of the band. I asked for a glass of water several times, each time draining it on the spot. Everything around me seemed to be moving in slow motion. I tried to ignore that, thinking it was due to no more than just the relaxing effect of the tannins. Besides, I was very tired. Leaving home at all put a great strain on my body. I kept checking my phone for calls from Ashley or Alexander. I didn't want to stay too long, nor did I want to drink too much, since I was only halfway through my day. I still needed to drive home, where dinner with my family awaited, along with so many tasks connected with the new businesses I had started. I still lived with my mom and aunt, but often with Alexander too. By now I had completely forgotten any of the seemingly silly commands I'd made the night before while deep in meditation. All that was still new to me. I brushed it off. Now I was in "active daily life" mode.

Meanwhile, time had taken flight. My phone rang. It was Ashley calling to say she was on her way and running late, but it seemed like hours had gone by already. I knew her personality well. She was one of my very best friends, and while I loved her dearly, punctuality was not among her best traits. If she really was running so late, she may not arrive until closer to midnight or at all if she got distracted. Who was I to blame her? In fact it was I who changed our lunch plans. I thought I should leave, otherwise I might get caught up in conversations with my friends and become too exhausted to drive home later. But my friend Jordan insisted that I come to the back patio where the staff often took their breaks.

As soon as I stood up, it was apparent I was in a radically unusual state. I could not be intoxicated. In fact I had never felt like this before. There was no obvious explanation. It was exactly like I'd awakened within a dream. There was extraordinary mental clarity, but moving my body felt slow and cumbersome, like being underwater. Anyone who has experienced lucid dreaming knows the heavy feeling in the limbs that can occur and the way the dream environment is heightened and sensations intensified. It's almost as though you're observing your environment but aren't really sure how to operate your equipment, having forgotten where the controls are, let alone how to manipulate them.

The cacophony of loud music and voices of patrons conversing between the gaps dividing their individual worlds was dominant. It began to cause a definite split in my attention.

The typical effects of too much alcohol were completely absent. There was no slurred speech, decreased coordination or lethargy. Nevertheless, the will to walk was hard to summon. This was more like ataxia. Incredibly, whatever was happening to me also didn't seem to be happening in that room but somewhere else. This didn't make much sense. Yet it was something I was acutely aware of. I remember wondering where else I could exist but in that familiar room and at that exact time. Even though I had just ruled out the possibility of my mysterious state having been elicited by alcohol, the thought was troubling because of no alternative explanation. I kept thinking the wine had to be the culprit.

Sitting at the staff patio table with Jordan, Mikey and the new guy who had just been hired, I said, "You know, Jordan, I'm feeling really out of it. I don't think I can drive. Maybe it was a mistake to come out tonight."

Jordan looked at me and replied, "Okay, let's do this: we'll play a game of cards, and if you win, one of us will drive you home in your car. We'll get someone else to follow behind to take them back here. Right, Mikey?"

Jordan was rubbing the rough stubble on his chin while looking down a little at Mikey, who was not much taller than me, and I'm only five-foot-three. If I lost, presumably they'd want me to stay out longer and socialize. In the short time I'd known them, they had become like family. I just looked at them all. Even the new guy seemed to have a similar disposition to Jordan and Mikey: a very nice, harmless young man in spite of his piercings, tattoos and shaved head.

"Thanks, that's very sweet of you," I said. "Are you sure? I really don't want to impose."

Jordan exhaled and made a gesture with his hand to indicate that it was no problem. The new guy loaned me his white uniform jacket, which had knotted cloth buttons typical of kitchen attire. Cards were shuffled.

My mind was clear, although it took every ounce of concentration to see the numbers on the playing cards. Earlier my hearing had become impaired. Now my eyesight seemed to be going too, but I knew the game well and won the first three hands. The game was called Big Two, popular where I grew up. As a player, your aim is to get rid of all your cards. As it turned out, the act of playing the game was more meaningful than I knew. In retrospect, the Divine was testing me. It is unable to interfere in your life without your consent and needs your conscious permission before certain experiences are allowed to unfold. One of the ways the Divine ensures consent to a mystical experience is by having you agree to participate in something mundane. Despite having an increasing number of faculties switching off, I won the game not once but three times. I believe that was significant. One instance is not enough, but three times is confirmation of agreement to what you are about to engage in, similar to a contract that requires multiple signatures and initials. Thus in a subtle way my soul was signing on to the experience that Power had chosen for me. In my subsequent research, I have also learned that the number three is associated with the ascended masters, of whom you will read more of in this book, so perhaps this was foreshadowing the adventure.

So far so good, it seemed, but I was reduced to significantly diminished motor skills. Control over my body soon started to fade. I wondered how I appeared to everyone else. No one seemed concerned or even to notice. Was it all in my head?

"You know, I hate to repeat myself, but I really need to get driven home." I was starting to wonder if I should have taken a cab much earlier. At the rate whatever was happening was increasing, I became alarmingly concerned that I might black out soon. Increasingly self-conscious, I did not want to cause even a minor scene, especially at a place where I used to work. I cared a lot about what people thought about me and always strove to present myself in the best possible light. I might even return to work there after I was healed. To pass out would definitely not be cool. I knew people would assume it was from too much alcohol and not from some health challenge.

Mikey said, "No worries, Sarazen, just be patient a little while longer. We have to wait for Jordan to get off work so he can drive me back here."

I fought a strengthening temptation to close my eyes – as if a giant vacuum cleaner was about to suck me right out of my body. There was no reason to feel so tired so soon either. It was only early evening. I'd had my quintessential quota of coffee already but wondered if perhaps more was required.

Instead I drank several more glasses of water and stood up to leave, thinking the hydration had helped. Instead, I tripped over one of the uneven planks of the old patio floor. Falling in slow motion, I barely felt the landing. Jordan and Mikey lifted me up immediately and walked me to the exit door of the patio, entering into the main area of the restaurant, each of my arms crooked in one of theirs. Everyone in the whole place seemed to be staring at us.

Before we got to the main entrance, Michael the bartender handed me a very inexpensive bill, still discounted even though I no longer worked there, bless his heart. Fumbling through my purse, I found my debit card, but could not remember the PIN to save my life. I sat down and tried every number combination that I typically used, but the error message was always the same: "Incorrect PIN." Michael, seeing my struggle, refused to charge my card. I did not feel right about not paying at all, so I offered to come back the next day. That too was refused and he seemed adamant that my debt was on the house.

Fortunately, Mikey, seeing my desire to pay, chimed in and offered to spot me the cash. My embarrassment had been increasing steadily. I wanted nothing more than to leave as quickly as possible. That did not seem likely, as I was forced to patiently wait for Mikey, who was saying many slow goodbyes, getting caught up in conversations that continued to delay our departure. The other guys did not want me to wait in my car, afraid I might try to drive home on my own. Since they didn't know me that well, I supposed that was a natural precaution.

My introverted nature felt the stress of overstaying my welcome, so to speak, and I agreed to give them my keys after they insisted on walking me down the steep front staircase so I could escape the increasing noise and commotion overloading my nervous system.

I sat down in the car, out of the elements. Finally, some peace and quiet. Over the next ten minutes, my body seemed to completely relax and melt into the passenger seat, slouching so far back into it that I seemingly had misplaced my backbone. Embarrassment now long forgotten, I entered into an empty state, free of any emotions, thoughts or feelings. I was no longer tired or feeling intoxicated, in fact far from it. I was so relaxed now that if anyone had got in the car with me, I doubt I would have noticed.

4.

Conversation *with a* Blue Being

ON THE WAY to my home Mikey and I had covered many topics in conversation. By the time we arrived I was getting a bit bored. It occurred to me, however, that I should be a more gracious host and entertain my guest. Maybe he was bored too. I didn't want to wait in the house. If my mother was up she would be likely want to make small talk. Besides, it was pleasant to be outdoors on such a mild winter evening after being confined all season.

"Mikey, when is Jordan going to get here to pick you up?"

He didn't appear to be especially concerned about it. "Another half-hour, I think – 10:15 or so."

Time had stopped flying and seemed to be crawling on its hands and knees. It was far earlier than I had thought, but it seemed so late. I assumed it was at least midnight already.

I really don't care for being bored, and boring others even less, so I made an effort to think of something to pass the time. Just then I had an idea.

"Hey, I'm super relaxed right now. Let's play *Drunk Psychic.*"

Mikey snickered. "What?! How do you do that?"

"How am I supposed to know? I'm drunk and never played it before. But there's no time like the present to find out." I laughed. I was in a playful, childish mood. "Anyway, what if I *am* psychic? Would that scare you?"

Mikey looked at me and laughed too, but nervously. "Um – I'm not sure. Is that what you want to do?"

"Well, not if you don't want to. You have ten seconds to think of something more fun." Giggling, I counted down quickly, but Mikey was either not thinking fast enough or just not that interested. He looked like he was wondering if Jordan would arrive soon.

"Okay, Sarazen, I'll bite. How do we start?" It was at that point that his manner changed, starting with something in his tone of voice. He appeared to become more intelligent in some way – though he seemed like a smart guy before – it was just that something was different now. He was like a different person. There seemed to be just *more* of him.

I lay back in the seat, which squeaked in response, and said, "I'm not sure how to start. Maybe I should try to focus." After lying there with my

13

eyes closed for what seemed about ten minutes, I admitted, "I don't think this is working."

"No?" he asked.

"No. Maybe I should just relax. Relax – mmm – that would be nice." I continued to lie back, now with my eyes open, staring calmly through the windshield into the bare trees that lined the visitors parking area. All of a sudden what seemed a lifetime of stored subtle tension melted away. I finally let go. "Wow," I exhaled. "I'm so ridiculously relaxed."

"Really? That's good." Mikey seemed to be finding the game only mildly entertaining. I believed he might be indulging me.

"Ask more specific questions, Mikey. That might help. Well, I'm just going to lie here because there is nothing else to do. Let's see where this goes." Just as I was about to fall asleep, my eyes started to burn. I thought maybe it was because I had been staring through the windshield too long. With my eyes closed, I saw red, yellow and orange. That wasn't so unusual, as I often saw colours when I tried to meditate. The red-yellow-orange blur moved to the left side of my field of inner vision and started to pulsate. I opened my eyes and thought Mikey must be flashing a light in my face. More precisely, it was like we were driving on a sunny day with the trees lining the road intermittently blocking the light, the sunbeams falling heavily on my eyelids. That was the closest thing I could compare it to.

Every time I opened my eyes, it was still night and still dark, almost pitch black. I was still feeling very out of it, similar to the feeling I had earlier when things were happening to me somewhere other than the restaurant. I thought, *Wow, I'm having a really hard time interpreting what's going on right now.* The colours in my closed-eye vision then became mostly orange.

Mikey asked, "Okay then, what do you see?"

"I see orange with a darker swirl forming in front of my left eye – that's strange – I just noticed that. Why is my vision so much better in my left eye? Maybe I have an eye disease. Maybe I have glaucoma. I might qualify for medical marijuana. That would be good." I giggled again.

"Your vision is fine," Mikey said. "I bet you could grab the dark spot if you wanted." Mikey now seemed to be guiding me through the experience. But how could he possibly know what I was seeing?

I said, "How do you know? You've never played this game before either. Anyway, I don't have hands inside my head."

Mikey was insistent. "Yeah, I know I've never played before, but I know you can grab that spot. Imagine you do have hands. Or why not try to grab it with your eye?"

I continued to stare at the black swirling dot. It began to grow. My right eye was now blind. It almost felt dead. My hearing was also changing. It was getting mildly fuzzy, and there was a buzzing like that of a little bee. Suddenly the black spot grabbed at me! I could feel it tugging at my chest. Reflexively, I drew back, all the while describing what was going on to my companion. I wasn't having much success in getting away from it. The black spot was strongly pulling at me and the buzzing was getting louder and more irritating. In fact it became unbearably loud.

"*Is there a bee in the car?!*" I was panicking.

Mikey said, "No. Open your eyes if you don't believe me."

Warily, I opened my eyes. Looking around, I now felt roaring drunk. The car seemed to be moving. Everything was extremely blurred. I could still hear buzzing, but there was no bee. Closing my eyes again, I was still being pulled by the swirling black hole, but unsure if I should trust it.

"Mikey, I've never done this before, so I'm not sure what's supposed to happen. I'm still feeling very relaxed though." How was this the same game I had started? It was definitely turning into something else. And why did *Mikey* know how to steer *me* so well?

"Why can't the spot be your friend? Don't be so paranoid," he insisted.

Unable to think of anything more witty, I answered, "Okay, maybe, but we haven't been properly introduced."

He laughed a little and said, "Okay. Sarazen, meet Black Hole. Black Hole, this is *Sarazen*."

"Great, Mikey. Now what?"

"Now you push in the direction it's pulling."

"What is it trying to do to me?"

"I think it's trying to get you out, Sarazen."

"Me? Do I want to be out?"

"I think so. You're the one who wanted to play this game."

I didn't know where "out" was, but for some reason everything he was saying made so much sense. It most definitely felt like there was some large, powerful black hole in front of my eye that I was somehow connected to, which was trying to pull me out of my body.

"True," I said. "Okay, I like your style. I'll play this game, but only if I can take someone with me. I don't want to go out there alone. It's scary enough in here."

Mikey looked at me. "Okay, who would you like to take?" He really seemed more like a *man* now, someone who had a tremendous amount of experience and knowledge. He had an air about him that radiated more of the father figure type.

I felt I could trust him. As I closed my eyes again, I became aware that I could now see through my eyelids, aware of both the black swirl in the orange field and the black car interior at the same time. That was definitely an ability I had never demonstrated before. I pretended to look around. "Well, I don't see anyone else here besides you, silly. And you seem nice."

"Okay, okay, I'll come."

"Wow, that was easy."

"It's your game. You're the drunk psychic."

"Good point." The game I had invented was the last thing that gripped my attention now. Hearing those words brought back the memory of my frivolous suggestion. The game we were playing seemed to be something else. I focused fully on the dark spot. It seemed to tug at regularly timed intervals. I then took Mikey's advice and pushed the next time it pulled, but nothing seemed to happen. I guessed my timing had been a bit off because when I tried it again, I immediately became the most awake I had been the whole night. Every cell in my body was on fire! I screamed for water, but Mikey insisted I was not burning, that there was no water in the car and that I should open my eyes. I insisted I really was on fire and that if he cared he would do something. He touched my arm and it stopped. Mystified, I was so certain I'd been on fire!

"Sarazen, look at me."

I didn't want to look at him, because I was getting scared, no longer sure who this person in the car with me was. I was beginning to question if I really knew Mikey that well at all. Maybe he'd slipped a drug in my wine back at the restaurant. What else could possibly explain what was happening? I kept my eyes shut tight.

"Don't think thoughts like that, Sarazen. They won't help me do what I'm trying to do. Think over what happened earlier tonight and you'll see beyond doubt no drugs were involved."

He was right. There had been no opportunity for anyone to slip something into the wine or all the water I had downed. But I was still confused.

16

How did he know what I was thinking? What other explanation could there possibly be? This friend had been in my line of sight almost the whole night. It would have been impossible for me to be with another person that was not Mikey – but looked exactly like him – an exchange would have to have taken place. If so, I would have had to have seen it. I'd thought we were going to play a fun game. Wasn't I the one in control of what I had suggested?

Just then a tremendous noise interrupted my train of thought, like a head-on car crash in the street, very loud.

"Mikey! What was that?" I still wouldn't open my eyes and felt very alarmed.

"What was what?" he countered.

"That loud noise – *a car accident* – at least somebody just lost their muffler or something. Get out of the car and take a look!"

"I didn't hear anything. We should move on."

His firm, abrupt tone made me let go of the alarming feeling about the loud crash. I felt that it had great significance, that someone could be very hurt and it was our responsibility to check. Nevertheless, he seemed to have great power of command with his words, so I felt compelled to follow his instructions.

Puzzled, I said, "Mikey, you never told me you could mind-read. I thought I was going to be the psychic."

He yelled: "*Open your eyes!*"

The face of the being I then saw was not the face of the diminutive twenty-something Mikey I knew, but of the most beautiful being I have ever seen. He was somewhere between thirty-five and forty years of age, his features perfectly proportioned yet somehow larger than life. *A perfect face*, I thought.

He seemed to be faking the appearance though, and not all that successfully. There was something about his skin that gave him away: it glowed. There were many subtle colours in it, but blue stood out most. The fantastic glow even shone through his clothes. He wasn't even sitting properly in the passenger seat, only pretending to sit, but really hovering slightly above it.

I only glanced at him briefly and thought, *Well, I must be really drunk. I better think about this. People don't normally float and glow.* It occurred to me I'd just discovered a good name for a toilet bowl cleaner and giggled involuntarily.

"Mikey – how – do you do that?" I asked slowly, staring fixedly out over the dashboard, afraid to look at the blue being again.

"Do what?"

"*Shut up!* That's a really good trick, Mikey the Magician. That should be your name. Who are you?"

"I'm your friend," he drawled.

"Well, I know that, but after seeing you just a second ago, it dawned on me: I don't really *know* you. I guess I've never really looked at you. You don't even sit properly. Did your mother tell you to sit like that? It looks funny, like it takes a lot of effort. You should be more relaxed, like me. I just learned how to relax. Did you know that?"

"My mother did not tell me to sit like this. I think it looks fine. It actually takes very little energy. You should try it."

"I can't float," I said, laughing nervously. "I never learned how." I then tried to hover, but didn't put much effort into it and gave up. "See? I told you."

His eyes narrowed. "You should look at me again."

Immediately terrified, I had only truly begun to admit that what I'd seen was uncanny. "No – I tried that – once."

He told me to stop being so childish, so I looked at him and – burst into laughter – he looked like he was in a Mikey suit. Apparently he had a sense of humour.

"If you spent more than a dollar on that suit, you got ripped off. Did you get it from the dollar store?" I teased, feeling a little less apprehensive.

"There are no dollar stores where I live."

Hearing this made me genuinely sorry for him for some reason. "Poor you. You can get some good stuff there."

"Tell me about dollar stores, Sarazen. I'm interested."

We talked a little about the items the shops typically sold, until I caught a glimpse of his eyes. I became instantly and absolutely terrified all over again. They were huge discs, perfectly round. When the light reflected in them from street lamps, they glinted blindingly yellow. I could not take my gaze off them, equally frightened and enthralled at the same time. Yet in some respects he looked so much like my friend Mikey who, I now thought, must be a sorcerer but hid it well. Or else this person was not Mikey at all. Had he replaced Mikey somehow? From my limited perspective, that notion was impossible.

Forcefully, he broke my train of thought: "*Stop staring at me!*"

"I can't! Anyhow, *you* told me to look."

"Well, I wanted to put you at ease by looking like someone you know," he said.

For some reason this explanation helped me to relax a bit. "Thanks. I guess." I was still unnerved and stared blankly into the space just above the steering wheel. "So, what *are* you?"

"I am not a 'what,'" he said firmly. "And I am now offended."

"Oh, you're offended?" I giggled in surprise. I quite liked his funny manner. "Well, you're clearly not a person."

"What do you mean?"

"Not a person like me!" I poked my legs hard with my fingers, but they felt significantly more squishy than anticipated. *I'm more spaced out than I thought,* I mused, *or else I need to work out more.* "See? I'm solid."

"You are?" He paused for a brief moment. "You can say whatever you want. This is a judgement-free zone. But you probably won't want to talk much longer, because soon you will start to feel even more relaxed. You might want to speak more to the point."

I silently worried that even thinking a bad thought would offend him. He might attack me. Even worse, he might leave!

He gently said, "I won't go until you're ready. And don't worry, there's not a thought you could think that could really offend me. I can see through you. I know your intentions are good. Otherwise, I wouldn't have come when you commanded."

"I *commanded* it?" I asked, dumbfounded.

"Yes," he answered. "You stated that you wouldn't go without a friend. So here I am."

I giggled. "Are you at my service, O genie?"

"You could say that."

"Well, you must not be very powerful if little old me could command you," I prompted, testing him.

"That would be a stupid assumption to make," he retorted. "Just because you commanded it doesn't mean I had to do it. I volunteered."

His tone dismayed me. Emotions in the state I was in were amplified enormously. "I'm so sorry. Will you be my bestest friend?"

He seemed delighted. "We already are."

"We are?" I wondered aloud, "You must have loads of friends if you travel a lot."

"I guess so."

"Do you have many bestest friends? Because you're my bestest," I confessed, amazed at how sentimental I'd become.

"You're the only one who's ever asked me," he revealed.

That seemed extremely odd. He emanated such charisma, making it impossible not to love him.

"You're not so bad yourself," he quickly retorted while beaming a toothy grin.

I pretended to blush, trying to be funny, and said, "So, come here often?" I reclined with my arm stretched towards the opposite seat, attempting to act smooth.

He either ignored the joke or did not understand it. He simply said, "Very."

Taken aback, I said, "Really?"

"Why does that surprise you?" he asked.

"Well, I would likely remember someone like you," I replied.

"You do." Then he seemed to utterly lose interest and changed the subject. "Back to a more interesting topic: What constitutes a person? Or as you most eloquently put it, 'someone solid'? Let's establish the criteria."

"Like solid versus non-solid?" I laughed.

"That's as good a starting point as any."

"Okay. Well, I can't walk through walls, but I bet you can."

"That's wrong, Sarazen. *You can.*"

"I have never walked through a wall in my life! Well, maybe in a dream, but that doesn't count."

"You have – countless times – and you know very well dreams count. You could right now if you tried."

"Well, easy for you to say, since there are no walls in here." Suddenly time flickered. Now I was back in the passenger seat, and that seemed more correct. How weird! Was Mikey somehow creating the effect, a way of taking control of our conversation?

"Well, I see a glass window." He gestured with his chin towards the passenger door window.

"Okay, funny man, watch this." Lifting my arm, I hesitated. *Then I pushed it through the glass!* Shocked, I kept my arm outside, marvelling at it, twisting my wrist and flexing my hand and fingers. "How did you *do* that?" The words came out very slowly.

"A better question would be to ask, how did *you* do that?" He seemed pleased with himself.

"I – I don't – know."

"Stop being coy. It doesn't suit you. So we squashed that one, wouldn't you agree?" he said, looking to me for acknowledgment.

I nodded slowly.

He continued: "Okay, so how am I different from you?"

I searched my mind, determined to put up a barrier which, I thought, should be very easy since there were so many differences between us. Finally, the obvious came to me. "My skin isn't multicoloured?"

He laughed and furrowed his brow. He looked like he was thinking, *What is she on about?*

I bounced his words back at him defiantly: "Don't be coy. It doesn't suit you." I thought I was being quite clever. A long, tense silence followed. "I know what I saw. It was only for a split second, but I will never forget it."

There was another pause, but still no reply from the radiating man.

I continued, "Look at yourself, you're fucking *glowing*. Nobody glows. They say pregnant women glow, but not like that. I bet you could power a small city! And that cheesy Mikey suit. You're wearing that for me? Who could you possibly fool with that outfit? A five-year-old could see through that trick."

I giggled again. This was getting ridiculous. "And look at your fucking eyes. They're like five times normal size, and yellow. Nice try, but I'm not biting. Can't catch me, I'm the Gingerbread Man! But I'm guessing you knew that, so it makes even less sense. Why did you bother? Nice one, but I don't travel with strangers, so if you want me to go anywhere with you, then you'd better show me who you really, really are. No mask. Do you see me wearing a mask? I think you want me to go with you more than I want to go with you, and I want to a lot, so that tells me I hold all the cards."

I was half bluffing, incredibly curious to see who or what he really was. He had said nothing of taking me anywhere, but I guessed his intention to do so and felt it was worth the gamble.

There was another long, awkward silence. He seemed deep in thought, and looked indecisive. But then he answered all my questions at once, preceding with, "How do you split a second? You can't. It's a stupid saying and you should eliminate it from your vocabulary."

I silently wondered, however, about microseconds.

He continued, "*You also* glow. You glow very brightly. Few can bear to look at you. You're probably right about one thing: I could power a lot more than a small city, but it's of little importance. And yes, I vaguely resemble Mikey, but it was your choice that I should look like him, though it could have been anyone. It's a disguise, true, but this is the way things are set up, all for your benefit. Do you think I like my eyes like this? Well, in fact I think they suit me just fine."

I was silent for a moment, greatly taken aback. "Sorry, I didn't think an all-powerful being would be so sensitive." My sarcasm ignored, I said softly, "All right, let's get on with this. It figures I'd get stuck with a being with a body-image complex."

That seemed to change his mood. He explained, "No. I was just trying to protect you. There are so many beings around me who think you're great and have so much potential, but I'm still sceptical. So I was sheltering you, but no, you want to *see* me. Fine, let's see what you're made of."

I resisted, nervously. "On second thought, I'm good."

"No. You wanted to see. Fine. I'm not embarrassed."

"Wouldn't that be breaking a rule or something?" I pressed my hands tightly against my closed eyes, but could not keep out the stabbing light penetrating the spaces between my fingers.

"I can break the rules," he said. After a long pause, he continued, "Oh come on, just look at me. Don't you want to know what's *out there?*"

That got to me. I was now too curious.

✳

I'd had a very active dream life since I was a toddler. As my abilities developed, I soon awoke within the dreams in a lucid state. In other words, I knew I was dreaming and had a great deal of conscious control of my actions in dream worlds. It was almost an avocation. There was my waking life, then my dream life, and they would seamlessly transition into each other. I discovered the freedom to create whatever I wanted because I knew I was not just a passive observer taking everything at face value. I could rewind dreams repeatedly to ensure they had the perfect ending. Sometimes there were dream-state tests.

My senses were always fully functional in lucid dreams, with the exception of taste and smell, which were only available from time to time. This made the authenticity of those experiences quite unquestionable, although I never confused waking life with dream life, at least not until that night with Mikey.

As I got older, I stopped reading for mere entertainment. I was looking for something deeper. Turning first to self-help books and philosophy, then popular metaphysics, I discovered the concept of manifestation using the law of attraction, a notion that held enormous appeal. I believed I already had a certain amount of mental control in my dreaming practice, so by extension I felt the next step was to create what I wanted in waking life. I thought there must be masters of the art somewhere, but if so, they must be "cloud-hidden, whereabouts unknown," as a Taoist poet once described himself. As mentioned, eventually I discovered the writings of Carlos Castaneda, which resonated with me for those reasons and more.

Fascinated, I was not, however, conscious enough nor had I acquired enough life experience to fully grasp the concepts expressed in the literature I was reading. My day-to-day life was very full – with college, a boyfriend and, before the traffic accident, three jobs. Distractions were abundant. The source of awareness within was elusive, masked by the chatter of the monkey mind. But if anyone had questioned it, I would have insisted I was already wide awake.

I had an intense curiosity about the levels of mind Castaneda described in his tales, although I'd come to understand that his books were considered fiction by academics in spite of having been published as anthropological research logs. I was driven to know whether he had just made the whole thing up to make money or whether there really was any possibility of experiencing similar altered states and visiting parallel realities. If he was speaking of something real, it would be possible to cast a new light on life and its meaning by exploring them.

So when the blue being challenged me, I could not resist, but there's no way I can do justice with words to what I saw then. I can say he was just the most magnificent creature. His features were humanoid and, unlike the Mikey I was familiar with, he was a man of tall stature. I had the impression he was greatly condensing himself in order to fit into the car at all. As mentioned, the Mikey I knew had a much finer bone structure and was not much taller than me. And the being glowed. Wow, did he ever glow. He had an immense resplendent light radiating from him that was in proximity beautifully warm to be bathed in. Apparently multicoloured at first glance, upon further inspection I could see that he actually emanated the most lovely soft blue extending out through his aura.

After seven years of much searching, I had given up hope that I would ever find further information about who I was sitting with then. But I was wrong. I have come to know that I am not the first person to be blessed with contact with this remarkable being. In fact he is very well-known worldwide. His Sanskrit name is Sanat Kumara, which I will use for him hereafter. He is known to theosophy as one of the Lords of the Flames of Venus. He is also the protector of our planet Earth, presiding over Shambhala, the mythical kingdom of the Hindu and Tibetan Buddhist traditions, helping us create our divine plans for embodiment and the achievement of our great freedom, since he already has his. He is what theosophy calls a powerful ascended master. All this information, however, was far beyond my level of spiritual understanding at the time and, like most people, I was unaware of the existence of mythical cities or beings that helped to blueprint our life plans.

✳

I yelled: "*Do you want to wake everyone in the neighbourhood with that freaking awesome light?!*" I imagined people coming out of their homes in pyjamas, then us getting arrested as aliens and finally studied in a top-secret lab at a hidden underground facility by scientists in white lab coats. It was an interesting theory, considering I was lumping us together as equals in my imagination.

"Do you really care?" he asked.

"Well, no." I had to admit it. I could not have cared less.

"Do you believe people could keep us where we don't want to stay?"

"No," I agreed, and really meant it, but didn't know why. I can hardly explain his effect on me. He was overpowering but uplifting, gorgeous yet uncomplicated. Fearsome but harmless, liquid, weightless but infinitely heavy. Iridescent, radiant, sublime, euphoric and dryly humorous. His character lacked nothing. He was superb yet unnameable. I could go on and on, but won't right now. Things will get more clear as the story unfolds.

"Unnameable. That has a nice ring to it," he said as his glowing waxed and waned in response to my thoughts.

I laughed. "It suits you, but we can do better than that."

He seemed genuinely flattered. "You know, no one's thought to name me before."

I could not tell that he was being sarcastic, that it was just his dry sense of humour. I had no idea at the time that Sanat Kumara had been given many, many names through the ages, according to the Theosophical Society, such as Sumara, Karttikeya, Skanda-Karttikeya, Ageless One, The Prince of Venus and The Ancient of Days. He is also listed as the leader of the Seven Great Brahmins.

In Vedic tradition, he is a *rishi*, a seer of truth, appearing in the *Chandogya Upanishad*, one of the oldest Hindu scriptures. He was also the teacher of the sage Narada, author of the *Bhakti Sutras,* an ancient but timeless Vedantic text on the nature of love.

Just as Jesus Christ has "appeared" to certain saints through the ages, Sanat Kumara has also appeared from time to time on the physical plane.

Since I was unaware of any of this information, I kicked around a few ideas for names of my own: Sky Man, Man of the Sky, Space Man, The Fourth Man from The Blue Man Group. He said he liked them all and that any I cared to choose would be fine. I felt, however, that perhaps I should get to know him better before assigning him a moniker.

Changing the subject, he asked, "You said you don't travel with strangers. Am I still a stranger?"

"I suppose not," I answered.

"Shall we then?" he said, motioning to get out of the car.

I was hesitant. My face must have shown it.

He asked, "What do you think you'd like to do first? I know you don't usually like a lot of assistance."

I answered, "I don't know. But you're right, I don't. No one's the boss of me! Are you sure I'm ready for this? Is there a manual I can read first or something? Can I take a course? You won't leave me, right? I don't want to get lost out there in hyperspace." I sounded so childish.

He exploded in the most delightful hilarity I had ever heard. It was enchanting. There didn't seem to be one tiny bit of badness in him.

"Even if there were a manual, you wouldn't read it." He laughed again. "You always like to explore first and ask questions later. I do miss that."

What did he mean by that? How could he miss me? I wondered. From my perspective, it was the first time we'd met, although he said he came "here" often and there was a familiar feeling of "home" about him. All at once I felt his deep affection for me. It moved me more than anything ever had, bringing tears to my eyes. It seemed impossible then for anyone to ever care for me as much he did.

Laughing, I had to agree with his observation, yet wondered about how to leap into the unknown. I then remembered a scene from one of Castaneda's books in which the Yaqui shaman don Genaro opened a big crack in the air. His peers had laughed and called it "the cosmic vagina." It made me laugh too.

"Well, that's a good starting point. Why don't we try it?" He was serious.

I was still unsure but determined to proceed. "Well, I guess if space is like fabric, and a human is a being like I've read about in books – there's more to us than meets the eye – maybe I could just imagine fabric and tear a gap or opening big enough for me to fit through."

"Just you?" he retorted. I watched his face actually morph into the face of a cartoonish, sad puppy dog.

"You know what I mean," I murmured, awestruck.

"I'm still waiting," said the cartoon dog impatiently while wagging his tail.

After taking a moment to gather confidence, I reached out my right hand. "Does it matter how far ahead I grab?"

"Stop stalling," he demanded.

"Can you freeze time so that this whole sightseeing tour will take only a few minutes Earth-time so I won't get back too late?"

"Sure, no problem." He smiled. "Now get on with it."

We exited the car into the cool darkness. With my hands outstretched, I grabbed the air. To my surprise, it was definitely substantial, like a transparent shower curtain but much softer. There was a ripple where I had just grabbed, revealing a surface that had the texture of a sheet of blank construction paper. Using both hands, I prepared to enter the opening I'd made. Looking back for a moment, I wanted one last reassurance.

Sanat nodded.

Then I gazed into the blankness, took a deep breath and tried to quickly make peace with the possibility of never returning.

The blue being could turn out to be the ultimate con man. *He could be the Devil.* I was beginning to see how suspicious I was of others. I really did fear the worst in people. But I'd already made my choice. It was a risk I had to be willing to take, although my intuition was that he was likely incapable of malice.

Diving head-first into the unknown through the folds in the gap, I was blinded momentarily by an intense white light. *Well,* I thought, *this must have been how Alice felt when she went down the rabbit hole.*

5.

Don't Travel *with* Strangers

MANY FRANTIC THOUGHTS went through my head instantly as I leapt through the portal: *I hope I'll be back soon because if not Alexander is going to find me asleep in my car either with or without Mikey. Alexander might think I drove drunk, which I would never do. My family and friends will be heartbroken if I fail to return. Maybe there's such a thing as astral predators who eat newbies like me for breakfast.*

But the blue being was at the forefront of my mind the whole time. I very much wanted to soul travel with him, but still couldn't shake my concerns. I seemed to be predisposed to give way to doubt. Given only the tiniest fraction of a second – *Why does he object to that expression?* – my decision had to be final. *Life may never be the same*, I thought, *and my insatiable curiosity could be the end of everything.*

During that infinitesimal moment, which paradoxically seemed to stretch out and touch everything, I also remembered my uncle Robert's story of how he once unexpectedly experienced an alternate reality while participating in a drum circle around a campfire on one of his wilderness camping trips. With eyes open, he was drumming in the autumn sunlight of Canadian mountains, but with eyes closed, he was drumming in shafts of moonlight beside a calm river in a tropical jungle. I remembered I had told him that if something like that ever happened to me, I would have no choice but to see where it took me. Remembering my words gave me the final push I needed.

It also seemed to me that destiny was providing an opportunity that may never come around again. I felt I must trust it to take care of me. As Einstein once asked, is the universe friendly or isn't it? The questions that had plagued me my whole life might be answered if I could let go and trust. So far, my seeking had been through only a small handful of books on popular metaphysical subjects, such as meditation, spiritual enlightenment and a variety of self-improvement topics. It had been a refreshing break after only reading physics, calculus and biology college textbooks.

While I loved those subjects, the information seemed to create an imbalance, as it was limited to a narrow paradigm. Despite looking for answers in many places, I never found much that I could really connect with in the New Age community. It all seemed highly speculative or opinionated. I wanted something much more tangible. Try as I may, I was unable to connect to anything powerful through meditation either. It really was Castaneda's book *Tales of Power* that was the first piece of literature that inspired me, and yet I still felt remarkably unprepared and had no idea of what to do when a girl finds herself face to face with an ethereal being who wants to take her on a cosmic voyage. I did not understand the connection between me and that book, if there was one.

To ease the anxiety, I wondered if soul travel might be an affordable way to see the world, but which world?

The threshold between the world I was leaving behind and the space beyond the tear I'd made in its fabric was like being on stage under a brilliant spotlight and not being able to see the audience. The light was extremely blinding and "thick," like heavy fog, but without the humidity. I had an intuition that my intention had to be strong to penetrate it. It was like it was challenging me to go big or go home. I dug deeper and somehow found just a little more determination to finally push through.

An extremely quick spasm in my diaphragm took my breath away. I felt something powerful stirring within my rib cage. I remembered the scene in *Alien* in which the baby monster emerges out of the astronaut's chest. My life had been exceptionally uneventful lately. *How could I not have noticed something that foreign having been inserted into my torso?*

I thought my mind must still be trying to control everything as usual, which felt like the beginning of an extraordinary anxiety attack. Or maybe I really was just drunk. If I was going to be completely honest with myself, I had to admit that experiences I'd had up until this day while drinking were quite the opposite: a dulling of the senses and the texture of experience, not a heightening. The effects of alcohol normally result in fewer memories or none at all, in extreme quantities, which I think is most people's experience. I had experimented quite a bit with drugs when I was younger, wanting to sample everything in life in case it was cut short. But this was different.

I had a rough adolescence. A short life, sadly, was a very real possibility, as I watched many of my friends die from numerous causes, ranging from car accidents and gang wars to disease and innocently being in the wrong place at the wrong time. During that phase, my late teens, I had very much wanted to find the meaning of life, to find a higher purpose than the wreckage that my friends and I saw too often nearly on a weekly basis. I was seeking God, you might say, although I didn't see it that way then.

On the one hand, I wanted to suppress the anxiety because it seemed tension was the only thing holding my body together. On the other hand, something inside was begging to simply let go and knew there was a friend close at hand to monitor things. I also knew I would never forgive myself if I didn't take advantage of the opportunity. Hadn't I already torn an opening in the fabric of space-time? That of itself was evidence of personal power. And I definitely did not want to wait until I had one of those near-death experiences I'd read about to find answers to my questions – unless in fact that was actually what was happening! But I had no idea of the price of admission. Could I afford it?

6.

Crocodile Tales

VAGUELY AWARE OF still being near the car, an immense pressure in my upper chest arose that made me call out for Sanat: "*Cut me open with a knife!*" It was absolutely critical: something that had been concealed or buried inside me had to come out. I thought it might be a bomb, but that just seemed highly improbable after a moment of clarity. All I knew was there was something explosive in there that wanted to get out and I didn't want it inside me. In fact it felt alive. After seeing that we could at least agree on that point, I realized that, in some weird way, I and this thing could communicate. We stopped resisting one another.

I tried to understand what the thing was by pretending to be it. As soon as I posed the question, I found myself crammed into a damp, coffin-like box. It was made, not of wood, but of bullet-proof glass of an unknown, indestructible, transparent material like Perspex, yet it had a familiar quality. I wondered where I'd seen it before. I could see something covering it, not muscle tissue and bone or even dirt, but something like dirt with strange stuff mixed into it so that its texture was inconsistent.

I was suffocating. What little air there was was hot and humid. In fact I was choking. I could not sense my guide. The only thing I could do was start smashing at the box from the inside, looking for a weak spot. It was, however, as if the coffin had been built about a foot too short for my frame, so I was too tightly constricted to exert any real force. *So this is how claustrophobia begins,* I thought, but hadn't the time to wonder how I'd been put in this situation. I had long forgotten my decision to leap into the unknown. The only question in mind concerned the source of the feeling bursting my chest. Driven by primal instinct, all I wanted was escape, even if the perpetrator was waiting for me on the outside. I'd take my chances.

Gasping, I flailed and bashed away as well as I could, but did not make so much as a scratch in the coffin. I stopped and tried to think what a survivalist might do in my situation, then remembered to conserve as much oxygen as possible. But panic resumed. All I could think about was getting through six feet of dirt to the surface. I struggled even harder, but then did something uncharacteristic: I prayed to the universe. I prayed that I could borrow strength from someone, anyone who wasn't using it just then, someone willing to lend it to me, to please see that I was worth saving.

Then I heard the most beautiful sound in the world: *a crack appeared in the box!* I fought for escape even more fiercely and didn't consider the irony of slashing my wrists on broken pieces of glass. Somehow I knew that was not to be my fate.

I imagined my fists as sledgehammers, and together they shattered the glass coffin, disintegrating it into a million shards that turned to sparkly dust. My worries of digging through the ground or if I would meet my captor at the surface disappeared, giving way to a new scene and a new challenge. I was shocked to find I was now face to face with a crocodile! *Wow,* I thought, *this predicament just isn't letting up!*

I contemplated riding the beast. Maybe then it couldn't bite me. There were still urgent feelings in my chest, but what was pain before was transitioning to relief, the letting go of a huge burden I hadn't even been aware of – my body. It seemed the whole enormous ordeal in the coffin was in fact my soul breaking free from the chains of the physical garment enclosing it. When I tried to focus on it, I felt I was falling, floating, spinning. Nothing else existed. I even forgot about the croc because now nothing was more important than letting go.

Lost in the relief a moment too long, I lost any advantage I may have had in evading the huge reptile. It approached stealthily and started biting me all over! The bites, however, did not have any of the expected effects. They were painful, yes, but did not inflict any damage. There were no wounds, no blood, just relentless, toothy, baffling chomping! Then I heard a distant voice. It seemed to be yelling instructions, but I couldn't understand. It sounded too far away to clearly interpret. The crocodile remained an incomprehensible but very real threat.

"Listen to me!" the voice insisted.

"*I'm trying!*" I yelled in pain, as loudly as I could. Then it seemed the pain was like that of a child bumping her elbow, who just before she really starts to feel the hurt is unsure if it actually will hurt. I calmed down when I realized I wasn't being devoured at all. It was just uncomfortable, not painful. I looked around. There were other crocodiles in the background looking ravenous, but awaiting a signal or command like well-trained attack dogs.

I listened for the voice in the darkness, but all I could hear was water lapping a shoreline. Where was I? In a swamp? Why would my guide let me be eaten by wild beasts? Something like the sound of cellophane ripping was heard in my left ear. After that I could hear the voice much more distinctly.

"Maybe you should let him eat you," the voice suggested.

Why? I thought. *For what reason? Don't crocodiles have a super slow digestive system?* I wanted to be home before dawn. They'd have to shit me out pretty damn quickly. I should have set better parameters for my experience.

"Invite the other ones if you want. It might go faster," the voice advised. The crocodile was still vigorously in attack mode, but his bites now felt more like pinching. He was no longer as menacing. In fact his nibbling reminded me of my cat Katie's love bites, only it was even more loving.

Well, I considered, *maybe there's a reason for all this.* My body felt numb, except when being bitten, which turned out to not be so bad after all. I decided to invite the other crocs to join in. My new attitude was, hey, there's plenty to go around.

They immediately surrounded me in a calm and orderly fashion. I thought they showed remarkable restraint when presented with a free meal. As they joined in, an extraordinary feeling consumed me, pardon the pun. Their biting seemed to be perfectly timed so that my whole body was bitten at once. The feeling was overpowering at first, but lessened by degrees. There was absolutely no pain from being gnawed by the reptilian predators. In fact I felt great, extremely aware and agile, even graceful, weightless, buoyant, lively, happy, peaceful and extremely awake.

I understood that I was a gift to them. It filled them with joy. I could not imagine that to them I was the best dinner ever, but I hoped it was satisfactory. Then a wave of euphoria hit me. Surprisingly, I actually loved them! How could I not have appreciated such ravishingly beautiful creatures before?

"They *are* you! They are your emblem," the voice in the darkness said as the crocodiles retreated towards the nearby shoreline I could now see against a backdrop of the most tranquil pastel peach-coloured sky. I wasn't quite ready to let them go and tried mentally to hold on a little longer.

If I'd been asked to choose an emblematic animal, it would have been a cat, like a cougar or a lynx. Or possibly even a phoenix, but never a crocodile. The southern Pacific coast of Canada, where I have lived my whole life, did not include such creatures among its fauna. Also, I think I would have chosen a totem based on land speed and furry aesthetics, neither of which to me are characteristic of crocs.

Mighty I AM, within and above, that we may be the fulfillment of the Divine Plan, we call to the Great Angelic Host. Beloved Angels, as we enter into a new dynamic relationship with the Angels, we invite your active Presence in our lives. Beloved Angels, Come! (3) into our lives and Blaze! (3) your Eternal Flames of your Sacred Fire Love, from out the Great Central Sun. Beloved Angels, fill and charge, the Immortal Power and Mastery of your Cosmic Christ Sacred Fire Purity, Power, Love, and Healing in Victorious Action, into our lives and worlds. Charge all our relationships, the personal and business activities of our lives and all means of transportation we use each day with your Sacred Fire Love and Mastery. Beloved Angels, fill our minds, bodies, and feelings with your Eternal Flames of Sacred Fire Love, Purity, Power and Sacred Fire Healing. We love you and we thank you, Beloved Angels.

"Well, they chose you. You don't get to choose. Take it as a compliment and don't be ungrateful. You saw them for what they are, magnificent creatures," the voice said.

"Yes, I did. They *are* magnificent creatures. I had no idea," I confessed. "What is it that makes them that way?"

"They are among the oldest species on earth, built to last. They are powerful and fearsome, able to instantly leap out of the water to snatch their prey. But they're also wise, good at conserving energy. They love the water and the sun, as do you. Can anything survive for so many millions of years without needing to evolve?

"They're tough on the outside but soft on the inside. They have a symbiotic relationship with birds, such as plovers, which pick off leeches and other parasites that feed on the crocodile's blood. They open their mouths wide so the birds can enter and act as dental hygienists. They can be generous, even protective. Sometimes crocs live under the nests of birds, where they benefit from the occasional fallen egg. The birds benefit from being safe from raccoons and other tree-climbing egg thieves, which to them are a bigger risk than the crocs.

"Crocodiles will still be around when mountain lions and humans have become extinct. Why prefer an endangered species as your totem?" said the voice, which I now recognized as my guide's.

I loved hearing this. Cats had always been so appealing to me because of their beauty, speed and agility, but now there was a lot more to consider. "But do crocodiles really allow birds to fly into their mouths without eating them?" I asked. I had never heard of such a thing.

"They're distant relatives, after all," he continued, "both more closely related to dinosaurs than other reptiles are. Would you eat a cousin?"

"No, of course not. I wouldn't eat a non-relative either," I said, trying to sound smarter than I was feeling. I still doubted him a little. "I just assumed that crocodiles will eat anything that moves. That's hardly being generous, though I guess it's kind of an equal opportunity thing."

He seemed irritated. "Did you ever stop to think that a crocodile has free will too? Every decision matters. There's a whole dynamic you may not be aware of. Maybe they're friends who would *die* for each other."

"Yeah, I guess I have heard of odd friendships between species: cows and geese, crows and kittens, orangutans and dogs, humans and boa constrictors," I admitted. The beauty and the compassion of it was intriguing. It was almost a rather romantic idea.

"You and the crocodile are not that different. In fact, now that he's eaten you, you are one and the same, with the same strengths. It is a great honour."

I agreed. Then I remembered I'd passed through an opening I'd intentionally torn in the fabric of reality. It had been my choice to take the risk, the difference between falling in and diving in. Maybe the crocs and I weren't so different after all.

7.

The Sand Chapter

MY GUIDE, THE blue being, asked me to give him a story.

"Are you a story collector?" I wondered.

"Not really," he answered. "I like to ask people who come to me for their favourite story because sometimes it helps me reach out or get through to them if they're having trouble, and for other reasons. Even though *you're not your story*, stories can be beautiful. If you have one to share, please do. If not, I have one from someone else that I think would be absolutely appropriate."

We were floating in space together, suspended in time. I could feel the energy from the stars, all alive and radiating towards us. Even though it was just the two of us having this conversation, we were not alone. There was nothing lonely about the feeling of life beaming from everywhere and everything. Some pockets of space felt more busy and highly trafficked than others, but the spot he had chosen was restful.

There was something so comforting about the darkness and silence that enveloped us. I felt all my previous fears about losing my body melt away. We were bodiless, so to speak, but that in itself is not entirely accurate. It only approximates what I was experiencing. We were also weightless. We glowed, completely self-luminous. Our faces had much more depth, detail and definition than the rest of our bodies. That is to say, however, if we had wanted to look different or show something going on with, for example, our hands, we could also immediately render detail. We did have a tangible form that was similar to a familiar body, but it was of a different type: a body of light, built to sustain travelling through the many dimensions of time and space, allowing freedom, enough to even venture into the higher realms.

I thought really intensely, searching for an appropriate story or memory to share. "I can't think of anything. My mind is completely blank," I said, sad that I had nothing to contribute. My personal history seemed to have vanished.

"Come on, think. Focus. Try harder," Sanat urged.

"I have nothing," I said. "Can't you just scroll through my memory banks and take what you want? You're welcome to anything you find," I offered.

35

I seemed to have guessed correctly. I didn't know how it was possible, but everything I had ever seen had been photographed and laid out in a scrap book in front of me, and immediately. I could see my guide flipping through the pages at lightning speed, pausing at some images and admiring others. He seemed thoroughly fascinated. We smiled, at times laughing at some of the funny memories. He did find quite a few stories that he said would be helpful in the future. He was welcome to them all.

I felt highly energized, like I'd drunk eight espressos one after the other. But that doesn't even begin to describe the feeling. I was vibrating at a very intense rate and could feel every cell of my body acting almost independently in the most euphoric manner, each one vibrating at its own rate while bumping into neighbouring cells. This friction created the most blissful, paradoxical, cacophonic blend of feelings. Transformation rolled through like a wave of lightning, if one can picture that. I could only surmise that the change of state was a result of flipping through the memories.

In later years I would come to understand that each of us is given an etheric copy of *The Book of Life*. It is your own personal story, where every memory, every nuance that collectively makes up your experience is stored in higher planes. Some people are very proficient at accessing this informational database, within the akashic records, or *akasha*, an all-pervading field in the ether. Some have travelled to the physical location called the Akashic Records in this universe. Many of these accounts have reported it being a grand library filled with nearly an uncountable number of books.

Nothing seemed to exist but the two of us, so I felt no need for concern about anything in the environment. Similar to being alone in the wilderness, except that there was so much more to it, was it that I was being filled with a sense of completion? I could not consciously pinpoint the source of my bliss. My entire attention was on our conversation. He was all I could see, but he was also losing more and more of his form the longer we spoke. This sort of thing didn't really bother me anymore, so I let it slide. It seemed so natural to be just talking and listening. He became more abstract somehow, less human-looking and more like pixels of illumination in suspension, which had an integrated awareness and potent energy. Just because his body was dissolving did not mean our conversation was diminishing. His colours intensified with his mood, chameleon-like, as he demonstrated ultimate control over his body shape and skin texture, which sometimes was like fabric, sometimes a little gritty and rough. At other times it became unbelievably smooth, especially when he was really happy.

His size changed frequently, but then I'm sure mine did as well. While we were looking at the book of my life, we were roughly the same size. Maybe it was the presence of a third item, the book, that provided a sense of perspective.

When I wanted to look at his face, or as I remembered seeing it back on Earth, he would no longer be faceless. It seemed to me I was creating my own perceptions and was able to focus or unfocus at will. I was the master creator of my own experience! Who better to entertain myself than me? Who would know better than me what I would find marvellous, magnificent and mind-blowing? Who better than me to know my own limits?

I knew my guide was real. I hadn't conjured him up, not at all. He existed independently of my thoughts or beliefs in him. That is to say I knew that he was separate from me and had his own individuality and volition. I did, however, a lot of creative editing of my experience just for fun. It was the ultimate freedom, like being the producer, the director and the star of my own movie the way I'd always wanted it. I thought this was what it truly must feel like to be the all-powerful Creator, one with everything, making instantaneous adjustments large and small to the field of existence by mere thought alone. Although I did not understand why, power of command had become so potent up here. Back at home, a command seemed to have very little influence on my environment, at least as far as I could tell.

Even taking into consideration everything I have revealed of the story thus far, it only accounts for what seemed like brief seconds in the whole of my experience. We are still at the very beginning.

There is so much condensed information available in the out-of-body (OOB) state that to accurately detail everything of the experience has proved extremely challenging, and frankly not possible given our current methods of communication. Non-verbal communication carries with it a vast amount of information that we do not have methods for transcribing on the physical plane. For example, when Sanat would send me information, I would receive an energetic bundle of data to absorb. This bundle contained within it a "movie," but it was a full-immersion movie that included taste, touch, smell, sound, beautifully detailed mathematics and the exact emotions he wanted to convey. It is a far superior form of communication because there can be absolutely no misunderstanding whatsoever. You fully and accurately receive what is intended, nothing more, nothing less.

I hadn't, however, been quite prepared for how challenging it was to even get started, meaning just being able to leave the Earth and my body.

It was my understanding that the entire purpose of the crocodile episode was the shedding of my skin, so to speak. Maybe everyone sets themselves up for this kind of breakthrough by overcoming obstacles, but somehow I'd set my threshold at maximum. It seemed to be my unique way of developing the will to make progress. We were sitting in what seemed like paused time, suspended in space, and I slowly understood that we hadn't even got started yet or travelled anywhere worthwhile.

As we floated in the nothingness, I felt the urge to do some exploring, but was a little afraid our time was almost up since so much had already happened. Even if the experience had ended then, it would still have been the most fantastic thing that had ever happened to me, absolutely incomparable and unforgettable. Yet I really, really, *really* did not want to go back to my physical body. It had taken so much effort to lose it. It was kind of funny how I didn't care for the old thing anymore. The idea of being trapped inside it again, just like that cramped coffin, almost made me feel nauseous and suffocated in spite of now having no stomach nor the need for lungs. I thought it would be a blessing to be rid of it and laughed at how I could have ever been so attached, never mind concerned. Maybe I foresaw how much I would love being free, part of the reason why it was so hard to let go of the physical world: because I would be highly reluctant to return to it. Clinging to anything seemed like such a human habit.

"So where can we go?" I asked.

"Where do you want to go?"

My ego interjected doubt: "Are you sure I'm ready? Maybe I haven't learned or read enough yet."

Sanat Kumara projected thoughts to me, such as, "*Don't be silly, stop listening to that side of yourself,*" then an image of the swoosh from the Nike logo, which I understood to mean "*Just do it.*"

Until then, I hadn't really moved my new body yet and didn't think I even knew how. We'd just been floating in space, motionless. He was watching me like the most patient teacher imaginable or perhaps like a parent in joyful anticipation of a child taking her first steps.

I couldn't think of where I'd like to go the most. I wanted to see it all because I had no idea if I'd ever have another opportunity like it again. I didn't want to wake up with the feeling of regret that I should have done this or that or what was I thinking? and so on. Since I didn't know where I wanted to go or which experiences I should wish for, it seemed logical to sample one of everything.

Then all of a sudden I was – for lack of a better word – warped, as in warp speed. I hadn't even thought of or pictured where I wanted to go yet, at least as far as I could tell. My mind was in an extremely sensitive state. No sooner had I contemplated the desire to travel than I began to feel a powerful force sucking me in some unknown direction at impossible speeds. I wanted to adjust the sensitivity of the controls, if there were any, like you do with a video game controller. The raw power of my brain seemed immense and highly suggestible.

I started to travel and felt like a rocket ship whose power was multiplying exponentially, even infinitely. I could just make out streaks of colours, which I took to be stars and distant galaxies, although this is just my interpretation now of what I saw. At the time I had no clue. There was no time for contemplation at that dangerous velocity. It all happened very silently, far too fast for sound to keep up.

It felt neither good nor bad, but potent and impossibly strong, almost too strong for my heart to withstand. There was also a distant, ancient familiarity, that I somehow had just forgotten how to do this. I believed that I had an instinct for astral travelling, and that part of my soul was trying to reawaken. Yet there was so much to relearn.

Then, just as quickly as it began, it came to a halt. I opened my eyes to a shocking sight: *I was in hell!* At least it appeared to be what perhaps I had programmed myself to believe hell was like. If I thought I had been experiencing discomfort before, I was gravely mistaken. There was a vast difference between how I'd just been feeling and what I felt now. It was the difference between sitting in a comfortable, air-conditioned jet airliner and then being dumped in the middle of a torrid desert in the middle of a sandstorm.

I was sandblasted with raging heat. Anything organic was rotten, although some small shrubs and trees were on fire. It was paradoxically deathly dry and smotheringly humid, an unbearable feeling. And I was all alone, but didn't have time to worry about that yet. I had to find my bearings in this strange world, a flat plane in every direction. In a desert on planet Earth, the sky at least seems like a dome. Not here. It was a casket lid, yet nothing at all.

No joy had been taken in creating this place, at least none I could perceive. There were no mountains, no trees, plants or shelter, just rolling red sand dunes everywhere in sight. The substrate seemed to consist of a flat sheet no more than an inch thick. I don't know how I knew that. There was an indescribable nothingness above the dunes, no atmospheric pressure, and yet somehow also nothing below, meaning it was "hollow." That was as close to understanding as I could get. There was no core to this planet, just endless fiery heat, with a strange, smoking flatness to the wind.

The scene was ominous and emitted a low vibration that made me feel very unwell, unsure if the body I was in was calibrated to endure it. I began to wonder how far I had ventured from my starting point. A momentary fear engulfed me.

Surveying my surroundings, I spotted crawling shapes and what appeared to be mangled human life forms. They were aware of me too. No threats were made, nor did they ignore me. They discharged a vile stench, and appeared to be in the final stages of decay. I continued to keep my guard up, thinking their behaviour could change from mild curiosity to vulturous hunger at any moment. Covered in dark, dusty robes, the stronger ones picked the flesh off some of their mates, similar to how monkeys groom one another. How could flesh even exist in such conditions, never mind anything else? My mind struggled to understand.

I'd had enough and wanted to be anywhere but this stinking inferno. My guide seemed to have misplaced me. Maybe I truly was on my own. I refused to succumb to fear and continued to focus all my attention on the present moment. Then I had a thought: if I had somehow accidentally thought myself here, I could also think myself out of it. I directed all of the mental power I could muster towards the seemingly non-existent space just above the planet. Nothing seemed to happen. I switched gears and started thinking of Sanat and his face, trying to tune in to his location. When that yielded no result, I tried one last attempt to hone in on projecting myself back to Earth. I could not accept the fact that I was stranded here, yet this place would not release me from its grip.

At the mercy of a planet that had none, I was trapped. The more I tried to escape the more I felt drained, and the more energy the vulturous creatures gained, like vampires. I tried to create some distance and started dragging my feet across a landscape that was like the most twisted sadistic vision Salvador Dalí ever created. My footprints shaped impossible depressions made of the most disgusting stinking filth, burning from the inside out. It looked like molten garbage that would twist and contort, then spontaneously combust into the ether. I felt I'd already been stuck here for aeons. Every moment that passed was longer than the next, until I could no longer remember a time when I hadn't been lost in a lost world. All the elements were trying to break my will.

I panicked. Had my guide tricked me? Was this place a kind of prison? That couldn't be true, yet I couldn't help wondering where the hell he was, pardon the pun. *Yes, this place is hell and it is real.* I asked myself: *If I were the super strong survivor type, what would I do to make it through this? Should I look for a cave, get out of this unforgiving scorching wind? But what if that's leaping from the spit into the fire? What if a predator is hiding in the cave?* Directing my vision to the sweep of the duned landscape, I saw there could be no possibility of caves in an absolutely flat plane. I abandoned that plan. I could starve. Yes! Death certainly seemed to be the only way out, although it didn't seem the place would even allow that escape. I'd likely just turn into one of the disgusting zombie vulture people.

My best hope was that my guide would eventually show up to save me. I reasoned that if I just stayed put, it would make finding me easier. I clung to that desperate hope, not wanting to spend one more second than necessary in this loathsome place.

Every ghoul that crawled by or moaned affected my spirit badly. I started to entertain serious doubts as to whether I had what it took to survive, cursed myself for going out for "just one drink" that night and repeatedly berated myself about it. If only I'd gone home instead, I wouldn't have ended up eternally damned to hell. When making my choice to go out for that drink, I never considered *this* as an option! *They really need to teach people how to fly these astral bodies properly,* I thought.

I saw a rotting, stinking corpse lying on the ground. It seemed to be breathing, but after closer inspection it was only maggots under its parchment skin creating the effect. I asked, "So what did you do to land yourself here?" No response. The maggots weren't interested in existential questions.

After a very long time, I was compelled to move on and did manage to eventually find a small cave in the side of a dune, but it looked much too dark and dangerous. My whole being told me not to enter, so I parked myself close to its mouth. In case something even worse came by, I might take the risk. I knelt down and picked up a small pebble to throw inside to see what would happen. It crumbled to dust in my hand and blew away. Each one I picked up did the same thing. I tried one larger than a basketball. It was really heavy. As I heaved it into the cave, just enough of it hung together to make it inside. Nothing happened, not even the sound of it landing. It was as if the cave was non-existence itself, a black hole that swallowed everything. I congratulated myself for testing it first and switched gears to begin looking for food instead.

Back on Earth, it had seemed a good idea to eat smaller fish because they would be younger and have accumulated fewer toxins. While there was no sign of fish, let alone water, I tried to apply that same logic now. Digging in the sand, I looked for small insects. I found a black beetle-like thing, similar to a scarab, something you might see in the Middle East. I decided to postpone eating for now, and instead chose to make a basket of twigs for all the dead bugs I planned to collect. I say "dead" because they did not seem to be alive as we think of life. While they appeared to be animated, they emitted a strange sort of vibration that signified decay. The task also served as a distraction from the thought of eating anything so incredibly gross. Maybe I could hold out.

As I was forming the basket, my imagination wove the sad idea of becoming a crazy sand lady for the remainder of existence, living in a twiggy hut, subsisting on nasty filthy bugs.

I wondered what was happening to my physical body. Was it still alive? How much Earth-time had passed during the aeons I'd been here? Had anyone missed me or noticed I was gone? I wished I'd said goodbye.

I tried to bolster optimism by thinking that my guide was still looking for me. *Man, if he is looking for me, he's sure taking his dear sweet time.* Utter boredom began to shrivel ability to withstand the torture, depleting any creative energy I had stored. Anything I did try to create was swiftly blown to smithereens by the gritty hot wind. There was absolutely nothing worthwhile, another form of torture the planet inflicted mercilessly.

My only good fortune was that nobody and nothing had tried to attack me – yet – but saturated with boredom, I then tried to start a fight by throwing dirty stones at some of the zombies in an effort to make something happen. No response, just complete indifference. They too had had their spirits broken by the elements. My attempt to provoke drama went unnoticed and unchecked.

Beating myself up for being so trusting as to go off half-cocked with only one friend I hardly knew, I felt like an orphaned child. I cursed myself for not even giving my guide my cell phone number. Then I cried because I remembered there was no such thing in this awful place. *What a stupid idea.*

I wondered if I could call my guide mentally and gave it all I had left, forcing it. No response.

After ages upon ages, the grind wore down any remaining patience, replacing it with dullness and lethargy. I could not even cry anymore. I just kept weaving twigs into sculptures: little people, little animals. I played with them like a child pretending to be God. I invented lives for them, gave them histories. I tried to make a crocodile. That was too difficult, although I did manage some cats, pigs, goats and one giraffe. Why was the crocodile so hard? It seemed they were equally complex. The one animal I wanted to play with I could not contrive. How strangely appropriate.

Whatever distraction I managed to derive from weaving was soon swept away by the relentless, maddening wind. I just didn't care anymore and lay flat on my back in the dust for a long time staring into the blank nothingness of what should have been a sky.

To my surprise, I could not bring myself to hate this hellish world, but only because I couldn't conjure up emotions. It was as though the planet itself had sapped me of vitality, along with manifestation power. I felt absolutely nothing except total boredom and bleakness. Slowly its weight overcame me. I succumbed to total despair. My guide should have shown up by now if he was ever going to. For a being that could go anywhere, he was not coming for reasons unknown. *What could he be possibly doing that was more important than helping me? Dropping off his dry cleaning?*

I scooped up some sand to look for one of the black bugs. One was trying to burrow back into the dirt, but I was too fast for it. Studying it wriggling in my hand, I saw the thing was in no way a good thing to eat. It hurt my hand just to let it crawl across my palm. Then I realized I did not actually need to eat at all. My body could remain the same forever. It was just my mind tricking me out of habit, making me feel like I was starving because I couldn't remember my last meal.

In need of some form of entertainment, I decided to eat it anyway. I'd already been here for eighteen eternities and there was nothing else for it. I tilted my head back and opened my mouth, prepared to drop the bug in. It was literally the most exciting moment on this planet so far. I closed my eyes and let it go, anticipating the writhing thing scraping my tongue. Nothing happened. For a split second, I despaired: *Oh great, I can't even do that much, everything just disappears.* But I opened my eyes to see Sanat Kumara's hand with the bug in it.

"Not so fast," he said. "Do you even know what you were about to swallow? And there's no such thing as a split second."

He was the most beautiful sight, a living oasis in the desert wasteland, too good to be true. *There is no way he can be real.* Yet I recognized his energy. My inner being felt its unique signature. I realized I'd been saved at last!

Emotions welled up and overflowed. I tried to cry, but the well was dry. I felt an array of positive emotions, including joy, excitement and something even better: relief. Just seeing him initiated restoration. My feelings had slowly become desiccated by the hostile environment. I had shrunk to far less than my true self.

His fingers twisted the bug, cracking it open. Dense, gooey, pure black ink dripped out. As it fell to the sand, a cloudy puff of dust arose before blowing away. "I thought you were health-conscious. You really should be more careful of what you put in your body," he teased as nudged me with his shoulder.

I was so happy to see a familiar face that was not in an advanced state of decay that I almost forgot to be angry with him. A storm of questions arose. I let one sift out as I croaked: "Can we please leave here?"

"Not just yet," he replied. He put his arm over my shoulders.

I didn't understand and was devastated with disappointment.

"Let's stay a while," he said, opening his arms and tilting his head back as if to soak up the sun on a beautiful day. "This ain't so bad."

I had to admit he was a great actor because for a moment I forgot where I was and even wondered if I'd been interpreting everything incorrectly, like an optical illusion. But then I saw his smirk.

"Maybe buy some real estate," he was saying. "Yeah, how about developing a big skyscraper right over there? I can see it now," he said, pointing over to a huge building arising from the sand, which poured off its dusty sides.

I laughed inwardly at how light he could make of this hell-hole when it had crushed my will to live. How could I embrace his attitude? It was just too difficult. The best I could manage was sarcasm: "Oh yeah, this will definitely be the place to be. I can see the billboards now: *Hell. Spoil your family. Lounge in front of the picturesque Sea of Nothingness. But hurry, units going fast!*"

"Exactly!" he said. "Think how wealthy we could be." His spirit was not dampened one bit. "Well," he said as he started walking towards the cave, "let's take a look at what you almost walked in on."

I panicked. "*No! Don't!*" I screamed.

I'm not sure exactly what happened next. I only remember him stepping into the cave's black void as though he'd done it a thousand times. He then called me closer as he shone a light on an extremely grotesque raptor, all messy sparse feathers and bald patches of wrinkled grey skin. I instinctively recoiled and fell back in fright, using Sanat's body as a shield.

"*No, no, no!*" Sanat yelled. "Come back here, Chicken Little!"

I had no idea what he was up to. If it was a lesson, I wasn't getting it. But I inched closer and peered nervously from behind his shoulder. From this vantage point I could see that the light I had seen him shine before actually came from his fingertip. That amazed me. I wanted to learn how to do that.

There on the cave floor was a small dust bowl. In it were several ugly hatchlings. How could anything reproduce under these conditions? It was somewhat touching that there could be the least little bit of maternal care and concern on this planet, even if it was only because the babies were as yet uneaten by the unlovely hen.

"Look at what you would've stumbled upon had you ventured in here. Oh, and she would have fought you! It would've been a quicker death than the bug though. She's probably the last thing to pick a fight with in this place. She'll only fight to the death. You really need supervision, don't you? I thought you were smarter than that."

"I don't know why you think that," I replied, frowning. "I was bright enough not to go in earlier."

"Would you like to hold one?" he asked, gesturing towards the nest.

"Not really," I said, looking at the damp, moulting nestlings. Their sharp beaks and claws looked menacing despite their small size. Maybe they would fight to the death too. All I wanted was to leave all this infernal agony behind.

"No, I think you should. The mother hen will insist. In fact it would practically be an insult, considering you woke her up for no good reason with that big rock you threw in. Here, take this one."

He passed a chick over to me. I reluctantly extended both hands, incredibly cautious. The thought of being pecked to death was more than I could bear. After all, I had already been eaten alive by crocodiles. Wasn't that enough for one evening?

"Put your arms out. He's ready to fly," Sanat said calmly.

"These things can fly?" I didn't think anything could take flight in this stormy place. But I did as I was told. The little bird flapped its wings, which were covered in a substance like mucus, which it flicked everywhere. Great. The wind picked up the fledgling, which quickly learned to take advantage of it, soaring out of sight. I heard small scratchy cawing sounds behind me and saw the other chicks leaving the nest. They followed suit and opened their sticky wings too. We picked up each one and let the wind take them away.

"See? This place isn't so savage after all, is it?"

"No, I guess not. I just needed to look around more. I spent all my time making baskets."

My guide bent to the ground and picked up one of them up. Its bottom fell out.

"I didn't say I mastered the craft," I explained.

"Well, I *could* leave you here a little longer then," he said as he stood up and turned to walk away.

"Ha ha," I said. That triggered all of my other questions. "So where the hell were you all this time? Why did you leave me here? Why am I here? I don't understand."

"You just went too far too fast. You got your new wings and hadn't even tested them before flying a cosmic marathon."

I silently repeated, *Too far too fast, too far too fast,* trying to fathom it.

"You're much like those little birds, you know. I think we've learned enough here, wouldn't you say? Ready for take-off?"

"I thought you'd never ask!" My relief was inexpressible.

8.

Flying

IT'S VERY DIFFICULT to describe the out-of-body state. Everyday waking consciousness relies on the physical body's senses of sight, hearing, touch, taste and smell, which are completely absent, as one would expect, at least in the sense that they are not present in the way we are used to experiencing them. This is not to say there are no senses, it's just that the physical sense instruments are not present. In other words, there is a faculty that is the eye of the eye, the ear of the ear and so on.

Imagine that you are a giant sphere, maybe the size of the one in the movie *Sphere,* about thirty or forty feet in diameter. Now imagine the only source of information about your environment has to be channelled through a pipeline the diameter of a drinking straw. There are not many receptors on the outside of your sphere, so you are very limited in how much information from your surroundings you can interpret. That's roughly what it's like to experience the world through the physical senses of the standard-issue human body. Everything is filtered and refined so that it will squeeze through a narrow opening. Anything that can't fit is ignored and rejected. Some philosophers have pointed out that the brain is a filtering mechanism so that we're not overwhelmed by the entire electromagnetic spectrum, hence only a narrow range of vibrations is available. As a result, the fundamental ignorance leaves room for much misinterpretation, inhibiting progress in understanding the true nature of reality as well as the development of the true potential of our being that is our birthright.

Now imagine that you're that same sphere, only *every microscopic point* on its surface is an open conduit. Each one of those openings acts both independently and collectively to capture data from your environment to deliver the largest database for the most accurate interpretation of it at any given time. With such enhanced ability, you are firmly connected back to Source in this state. Whether you call it Source, or God, or Universal Mind, it is all the same. It is the central spark of the Creation and the focal point of energy in the universe that collects the data from all of our combined experiences simultaneously. It is the greatest computer server in the universe, if you prefer to look at it that way. This is the locus of omniscience.

When you are in the out-of-body state, your being is continually reporting, sending signals from all the data you are interpreting back to the central Source. With that connection, you are also able to access the database and download the answer to any query, just like using a search engine, such as Google. All of our technology on Earth is a weak impression of something much more complex that already exists in the universe. Google, cell phones, GPS: there is the divine version of almost anything you can conceive of. Unlike Google, however, it is not limited to human knowledge. It can access the knowledge of the Whole – what was, what is or ever will be – because it is all of those things.

That's what it's like being in the out-of-body state, able to access and travel multiple dimensions beyond the physical plane. It is indescribable in words, because there's nothing to compare it with in everyday experience. It is like trying to communicate to a newborn the concept of compound interest or trying to teach a puppy how to drive a car – it just can't be done! That is also how you can tell if you are experiencing something truly divine. Its effect on you can be felt profoundly, rendering you completely lost for words. Even trying to attach words to it seems degrading because it diminishes the grandeur. And this is how God works through each one of us, revealing His secrets one by one as we each demonstrate that we are ready. It's the failure of language that makes it seem unnatural from the usual perspective. But the truth is just the opposite. Unless one has experienced being out-of-body, all words can do is point to it, and we attempt to define it as best we can.

When my guide and I left planet Hell, the way we travelled was by mere impulse, that is, the moment I thought about not being there anymore, I vanished and reappeared somewhere else immediately, like switching to another television channel. I wondered why I hadn't been able to do that in his absence, although I certainly tried.

The planet we left behind was not actually hell in the way many theologians have programmed some of us to believe, that there is a place of punishment and suffering we go to if we commit unforgivable sins. One could even argue that the process of reincarnation is the hell they speak of, and depending on your karma you either will experience more or less hell in your subsequent embodiment, depending on the deeds you choose in your current life. That hell planet was just another creation of the universe in its exuberant quest to express its limitless nature, otherwise it wouldn't be limitless.

Everything in our reality is always open to interpretation: we project onto the screen of awareness our thoughts and feelings. This is known as superimposition in the most ancient teachings. To me, that planet was an absolute abyss that was like hell. I would never want to go back, at least not unaccompanied by a chauffeur. But to the creatures living on that planet, that is all they might ever know, and the only thing they could ever interpret as "home."

I am not sure what the role of those humanoid beings was. I do understand now that because we create everything in our reality, in some way they had created that situation for themselves. Perhaps they had evolved there and accepted it as their "normal." Nevertheless, if they were suffering, that could mean there was resistance. There may be pain in a situation, but suffering is optional, an indication that at a deeper level there is freedom from it. Maybe that was their difficult lesson.

One thing that quickly became apparent was that operating my new wings definitely had a steep learning curve. I seemed to have accidentally shot off in the wrong direction alone very powerfully, then either due to the natural forces of the planet or from the sheer exhaustion of burning myself out prematurely, completely depleting the explosive energy that appeared to be a prerequisite for flight, I'd accidentally and quite literally landed in a sticky situation.

Although it seemed I'd absorbed years' worth of knowledge already, only the most recent memories remaining near the surface stayed with me. Maybe other travellers are able to retain even greater detail while moving between worlds, but for me it was an instantaneous and shocking transition from night to day, from hell to heaven.

Yet there was still vision in the velvety darkness. Outer space was our backdrop, its unfiltered points of starlight shining from every direction. Of course I was weightless, seemingly bodiless and eyeless, having much less of a definite form than I'd grown accustomed to. I could nonetheless at times see intense light coming from everywhere. I still felt in possession of a mind and still felt like "me" as I gravitated towards a distant luminosity, gradually moving towards its centre, not noticing I had now branched off alone, silently seeking my own experience.

There I came to rest on a brightly glowing, web-like bed that extended to the rim of a vast transparent dome. In the centre of the dome was a gigantic glowing white sphere. It was impossible to look at it directly for too long. Its powerful beauty began to overwhelm my vision. I could feel part of myself melting into the web. I was dissolving. It felt like being suspended on the surface of a trampoline with a circumference many times larger than that of our sun. I wondered, *Is this nirvana?* Nothing else existed. I had reached the Centre of Creation. It was Source.

My every pain and fear, no matter how great or small, was completely absent. Wrapped in utter peace, the joy of the entire universe arose within me, like the feeling upon awakening in a warm bed on a cold morning multiplied by ten thousand, like finally feeling all the warmth of the sun invigorating every cell and nourishing every molecule of my being, parts of me I didn't even know needed it.

I was alone there, although not truly alone. I was connected to the web that formed an interconnected superhighway of information just below, that gave me unlimited access to anything and everything communicated through this living web, which had a separate intelligence from my own.

Though the level of peace and joy I felt was euphorically fulfilling, I did not want to stay, a desire that seemed strange to me even then. I had just come from an eternity in hell. It now had transitioned to its polar opposite. I thought I would have loved to rest there forever or even just a bit longer, but the idea was somehow oddly unsatisfying. Perhaps I took from the experience all I needed to become fully recharged.

The state I was in, fully connected to Divine Love, seemed so natural yet in a way boring, similar to when you have taken a restorative vacation, but then naturally return to the desire to be productive and experience new things. The idea of resting forever seemed stultifying.

Just then two angels came to my side with great speed, lifting me up and carrying me away from the warmth of the immense white sun. They had seen me resting in Source for too long and came to save me. I had not known I needed saving, nor that one could spend too much time at Source. In retrospect, that great feeling of warmth was actually facets of my personal awareness breaking down and returning their origin. One would never realize it was happening, because it was so euphoric to simply rest. Everything was more than okay, soaking in the universe's best sedative. I wondered if taken in very small doses the experience might be best utilized as a highly restorative exercise. If it was on Earth, people would probably ruin it by erecting a spa, with lots of shops and a charge for admission to view the sphere. I couldn't say, however, they would be too wrong in doing so, as it was the most magnificent thing I had seen yet.

The angels seemed to play a specific role. It was their job to prevent beings from accidentally deleting their individuality like moths attracted to a flame.

I was grateful for them and felt I had a lot more to experience and learn. It seemed almost lazy and irresponsible to hide myself in peace, in complacence. I could become addicted and fall asleep within it, just as I had fallen asleep in human life. It also seemed that kind of narcotic nirvana might appeal to some as their version of heaven, but for me it was too simplistic. I felt an obligation to my soul, a certain esoteric mission to complete. I felt the pull to continue moving forward in some direction, any direction, and hoped my soul would guide me to the most important path. Overconfident perhaps, somehow I knew I could do better than simply bliss out.

To rebalance, I asked for and was granted the experience of feeling all the pain and suffering in the universe. I'd already seen what I interpreted as my own personal version of hell, so I was unafraid. I was beginning to understand how the universe operated, and indeed the contrast of light and dark was fascinating. The darkness added great interest to what otherwise was a love-filled, benevolent, rather uneventful and monotonous placidity. It added the capacity for change and growth, which would be absent but for the challenge created by the darkness to take the opportunity to advance towards the light. I wanted to understand the concept further.

A rapid stream of images of people in different situations, hundreds of millions of them, passed through me like frames from old-fashioned movie reels. As they did, I was projected into the experience of each person's pain exactly as they were experiencing it, but was pulled out again quickly to enter and experience the next frame. I was able to remain unbiased throughout the process, and while it felt very heavy, I seemed to have gained much strength from the planet I had just left. I tried to understand those experiences from a higher point of view, to interpret their significance in relation to the grand scheme of things as well as possible. I wanted to understand each role. After some time, I felt I had gained a very good overview of human life by seeing both sides of the coin, light and dark.

Aided by the angels, I lifted myself out of bed, so to speak, and shot up through the transparent dome, feeling a kind of paradoxical undulating vibration originating from the bottom of my spine up towards the top of my form, which now resembled that of the angels as I passed through the barrier, almost like diving through water, except it was a sort of semi-liquid gas similar to plasma, but more like a non-electric, dense, wet vapour in consistency.

High above the dome, I began to take on a slightly less substantial form, like that of a fluttering sheet. Alone, peacefully hovering, I felt very satisfied with my choice of experiences. My guide was either watching over me invisibly or allowing me to explore on my own, like a parent who knows its child needs freedom to learn.

Looking around, I sat on a transparent energetic perch I found, perfect to overlook the stars. I remembered the fantastic experiences of explorers of the unknown I'd read about, and wanted all of that. In spite of recollecting many of my previous much shorter journeys out-of-body during dreams when I was younger, I felt there was still so much more to learn and see.

Unsure of where to go next, I automatically started to drift towards planet Earth. Many planets were in plain view, but the human home world was such an exquisite, glowing blue sphere, so attractive, bewitching. I made a couple of high-altitude orbits around it, entranced by the radiant blue glow. I dived down towards the hemisphere in night's shade, intending to visit some of its inhabitants without actually returning to my physical body. I wasn't sure how my "other half" was doing. I really didn't care.

In Earth time, that decision was made after experiencing the body's disappearing state as it waited in the car with Mikey. I did not understand it while the process was happening, but all the confounding bodily reactions I had mistaken for inebriation, such as lack of coordination, were a result of my body adapting to withstand the power of the experience.

Theoretically, it would seem that I had in fact been killed by the huge truck crashing into my car in one timeline. That is what gave the Divine priority permission to pull me out of my body and reveal so much of the greater reality of life, sights which until recently very few have glimpsed or even intuited. Most near-death experiencers do not report seeing or remembering a great deal of the other side. Of the few books that have discussed visits to Shambhala, the memories reported are very indistinct.

So it would seem that I was being held in some sort of temporary stasis to allow the learning to continue. I didn't want to get sucked back into the world just yet, but at least I knew I was still breathing.

I chose to visit my uncle Robert, whom I had affectionately nicknamed Uncle Orbit while learning to speak, when pronunciation was still a work in progress. Sometimes children are most intuitive, and that name matched his persona quite perfectly, so much so it became synonymous with his name from then on, at least to me.

We met in his second-storey living room, probably less than an hour before midnight, but the room was saturated with light, almost like daylight. His physical body was downstairs in his design studio, where he was working at his computer workstation as he so often did.

"So what's happening, Uncle Orbit?" I asked, speaking to his spirit while his Earthly self continued to work on a graphic design project he was near to completing.

"Well, Sarazen, I'm very close, but it's hard to fully let go of attachment to human existence," he replied. "It seems so full of promise. There's still the merest thread of my being hanging on."

I'm presenting our communication as conversation, although we didn't really speak in words. Calling it telepathy seems to dilute it as well because it was encased in sound, images and colour, which of itself is able to convey vast amounts of information as I have mentioned previously regarding non-verbal communication. In attempts for me to give it a human name by means of differentiation from basic telepathy I created the term higher-dimensional Communication (HDC). I have also, however, been given the divine terminology that the ascended host use with regard to this manner of communicating: Lumaelia.

This is the same type of communication I shared with my guide. When communicating using Lumaelia, you are directly connecting to another being's soul. In this expanded state, it is as though you have taken your laptop and plugged it directly into their server, or their consciousness. Through this connection, which is facilitated by light energy, one is able to receive and clearly interpret everything, from complex mathematics, movies, images and memories to smells, tastes, delicately nuanced emotions and other types of auditory and sensory experiences that are received by a more advanced body than your physical one – all from a single millisecond of data.

HDC, or Lumaelia, is free of error and miscommunication as well because there is no room for misinterpretation as with the spoken or written word. That is not to say that you aren't still learning. If a being shows you something you've never seen or conceptualized, you will still need to learn it. It will just take dramatically less time than before.

I then noticed and began to study my uncle's purple and green aura. I observed that mine was purple and blue, although I drew no conclusions from that. Unfamiliar with auras, the meaning held little significance for me.

Nicknames often unwittingly reveal essential traits. I saw that Uncle Orbit is the Travelling Man, and that we had spent many lifetimes as friends, like schoolmates. I even saw one lifetime when he was my husband, which was weird to ponder, along with several others in which more friends joined us to see how each other's evolution was going. Each of us had our favourite pastimes. His preference was to stay close to planet Earth. Uncle Orbit's thing was to fly at impossibly high rates of speed, boomingly fast.

"Show me what you like to do," I suggested.

We went down the stairs into the street in front of the house. There we ascended about eighty feet into the night sky, straight up. From this vantage point we could see the neighbourhood, the ground illuminated by street lights. We rose higher. There was a brief moment of eye contact when I saw a glint in his eye, the signal to go, then a silent countdown. A sonic boom rippled shock waves out from our starting point as we raced each other at Mach 10 speeds, flying across shining seas and vast continents, then down the coast of Africa, where we witnessed a sunrise. Top speeds had not even been approached yet, but that was only so we could savour the magnificent view. We paused. He seemed lost in contemplation.

"Sarazen, I know this is your final life here in the Earth-dream," he said, gazing into the solar glow cresting the planet's curved eastern horizon beneath its backdrop of soft starry black. "My house is near yours so that I can see how things unfold for you. And so that I have the opportunity to say goodbye."

"I don't know what it means to live a last life," I said, "how many lives you have to live before the last one or how many it takes to resolve your karma. I only know I've accomplished a lot and this one is a kind of final victory lap." I do not know how I knew this information, which was news to me. My soul appearing to be doing the talking.

Pensive, I continued, "I just wanted to stretch things out a little bit longer because I've discovered I'm more interested in human beings and human life than I thought."

On the return orbit to the house, I arrived to be greeted by Uncle Orbit's guide. In fact I met two guides. One was a tall man, his face obscured by a wide-brimmed fedora and the upturned collar of his trench coat. His clothing was very neutral in colour and retro, from the 1940s or '50s. Though he showed himself to me, he was only a silent presence. Was he a detective? An investigator? A spy?

The other guide was an Indian yogi, whose name I was only able to discover much later when I'd returned to my physical body. I felt a reverential respect, the strange mixture of fear and wonder known as awe, not that anyone of his spiritual stature could be corrupt or evil – that is not possible – it was just that his eyes radiated such incredible power.

Though I'm describing all this in linear fashion, my encounters with him actually occurred at the same time, as I toggled between several experiences simultaneously and in varying situations. The yogi/guide always appeared as a formidable figure. I asked him why Uncle Orbit still seemed so earthbound.

The yogi told me, "Once the urge to awaken arises from within, it's only a matter of the right time. You have no duty in this regard, so there is nothing for you to do. Besides, the Earth and the entire cosmos is but a dream, and the dreamer is the essence of stillness at its centre. The illusion of motion is in consciousness only."

I appreciated his mystic words tremendously. He seemed a strange sort of guide, such a force to be reckoned with! And I was very, very scared of the power I felt emanating from his presence. Although he gave me no reason for fear, being awestruck made me highly uncomfortable. I was happy I wasn't so frightened of my own guide. One could argue that the feeling was only subjective and that others would find Sanat Kumara and his power absolutely terrifying. Nonetheless, I was thankful for my particular pairing.

The yogi's tone gave me no opening for a response, but I did feel he was watching developments closely. He was apparently only visible to me. I then asked him for his name, but he kept flashing to me images of the cartoon character Yogi Bear. It made no sense. Later, I came across his photograph on the internet and that's how I learned his real name, Paramahansa Yogananda, and discovered that he, in 1920, went to the United States as an emissary of his monastic order in India, introducing many Westerners to yogic philosophy and practice of meditation through his classic book *Autobiography of a Yogi*.

Uncle Orbit later told me that early in life Yogananda had been a presence, although the guru had died when my uncle was less than a year old. When my grandfather and he were walking in a street of the town where they lived, passing a bookshop window display, he was immediately drawn to the portrait of the long-haired man with soulful eyes, the author of that book. My uncle had been only just tall enough to peer over the low window sill.

As a young man in art school, Uncle Orbit was encouraged to read that book at last by a fellow student who had grown up in England, then travelled to India in search of Meher Baba, another well-known spiritual teacher, as well as to visit Sri Aurobindo's ashram. Soon my uncle had a dream in which he was back in high school, in the basement of the gymnasium, lifting weights. He only realized that the dream was in black and white when the doors swung open. There stood saffron-robed Yogananda in living colour, beckoning my uncle to follow him outdoors. Together they flew high into the starry sky above the circle of the Earth, then dived deep into the sparkling sea, which strangely did not impede their flight. Maybe that's when Uncle Orbit first acquired his love of flying.

9.

The Cycle *of* Reincarnation

MY GUIDE WAS waiting for me when I phased back into the astral plane. But how I arrived back there was another story. No sooner had I the desire to see him than did he appear. I seemed to blaze at the speed of light through a large wormhole-type structure. It felt like riding the fastest roller coaster in the cosmos, seeing so much race by much faster than the eye could catch, which created a beautiful streaking rainbow effect. I felt I had seen enough of Earth, but I still had a lot of questions for him. It seemed with every question I was given an answer to, ten more arose in its place. I still didn't know who or what he was. I even wondered whether he was a manifestation of the universe in the form of an answering device, a special interface just for me. I just wanted to know the truth.

It is important to point out that in the out-of-body state truth cannot be concealed, although it remains hidden in plain sight until it is perceived. Insights and answers to questions have a certain obvious quality that resonates immediately within, once explained. One can also see visible changes in the being that is responding. Sometimes this expresses itself in arrays of varied colours fluctuating in different regions of their body, primarily the solar plexus, but also radiating from the eyes and crown of the head.

There also were lines of light that from time to time emanating from my guide. Sometimes they would connect to me or lightly touch me, transmitting much information. These "cords of the universe" were not limited to only my guide and me. I began to see them everywhere. It was a great way to learn the truthful answer to anything directly because words were completely subtracted from the equation.

Once reunited with Sanat, I began to ask a lot of questions. Finally things started to make complete sense. Some of the questions I asked seem kind of superfluous now. He didn't directly respond every time, but would only stare at me as if to say, "You already know the answer."

I asked about the meaning of life and was shown a rapid-fire, endless stream of visual images. It seemed like the output of an enormous database I was temporarily granted access to, revealing many universal laws my human self had seemingly forgotten. This was greatly refreshing. I tried to absorb it all as it highlighted countless interactions between people – both happy and sad – showing the full spectrum of emotions and every kind of interaction.

It showed the harmony of nature, how it will always seek healing, wholeness, to balance itself if disrupted. I was also shown the evolution of human relationships, nature's relationship with humans and nature's unfailing adherence to the rule of cosmic law, how these relationships relate to the universe as a whole and higher cosmic laws. I cannot do justice in words to the impeccable logic, reason and common sense of this harmony, especially in the minute detail they were displayed.

Bringing that same level of detail back with me into the three-dimensional plane, however, has proved challenging, going from having been shown the answer to everything, knowing complete fulfillment and understanding, then slowly day by day feeling the answer become more obscured as it dissipates in daily life. It has been an effort to exercise my brain like a muscle to continually build upon my knowledge of the laws of the universe so that they do not fade away altogether.

I had to admit, my guide truly was a master teacher. Instead of telling me his opinion or simply stating the way it is, he took a far different approach and uploaded thousands of experiences, visuals and intuitions into me, allowing me to form my own opinion. I arrived at few intellectual answers to my questions, only a deep feeling beyond the power of words to articulate.

I asked about reincarnation, how many lives we get, how it all works. I was very curious, as I had never studied the topic and held no set beliefs about it, nor of my views of God. My entire life had been a contemplation of the meaning of life, but no specific religion ever seemed like the one. To me, all were limiting. I opted to view myself as spiritual as opposed to religious because I believed any religion that condemned another one in any way was clearly not the path. So I adopted all of them, taking little bits from each, including the idea of reincarnation. God, however, had remained an illusive figure, obscured by some unknown quality that I had not yet understood, although I wanted to. I just hadn't had any personal experience of "God" yet, so there wasn't really much I could say on the subject. I held every option open on all those questions until my personal experience could provide the answers. I trusted they would come.

I again was not given a direct answer to my question about reincarnation. Instead, I was shown what can only be described as an endless list of souls awaiting the opportunity for Earthly existence that was so long it wrapped around the Earth several times and trailed off out into space as far as my eyes could follow. It was as if planet Earth was the most exclusive club ever. The beings waiting to take form on the Earth held it in extremely positive and warm regard. As they waited, I sensed no jaded or hardened feelings, unlike so many of us after a few dozen years here. There was no lethargy or animosity, just the sheer exuberance of strong desire to tackle each and every one of their goals for their upcoming lifetime head-on.

I learned the Earth plane is also the most challenging battleground, to use another metaphor, because its limitations are so strict. Outside of those limitations, in the out-of-body state, creativity is effortless. There is no resistance, hence no frustration. You are able to easily manifest exactly what you want and quickly because creation is as instantaneous as thought.

We have been given something very rare, participation in Earthly experience, and, moreover, *free will*. This is not to say that when you're in your fully connected state you do not have choice, only that we have the ability to violate universal laws, the freedom to use our will constructively or destructively during the more limited reincarnation cycle. That is not always the case in the infinity of worlds manifesting in the universe at any given time. In fact it's extremely rare, which is why there is such a line-up to take birth in the demanding Earthly environment. In other words, Earth is one of the most, if not the most, difficult condensed sensory learning system there is in this universe, at least at this time.

The challenges that free will poses are enormous. The level of difficulty of the game has become so high there is a very great risk that we could all fall completely asleep and remain that way. As inferred, each of our souls voluntarily signed up for the experience. I have since learned that the vast majority of the population evolved on Earth, their original home. This was a crazy notion to me, as I had assumed we all were born of seeds from distant star systems and somehow got stuck in this collective game or dream together. The people of Earth, meaning the people that have always been from here, are called the I AM race. This is not to be confused with the "I AM," the Creator of all. The I AM race lived in blissful perfection for a great many millennia, but at some point decided that became a little too dull. They decided collectively to try a very challenging experiment together: to cut the cords to their divinity, then see if they would be able to reconnect to everything that they are.

Could they remember who they really are? Would they be able to figure out there are universal laws that operate everything? Would they be able to figure out they're not alone, that the universe is brimming with life, once they had lost the ability to see and know all like they had always been accustomed to? If given the choice to do right or wrong, what would they choose, especially if they believed that no one was watching? Could they find a way reconnect to their true selves or would the true powers that are their birthright lie dormant forever? Like a long-lost dream in which you feel you can fly, but upon "waking" you dismiss the memory, choosing to reinforce the comfortable view of the world as you know it, you forget that you have participated in creating something wonderful with your own consciousness.

There is the well-known question: Could God create a boulder so heavy he could not lift it? The creation of this game also satisfied an interesting question from the perspective of the Creator: Could God create an experiment so challenging and unpredictable that even he couldn't predict the outcome?

Remember, the whole premise of this experience was to answer the question of what would it be like to live in a world without the Divine. Together, using our divine mind and its powers, we created a godless world. As evidence of our success, today there are very few traces of divinity anywhere. An atheist should congratulate themselves on the divine ability to create an illusion so strong it could fool even themselves. Mainstream science sees the universe as essentially random, the result of a set of arbitrary physical laws that form the galaxies, stars and planets, as well as the accidental creation of life which somehow reproduces its amazing variety of complex forms. These processes appear to be mechanistic and self-sustaining. Imagine a world that started out totally differently, in which acts of spontaneous materialization, divine creation, instant knowing and expanded states of consciousness were the norm. It would actually be very difficult to create a world that appeared to be nothing but a machine operating haphazardly, that is, devoid of all those things. It took divine intelligence to even conceive of a world that can appear so random. Regardless, there are still glitches and clues if you look for them. Human reproduction might appear mechanical because the infusion of the spark of life in a newborn is hidden away so cleverly as to be nearly invisible. Yet with all of humanity's technological advances humans are nowhere near being able to create a human being from scratch. Even cloning would need pre-existing eggs that contain all the necessary instructions in the form of DNA.

Being human is not a natural state for any of us. This is part of the reason why many humans experience discomfort much of the time, something we have created solely for this human experience alone. No soul is created as human. The human form is temporary in nature. It lives, it dies, it succumbs to illness. It is the avatar body, to borrow a term from gaming, created to allow us to interpret this experience. Our true origin is eternal. That is our true nature. Looking around past the small sandbox that is our planet, we can see that all the cosmos is created in divine perfection, with not a star out of place and with enough energy to sustain its light forever. Our light is one and the same.

We are created as beings of light within the Great Central Sun. Through natural mechanisms dictated by the higher powers, a planet is chosen for us to live on with our soul family. That planet becomes our native planet. Our soul has a structure that matches that of our soul family, who also simultaneously must broadcast an invitation for our incarnation to occur. The desire of the Divine is partnered with the desire of the family. After we finish our great work here on Earth, we will all drop these uncomfortable bodies and be our true selves, free of the heavy physical form.

The longing for freedom makes many of us manifest terrible diseases. Quite frankly, we don't really know how to take advantage of these bodies we've been given and end up storing much toxicity, which leads to the rapid decay of our material form.

The majority of life is spent making sure your body is okay, that it is fed, has shelter and clothing to protect it from the elements. We don't even really understand our bodies, yet we are born with a strong desire to reproduce and create new bodies for strangers who don't even know they want one yet! This survival imprint is something that was placed in us to ensure our own game would continue. But we are so much more than the need to survive.

With great risks come great rewards. Because of the great challenges facing all of humanity, we each stand to gain an incredible degree of soul attainment once we have learned all the lessons there are to learn in the Earth school.

Cutting our cord to divinity and starting the reincarnation process makes possible a wide range of sensory experiences that were not available to us before. Some of us are drawn to the tactile: the taste of food, the aromas and fragrances. Food was never such a necessity as it is for us now. Originally, energy from Source fuelled all our cognition, drive and momentum. I have had the opportunity to experience this first-hand. Some of us are strongly drawn to the challenge of being stripped of all our powers and knowledge, then the chase of acquiring them again, thus creating in fact a giant game of hide-and-seek with our Higher Selves. Coming to this understanding was such a personal relief because my deep depression before my out-of-body experience (OBE) was created by my assumption that there might be nothing more to life than a brief string of meaningless experiences and suffering.

However, we've been in this game a lot longer than we think we have, a flaw perhaps attributed to the rebirthing cycle, causing us to fall asleep all over again each time. In actuality, we have long surpassed the allotted time to solve our collective problems, and granted many deadline extensions to save ourselves and our planet. This is not an experience that will be allowed to continue indefinitely. We are required to show a certain collective progress. For example, we are not permitted to destroy a planet that has been given to us. The results of such careless destruction would create far-reaching cataclysmic events, not only for our own planet but throughout our solar system and the universe, potentially creating a black hole in one probability. Thus the ascended host is given permission to intervene if we are seen to get too close to our own annihilation. New end dates have been instated, along with backup plan after backup plan to ensure we all safely wake up from the never-ending twilight zone that seems like the only reality.

I was shown that some souls perhaps were a little overly optimistic about how long it would take to become whole again. Many more incarnations were needed than initially planned. They had underestimated many factors when drawing up plans in the higher realms. It is hard to imagine that your God Presence, or the Divinity, could be capable of making mistakes, but free-will systems are by definition unpredictable even to God. It too is learning through these experiences with you and gaining greater intelligence as a result. Mastering life is so challenging, with doubts continually cropping up. We are tempted to give up in futility. Every day as soon as we step out of the door we are bombarded with the beliefs systems, or lack thereof, of everyone around us. Progress is not guaranteed, even for the most determined. Everything on the Earth plane seems so convincing in appearance, so permanent. Most of us cannot easily see how insignificant nearly all our problems are and how no harm can ever come to our essential being.

All difficulties aside, the cycle of reincarnation is potentially most rewarding. Over lifetimes we advance towards the light, towards truth, as veils are lifted. As our karma gets resolved and we begin to let go of our attachments and all unfulfilled desires, we are no longer bound to this plane, we are no longer blocked from promotion and finding True Love, as in the Divine's version of Love, not the greatly diluted quality that we more commonly refer to as love.

As Robert Monroe, a great pioneer of OBEs, was shown and wrote about in his books, very few of us have ever experienced Divine Love, even though we may think we have. This is also part of the reason why healing for the planet has had trouble gaining momentum. In the process of cutting our cords, we consciously also severed our ties to Divine Power, Divine Mind and Divine Love. As it turns out, Divine Love is far more difficult to live without, nor is it easy to reconnect to. Many of us did not foresee this loss of the Mother's Love impacting us so greatly and have spent lifetimes trying to find that source of Love in others, often coming up with greatly unsatisfying experiences and wondering why, constantly seeking that same level of unconditional acceptance that only the Divine can provide.

As each of the experiences in which we sought love are healed, we heal deep emotional wounds incurred during lifetimes in search of the Divine connection we are missing: Love, Abundance, Power and Manifestation. As we realize we have been given the capabilities to assimilate and integrate all of our lessons, the level of healing we experience allows our connection to the Divine to be restored and for us to reach the last Earthly life. In this we are given the greatest opportunity to help humanity, to set an example.

It is at this end point on the path to wholeness and maturity that the individual has the realization that life is truly about how they can be of service to others. It is no longer about the accumulation of objects or seeking relationships that are really designed to deliver lessons. There is a knowing that arises from within, that one is but a small part of the whole. In that connectedness to help the "other" is ultimately the greatest way to be of service to the self.

Many before, particularly theosophists, have called this process the great "ascension." Through hard work and diligence, we earn the capacity to merge with our higher self. Long study is required, although beings like Ramtha are said to have completed the feat in one lifetime with no guide. Even so, he was a humble student of the greatest teacher, his higher self. History books are filled with references to the ascended masters, such as Enoch, the Buddha, Quan Yin, Saint Germain (also known as Merlin, Lao Tzu and Shakespeare), Maitreya, Milarepa and many more. The most famous of all was Jesus Christ.

Jesus accomplished something much more difficult.

To complete the ascension means you will have learned every core lesson, mastering your life in this plane through experience, and are very close to being fully healed, so close that another incarnation would be unnecessary.

After all, there is that long line-up. Incarnations are valuable and in great demand. Since there is a limited number of births, there is also a limited number of souls that can incarnate at any given time.

To ascend, you must pay off all your karmic debt by means of in-person remuneration or more advanced methods, such as invoking the Sacred Fire, an alchemical transformative process by which the powers and energies of higher-dimensional flames can markedly transform a person. Tears of gratitude is also another method with which one can burn their karmic debt off and sometimes even release the individual from a debt. To still have a balance of negative karma means you have incurred a debt. While our free will allows us to seemingly violate cosmic law unchecked during our stay, settling that debt is a requirement during your last life. You have corrected your manifestation process and are easily able to *get your life in order*. This level of mastery also means you are not provoked by the actions of others, because you are able to see situations for what they are, showing nothing but mercy and compassion for others.

Lastly, you have to have awakened to the fact that your human personality is only a small fraction of your larger self – your soul. This knowledge provides the opportunity and permission to become one with it. Completing the ascension enables one to drop the body, allowing the help of ascended master realms in the fifth and sixth dimensions.

The ordinary five-sensory, three-dimensional realm is what we have grown accustomed to as our reality. It is of much greater density than the higher realms, as it is bound by linear time. Structures that exist in the three-dimensional realm and lower have increasingly simple forms and lower vibrational rates. Likewise, the higher the dimension the more complex the structures because of the increase in vibrational rate of energy. The lower the vibrational state the longer manifestation takes. In higher dimensions than ours, consciousness is more freely expanded, more advanced. Instantaneous manifestation is possible without the impedance of a dense physical body, as it is replaced by a faster, lighter, more harmonious one that responds easily to conscious command.

The three-dimensional realm is largely unpopulated due to the comparatively low vibrational frequencies.

An ascended master is a being who has graduated from the human form because he or she has achieved total mastery of thoughts, emotions and feelings in the Earthly plane. It is not because he or she is *your* master and you are the slave or that they think they are *superior* to you in any way. On the contrary, they are completely humble and view every soul as powerful and as beautiful as the next. They have become whole. Having fully restored their connection to Divine Love, they see you as you really are: pure, whole, complete and unlimited, just like them, although you may not know it yet.

It is the act of removing everything that is not the True Self that allows for one to see what has already been there all along: your pure, divine nature and your inherent connectedness to everything that is.

Ascended masters work alongside the angels in angelic and other realms. They are particularly capable of astounding feats of power. However, they are only able to demonstrate these powers with the Divine's permission. The Divine does not interfere in our self-created simulation, which is why there is usually no clearly visible sign of them in our daily lives. Yet people who are awake enough and believe in higher realms are granted the ability to see, feel and have experiences with these divine beings directly and are given support when they request it.

One has to *believe* before one is allowed to see. That is just the way it is set up. These beings are not allowed to interfere in our lives without our belief systems in place first. For an angelic being to appear to a non-believer would be a violation of the laws that govern each person's awakening. The ability to see them may also be connected to attainment from past lives, especially when one is approaching the last earthly life. Achievements in past incarnations carry forward, allowing a person to come into existence with seemingly unmerited "gifts." In other words, these higher-dimensional beings exist all around us, independent of our conscious beliefs in them, but our faith in them gives them the permission necessary to help.

Since they vibrate at a much higher frequency than we do, we are not able to detect them with our physical eyes, as we are able to only interpret a narrow range of the entire spectrum of light. Remember the description of how you are like a large sphere trying to pull things in through that tiny straw! Most of the data around you is filtered out.

Jesus chose to stay long past his ascension to integrate his higher self into the game without discarding his body. That act was far more difficult than dropping the body and serving from higher realms, but of far greater service. It demonstrated to humanity what we really are and what is possible for us all. Jesus in his original teachings taught his followers how to become like him, to complete the "resurrection" and become a living god. Yet, over the millennia ignorance would corrupt his teachings and distort their true meaning, removing nearly all references to the fact that we are essentially gods in disguise.

It was many centuries before the Bible became widely accepted. Yet due to the inferior motives of men, this edition included the concept of a God that should be feared, with all references to reincarnation removed, as well as the fact that you have a God Self and your own God Potential. This made it appear that becoming a living god was only worthy of Jesus alone, yet at the heart of his teachings is the idea that the same potential is available to us all.

The Sinister Force working through the editors of the Judeo-Christian books of that period, as they removed all mention of that, made Jesus' demonstration a strange anomaly. Their censorship is also the reason for so many contradictions in the Bible about how we are supposed to live our life, causing much confusion and debate. For example, it condemns divination, but also shows examples of great ones like Moses and others having done exactly that.

The Sinister Force is the collection of all the dark thought forms and emotions that have ever been created by us, since the beginning of time. Essentially, this force is all our collective imperfections. When a manifestation is created, a person unknowingly sends that energy out into the universe, where that energy resonates with compatible frequencies. This collective group of imperfect manifestation has essentially gone out, made comrades and come back to the source of its creation to teach us a lesson. Whether the result is positive or negative, the infallible laws do not discriminate. This force has existed for so long and has gained so much momentum it is increasing our slavery. Among dark human thought forms is the fear of death. Since the Sinister Force is the accumulation of human negative emotions, it also fears its annihilation, thus instinctively protects itself by working through people who consciously or unconsciously ally themselves with it. Some small part of them has to be willing, otherwise it would be a violation of free will. However, that part could be so small that consciously they might not realize the interference they invite.

Enter the powers that be, or what some have named the Illuminati, the finest example of the Sinister Force on Earth today. Whatever they are called makes little difference. The fact remains that there are cool, calculating criminals who have gained financial control over the world using unlawful means. This increased level of control started around the time of World War I when they profited from the manufacture of armaments, supplying both sides of the conflict. They set up the private institution which is now the

Federal Reserve in the United States, and in other countries, placing them in control of international monetary systems. More recently, Vladimir Putin took back control of the privatized banking system by force of arms. That stranglehold seems no longer as prevalent in Russia. This was not mainstream news but is easily accessible through alternative news networks. These are only two examples, but there have been scores of others, establishing the little known most wealthy and powerful seven families on the planet. Being out of the public eye and influencing the passing of laws behind the scenes is designed to protect their fortune, ensuring the masses will never approach their level of financial and political freedom. After all, how could the dark powers control the world if it were populated with honest, open and transparent divinely connected beings like Jesus?

All manifestations start with something as simple as a thought, whether it's a constructive thought or a destructive one. For example, the world's most advanced supercomputer started out as a concept in someone's mind. Anything focused on with intention long enough will become something in the material plane eventually. A second example: spiders and other insects that are not of the light, meaning they are not purposely created by the Divine and have not been on the planet that long compared to the majority of animals. We recoil at the site of them because instinctually some part of us understands they are a collective manifestation of our dark thoughts and nothing more. We can determine how much light is in these creatures by the specific responses they illicit and by examining their purpose in our ecosystem. A bumble bee has a lot of divine light and serves an important divine purpose in aiding food production. Next, consider mosquitoes – which serve no divine purpose. They spread disease and their blood-sucking stings are so irritating they can ruin outdoor fun. There is very little light in them at all. The only animals that feed on them typically only have slightly more light in them, as a being with a high vibration would instinctively understand that these are the equivalent of junk food. Spiders, a more dense creation, also primarily consist of darkness. One could well argue they are needed to consume other insect pests. In fact that is a very valid argument and supports my point, as it is typical of the darkness to turn on itself.

There is an iota of light in them, however. There has to be for a creature to exist, but they are not created as nature intended. In time the cycles of our dark thinking, with any luck, will correct themselves and our environment along with them.

Unlike these creatures, humans are meant to be and are naturally psychic. We have all had glimpses. A friend calls when you were just thinking about them. Or someone says something to you and you feel they have "read your mind." When in our natural state, that connection is vital, for eternal existence tells us everything we need to know in advance. That said, there are very few souls that walk this Earth who have chosen resurrection as a part of their plan, primarily because of the vast amount of hard work and skill that is required. The simple truth is the resurrection is such a great undertaking that has not occurred in so long that most souls choose the path of ascension instead. While resurrection is not a prerequisite to leave the game, the rules governing our experiment are clear: everyone living on Earth must ascend in order for the simulation to complete, each part returning to the Whole. The experiment cannot complete if someone is left behind, hence those who have already ascended will stay and continue to help from the other side until the last person is free. We will then have earned our right to rest and recover, pursue other interests and begin to plan the next great adventure.

It may be more accurate to say that all of Creation is waiting for each soul to achieve its ascension, the point at which we become reunited with our eternal being. Creation is within each of us, only appearing to be an outward manifestation reflected in our surroundings through the magical power of the unconscious mind. Buddhism refers to the external as the phenomenal world, that which appears and disappears like a phantom. Remember, the desire for this experiment arose from the idea of separation – duality – and the desire to experience light and dark, good and bad, happy and sad, etc.

The universe also works in cycles and loves completion, allowing us to evolve and start new soul journeys to even better worlds. The more attainment a soul has, the more choice it has in what it enlists in. It is like a very well-qualified job applicant who has the requisite education and experience.

The universe, however, does not tolerate stagnation. Things are either moving in the direction of advancement and healing or in the direction of incurring negative karma, resulting in additional lessons, i.e. regression, devolution.

In between incarnations, souls are given a break and taken up into the Planes of Bliss, where they are able to process their experiences, gain greater perspectives on their life lessons and whether their course went well – or not. The movie *Astral City: A Spiritual Journey,* based on the book of the same name channelled by the beloved Brazilian medium Chico Xavier, is the most accurate rendition of the process of reincarnation that I have seen portrayed in film. It illustrates the advanced ethereal city that is Shambhala and shows how divinely guided Chico was to portray it in detail.

I believe that Robert Monroe had been shown a similar place, which he called The Park, where he continued to be of service and even trained others to reach while in the out-of-body state. In the Planes of Bliss, a soul is able to relive all the experience of their previous lifetime, but in the way they wished it had happened, providing a sense of closure to the soul and effectively cleansing the emotional body as much as possible before the next incarnation. This service is in place to give each of us the best chance possible to actualize our plans in the next life, carrying forward the least amount of emotional baggage, yet this isn't always the case.

Once a soul has completed a life, they take up the task of planning their next one, assuming the soul has a substantial connection to the Divine. Many souls have little input in deciding their next life, because their lack of belief prevents that bond from forming. How can you work in harmony with your higher self to design your life if you are in denial of its very existence?

For the connected one, this planning is carried out primarily by the larger extension of ourselves, the Great God Presence within the Great Central Sun, a large star that is the main processing centre. Essentially your level of understanding and connectedness determines the process. Many beings reside there. It is the main focal point, the hub of the workings of the universe. For very advanced beings, the planning is extremely meticulous and takes a great deal of time. Precise details ensure that their soul has the chance to meet all the people they are supposed to, creating windows of opportunity for lessons that will allow for specific realizations to arise. This may include choosing where you are born, what career path to pursue, selecting children or spouses, if any, or planning an illness that may serve as a useful tool to advance your learning.

Most souls, however, do not seem to have that level of control. This trait is also reflected while in embodiment, neither knowing why they are here nor caring. Their incarnations are largely unplanned, due to their disconnected state. They have little or no inkling of who they really are, accepting all of life at face value, although there may be a far-distant memory of some very important mission that got drowned out by aeons of mental noise and the tendency to drift back to sleep. Millennia in the sleep state (which some would argue is waking life), in fact millions of years, has resulted in a thick layer of psychic dust and grime that conceals their natural gifts and innate knowingness, blocking any connection to their greater self.

The seventh Golden Age we are living in is not permitted to fail, as far too much time has passed for what was supposed to be a short experience. Most of the previous Golden Ages have been near-total resets of the Earth simulation, hence very little evidence of them or the structures they created remains. A clean slate was needed to try again. In most cases any archaeological findings from those times were intentionally buried for later generations to discover. This occurred when it was seen there was no possible chance of us completing our plan.

That is to say the Earth is like a stopping point on a journey, an educational training ground, a learning lab. There is one version of Gaia, the name of the Earth personified as a goddess in Greek mythology, in which she is as pristine as the day she was created, before she had been touched by humans and the destructive imbalances in climate that have ensued. This is the planet's authentic state of being. However, our reality exists as well, the version of Earth that is projected like a hologram onto the planet through the lens of the universe to facilitate our learning and growth. In fact some have even stated to have seen other simulations in higher dimensions on Earth, inferring that a different hologram coexists in every dimension. We are not the only peas in the pod.

One could say that the process of incarnation was developed so that we could play the human game. There had to be bodies created and a reincarnation cycle, as our eternal bodies do not exist in the three-dimensional plane. Death was also an important factor because if we lived forever it would be too similar to our natural state. That would not aid the type of learning we were seeking.

Many souls have acquired a great many attachments and entanglements while playing the game. But what fun is the ride if you can't sample all the experience has to offer? The difficulty arises when the person becomes attached to what it sees as external to the self. The concept of family is one example. We are born into a family. That seems like the reason why we are here. In part this is true. Yet suffering arises when people cling to one another. When a loved one passes it can cause a traumatic chain of events powerful enough to derail the plan for one's life.

What many fail to recognize is that their true family, their divine family, misses them tremendously. Often we only include the newly introduced souls around us as relatives, who may have been selected for us by our karma if we did not have a hand in our own selection. If our family originated on Earth, like most have, then they are likely also asleep, with no remembrance of their divine connection to us. More advanced beings do reincarnate with a soul family repeatedly, but seldom is that actually one's true divine family. A soul family is like a very good friend you have often travelled with. There is a strong familiarity. Nevertheless, it is very comforting to have a familiar face nearby, especially in an experience as challenging as incarnation on the Earth plane, even if they are not of the divine family you were born to. Just like life on earth in general, soul family is what you make it.

Faith in a benign universe is lost and the deeper meaning of life is hidden for those still in slumber. Seemingly awake, but lacking the drive to accomplish anything worthwhile, let alone ambitious, they have exchanged insight for so-called security, choosing the first occupation anyone suggests they take when the thought of gainful employment arises.

In this situation, the being's God Presence is pushed so far back due to lack of awareness that it retreats into the Great Central Sun, giving the individual, or the individualized God Presence, just enough energy to animate their physical garment. The person is left walking alone through life with no guidance, because they have willingly shut themselves off from it, essentially suppressing intuition. Despite the thick haze of ignorance, it is up to them to try to advance, often through encounters with more advanced souls who can help facilitate a shift in the trajectory of their life.

After their lifetime has come to its natural end, they again return to the Planes of Bliss to process their lifetime, and are more or less randomly placed in the next body that becomes available, with no careful selection of family and circumstances. Karma, an impersonal force, will greatly influence all elements a person enters into in the subsequent life, even when the higher self is apparently not present.

The irony was that, while in the OOB state, I could see that the majority of souls on Earth cursed their existence as a burden in spite of the precious opportunity they'd been granted, while so many others lined up behind them hoping for a vacancy. They didn't see life as the strange, bizarre, impossibly wonderful manifestation that it is.

The souls waiting for their chance to be born were as if shaking their heads in wonder at the lack of initiative on the part of the humans unaware of their good fortune and lack of desire to evolve towards enlightenment. From this perspective, it seemed as if the vast majority just spent their lives mechanically, breeding and dying like mayflies, never considering that their world was a gigantic playground to experience.

Yet there are no rules, or so it seems. The whole simulation is a freely willed system. This allows individuals tremendous power and the option to choose anything they want, even to waste the incarnation they have been given if they so choose.

Yes, our system is based on free will, but that is not to say it is devoid of order and the balancing forces of universal laws. If a person steals, karma will result as a balancing measure, but the process is slow, complex and seemingly invisible, making it difficult to understand. For example, someone could earn a tremendous amount of money at the expense of the health of a group of people or even a nation. Free will allows that option, yet no one can escape the laws of balance. I saw some become exceedingly angry and frustrated at the world during their incarnations as they repeatedly chose to harm, then time and time again pay the price but curse the world for being so cruel, thus failing to understand the law of cause and effect. One could argue it would be a lot better if we lived in an environment that obeyed instant karma. But that in fact is precisely what we got tired of living in long ago, during our time in perfection.

This long delay in repercussions has its advantages, the potential for soul attainment due to the difficult nature of navigating a free-will system being one. I was also shown that the beauty of this is that there's no limit to how far a soul could advance in any particular lifetime. All the same, it was possible to just tread water too, not moving ahead for aeons.

From this divine perspective, I could see individual trajectories displayed graphically, like waveforms which could be charted to reveal a wide variety of contrasting features, all related to personal development either towards merging with their higher self or *retreating* from it. The sight was similar to a very advanced, three-dimensional mapping system controlled by my consciousness, yet it had a tangible external structure, a flat translucent screen that could stretch or condense based on what I wanted it to display. I simply needed to think of the quality I was tuning in to, such as finances and financial lessons, and a wide range of data would appear.

I could see all the intersecting windows of opportunity in a person's life for financial growth. I could see all of the people who were carefully selected as candidates they would meet along the way, who would help trigger their deep pains and outgrown behaviour patterns needlessly carried forward again and again into each life. It brings a new definition to "the skeletons in the closet," dragged along from house to house.

There were many "windows" and "doors" displayed in each graph. If a person was able to walk through one successfully, passing their lesson, then I could see the wonderful set of new paths waiting for them on the other side. If they failed to take the opportunity, then the same set of lessons would repeat with increasing tension until the cycle had successfully been transcended.

These graphs had a tactile, sensory quality that was so immersive I could extract far greater information as well. I could feel the mood and the tone of each of the "spiritual intersections" on each graph, along with the desired "realization" of what was *supposed* to happen. It was such an engaging experience that I could have become lost in time just playing with that one device alone, as I longed for a far greater understanding of how the universe works.

10.

Questions *and* Answers

"WHAT HAPPENS WHEN humans die?" I asked. "Where do they go?"

"After the body is dropped, there are several different levels that can be reached. It's possible to get caught in the trap of wandering aimlessly without finding the way back into the human world or to progress beyond it, just waiting for something to happen. Are you thinking of someone in particular? You can see for yourself if you like," my guide suggested.

In fact several people I'd known had died, some quite recently. I turned around and, through a mist, saw my friend Anthony, who had hanged himself. He was a very close friend while we were growing up, part of a large group of childhood friends. He had left a huge impression on me. We always had classes together, shared a similar sense of humour and had gone camping more times than I could count. He was dearly missed. His passing had been hard, as outwardly he had always put on such a happy face, making others smile too. We had drifted apart in recent years, but I was incredibly shocked when I learned he'd taken his own life. I thought that to do something so extreme he must have had a very powerful reason. He seemed very surprised to see someone he recognized.

"Sarazen – are you dead too?" he asked, amazed.

"No, just visiting." I went straight to the point: "Anthony, why did you take your own life?"

As he lightly touched my arm, I was shown, and felt, all the events that had led to his final moments on Earth. Caught up in a lot of trouble near the end of his life, he had concluded there was just no other way to escape all the problems that had ensnared him. Selfishly, he hadn't foreseen the magnitude of pain his final act would inflict on others. I felt the regret that arose as he died, after the realization that it was too late to change his course.

We sat together for some time. Then I said, "You know, Anthony, you really, really need to let go."

It was obvious that he was guilt-ridden, consumed by the grief he'd put his family and friends through, tormented by the futility of attempting to influence them to feel better from this far-distant realm, unable to communicate. I think our talk must have helped him because when I returned at a later time, he was no longer waiting in that purgatory-like space.

While I had been visiting with him in what looked like blackness, a plane devoid of any background, I wondered if I was in some type of lower realm. I was unable to see their environment as they saw it. They seemed to be interacting with scenes invisible to me.

I turned and saw another man, Stu, a close friend of the family and like an uncle to me, who had lost his battle with cancer. Unlike Anthony, he didn't seem surprised to see me. Like Anthony, he was sad. I again was privileged to see all the events leading up to his last day. Stu had been fighting cancer for years, slowly and painfully. Towards the end he had gone into remission, but eventually succumbed. It was difficult to see such a tall, robust person, who seemed strong as an ox, fall. When I was younger, I looked up to him and assumed he must be invincible because of his firm handshakes and hugs.

I saw that he had left his body during the first time he had been hospitalized, but it led him to believe he was losing his mind. While he was alive, my impression was that he was not interested in spirituality as I understood it. He had concrete beliefs that he lived by, and seemed quite okay with them. That belief system was in direct conflict with the notion of being out-of-body. It seemed he had no way to cope with it. Afraid to appear foolish, he spoke to no one of his strange experience, instead trying to find solace in denial. Then I was shown a remission had come about shortly after being discharged as a result of finding ways of living more harmoniously.

When the cancer returned, doubt returned too, tenfold. Stu no longer believed he could really be healthy again. He focused on the pain, and the universe complied with the signal he was broadcasting. Stu was burdened as well by guilt. Even in the post-death state he tried to remain close to his still-living wife, hovering over her because he knew he had left her with many burdens. He punished himself needlessly for his acts and suffered far beyond what could be considered conducive to learning. In short, remorse prevented him from moving on.

Anthony's and Stu's situations were the same. Both were stuck trying to process the tremendous amount of pain they had caused, which in turn prevented further development. I tuned in and offered a similar message with the intention of helping Stu move on. But he seemed a bit more set in his ways than the young soul Anthony was. He seemed to take everything I said into consideration, but needed more introspection to validate things for himself.

While still in that zone, I saw a few other old friends who had not died as far as I knew. I concluded they must be high on drugs, possibly psyche-delics, because they seemed quite incoherent compared to the departed. Their responses were erratic, their presence not as "solid." They even looked translucent. Later I confirmed they were still numbered among the living. Astonishingly, however, they also remembered seeing me while they were under the influence and had the same question about me! That amazed me because they had appeared too groggy to remember anything from their time in the out-of-body state.

My next questions concerned diet. "What kinds of foods should my physical body be eating? What's beneficial and what's not?"

My guide responded, "Each person has a vast array of compatible foods. In your case, you can eat anything you feel like eating. In fact avoiding meat as you've done for the past year or so may not be such a good idea. As far as food goes, you're also allowed a vice. Pick one."

"That's a no-brainer. I choose caffeine! Coffee."

I loved coffee so much, although it had taken a while to grow on me. It was something I felt greatly lifted my mood and was such a wonderful accompaniment while painting in my studio.

His comment about eating meat confused me. I had just spent a year adapting to being a vegan and had met someone who was sharing with me their spiritual insights about that. I had always been what I referred to as a "conflicted carnivore" and when I did eat meat it was typically very little. I could not argue though. At this juncture my body seemed to be missing something. I was not feeling completely healthy and had actually gained unwanted weight, even though I was exercising and supplementing with protein. This was highly confusing, as there was much to learn about how to properly balance a vegan diet. I was trying to accomplish that on an all too limited budget, which was only making matters more challenging.

Immediately my mother and one of her best friends came to mind. My mother had always been the most supportive person in my life, the rock in my family. Nevertheless, I saw that she and her friend should never drink alcohol. No one would label them alcoholics, but I could see they both lived in social settings surrounded by people who really enjoyed wine. Yet alcohol was the detrimental factor clouding all aspects of their lives, more than either of them could understand.

I was also shown that their bodies needed a significant cleanse once a year at a minimum. I saw their eating patterns were irregular, portions were too large and they weren't getting enough exercise. In fact it was shocking to see how their whole lifestyle needed a revolution. When in their presence I had never seen the direct effect of their lifestyle choices, nor had I come to any of those conclusions. Seeing this information intrigued me and I wanted to understand more about the effects of food.

In the same way that each person has an aura with unique colours and patterns, each food has its own aura. Because each person's body chemistry is unique, each food thus has its unique interaction with it energetically. Just as a person can wear a perfume and their pheromones commingle with it, creating a unique fragrance, there are thousands upon thousands of similarly unique reactions going on within each of us every day. Each food also has psychoactive effects, although often they're overlooked because the effect of each is so small. In my case, pasta makes me sleepy but stimulants relax me, which is not the case for most people, although many other foods affect us in ways below the threshold of normal awareness. Nevertheless, they are potent modifiers of consciousness and have a greater interaction with our system than we realize.

I then wanted to know about other people, that is, who was beneficial for me to associate with and who was less so.

All I had to do was think of a particular friend and I could immediately feel the full range of their feelings about our friendship. That turned out to be both pleasant and unpleasant. I saw that some people did not have the best intentions towards me, although none were outright malicious – after all, these were my friends – but mostly they just weren't that genuine. We just didn't have the kind of relationship I had previously been under the impression we had. I resolved to put some distance between us. One of my friends stood out though: my long-time boyfriend Alexander.

I felt his love for me and it was the most amazing feeling, somewhat of a pleasant surprise because I didn't know if my feelings for him could even equal it. He had pulled away from me a long while before, and I had been trying to restimulate his love for me for some time. Our relationship had been on the rocks, and although we'd had a whirlwind romance for the first four years, we had recently gone through many tests. I wasn't sure that we were growing together. I hadn't, however, correctly gauged the depth of his love for me. It was a wonderful discovery.

✳

Next, I looked into my own past. It's said that when we die our whole life instantaneously flashes before our eyes, a replay of every event, every thought, in the most minute detail. Something similar happened to me then, a life review. I found some discrepancies between what my mother had told me about my early childhood and how it really was. She had given me the impression that I was the most angelic baby, so easy to care for, never a problem. Such was not always the case. I cried a lot, I yelled a lot, I was very frustrated much of the time. It must have been rather exhausting to look after me because I didn't sleep enough and demanded a lot of attention. I thought it was strange that the need was felt to portray things otherwise. I guess I'll never know for sure, but I don't think my life would have turned out differently if I'd been told the whole story. Conversely, if I was told how difficult I was as a baby, I may have grown up to be an even more difficult adult. In either case, perhaps she was guided to say differently. I felt my mother's intentions were good in her spin on the truth.

I turned to my guide: "Are you God? What about religion? Is there one that's more true than another? Is there a right one? There's just so much conflict in the world because of belief systems."

"As you say, they are just beliefs, about an imagined reality. Earthly life is itself an imagined reality."

Sanat's words rang a bell because I had already perceived that Earth exists only because of its inhabitants' beliefs, a strange thing indeed, but it was quite clear. The planet itself was real, in the sense that it could be experienced – it exists independently of our beliefs in it because it is something the Creator has imagined into existence. It was like a way station, a stopping point on a long journey, changing its features as the thoughts of its inhabitants changed. I assumed other planets might be similarly affected.

"It doesn't really matter which beliefs are chosen so long as they're uplifting, offer solace, encourage equality and are basically positive. It is possible to construe things in such a way that it twists perceptions and skews morality. Yet that is a very human way of thinking. There is no such thing as misfortune. There is only *what is.*"

Again, his words rang true. While I was out-of-body, not one being I encountered evoked pity as I looked into their souls. In that state, everything that manifested had the exact same weight, value or importance as every other manifestation, including what is most often interpreted as misfortune, a human judgement based on personal likes and dislikes. Ancient Eastern tradition calls this state "*samadhi.*" There is only *what is.*

Every person was of equal importance. I felt love and compassion for each equally. This was an important insight, the fact that equality in love did not mean indifference to some in favour of others. In life I had resonated with some and loved a lot of people, but definitely had not found kinship with all nor valued every relationship equally. Idealistically, I aimed to love everyone, but how that played out in daily life was not always perfect.

Looking down at the Earth, there was also a huge number of forms of consciousness other than human. I was not quite sure what they were and did not spend much time analyzing, but my impression was that they were foreign, not from Earth. They did not seem like they were an initial part of the plan we created so long ago, yet somehow had gained permission to interact with us and seemed adhered to the outer surface of the simulation in some way. There were large clusters of them that formed all over the globe, gathered in greater numbers in some locations more than others, sticking mostly to inhabited areas and less so over bodies of water or the uninhabited regions of each continent.

In contrast to the other realms I had seen, the Earthly realm was an extremely concentrated, complex situation with many facets. In the light of all my questions and newfound answers, most of my other queries about human life and its relation to its source faded away eventually because they no longer held much importance. Everything I once wanted to know so badly was now obvious and self-validating, permeated with a deep inner knowing.

11.

The Witness

ON THE OTHER hand, I had seen beings on other levels of existence whose roles I wanted to understand. The most pressing enquiry, however, was directed towards my guide as I resumed the interrogation: "Who *are* you?"

"I was sent here to be your guide," the blue being responded. "I volunteered for the position because I feel indebted to you. You helped re-establish something I needed, but you haven't been back in human form for a very long time. So now I have the opportunity to repay you. I have no obligation, it's just that I really like you and want to return the favour."

I didn't understand. It most certainly was not what I anticipated nor was it congruent with his other responses. I had so many questions, but every time he answered one, many more sprang up like dormant desert blossoms after a rain. Yet in the timeless space we were suspended in, I couldn't explain why I felt so pressed for time. Part of my soul understood the significance of the entire experience and knew it could come to an end at any moment the Divine chose, therefore every question had to be among the most important while the window of opportunity was still open.

I paused for a moment to consider how to proceed. He felt indebted to me? What could I have possibly done to earn the debt of such an amazing being? I rejoiced at that thought, as far-fetched as it was, and thanked my lucky stars for some unknown past deed that had earned this out-of-body experience. And what did he mean by saying I hadn't been "back in human form in a long time"? Did I take a break to help accomplish something for him? What constituted a long time by his standards? Since time was non-linear, and we could pause time up here, I believed he was not speaking of the human passage of time I was accustomed to. I circled back to the most pressing question, regarding the true nature of my guide.

"But you seem so all-powerful and all-knowing," I said.

"You're much more powerful than I am. You just haven't awakened to that fact yet."

Again his answer sidelined me. I was unprepared for it. "But you – are you – *God?*" I was still unable to absorb the magnitude of what he'd just said.

He laughed. "I guess you could look at it that way. I surely wouldn't be insulted!"

"Well, then – what is your – *job* in the universe? And do you have a personal assistant or what?"

"There are openings," he stated cryptically. "Listen, you are the Witness, that's *your* job."

Hearing that provoked disappointment. It sounded very familiar somehow. Something very faintly far off at the boundaries of awareness sparked with recognition. How did he keep turning the conversation back to me when I was really more fascinated to learn the truth about him?

My initial reaction was that it didn't sound that interesting. He continued to show me that Uncle Orbit was the Travelling Man. Now that sounded like something interesting, like someone on the way to a destination, a destiny. The "Witness" just sounded so uninvolved, like someone passively sitting on the sidelines observing passers-by. I wanted my role to be interactive and more dynamic. I didn't know what I had expected to be called, because I hadn't been anticipating being given a role at all. If I had been asked about it, perhaps I would have said the Visionary.

Seemingly changing the subject, Sanat Kumara began to show me other people I knew. Their colourful auras were plainly visible, but more than that, I could see far beyond their DNA into the energy signatures that defined their being. Each pattern was more unique than faces or fingerprints, and displayed a beauty created by the universe that was a genuine work of mathematical art, incredibly precise. I couldn't help but see and feel the power of whoever the Creator was at that moment and longed for a greater connection.

The dozens of "jobs," positions or roles I saw that the universe offers, really more like archetypes, were perhaps only a small slice of the total available. I was enchanted with the idea and wondered why I had never before come across any of that information in my quest to learn about spirituality. I had never heard any mention of specific roles we are assigned and graduate from after a series of embodiments, such as Time Traveller, for example, and got excited at truly brand-new information that I alone seemed privileged to receive. But then I felt slightly crestfallen. Even if it was new data, who would believe me? In my daily life I still felt very small.

Continuing, Sanat revealed that my boyfriend Alexander was the Builder, whose aura was red on the inside and yellow on the outside, complementing mine, which was blue on the inside and green on the outside. This was a different aura than I had earlier while travelling with Robert. I saw that

Alexander did not have to be in my life. We chose each other. He appeared as a very young soul with so much to accomplish, highly motivated and very driven. He was actually revealed to me as an infant, a baby, which was quite surprising because ever since I had known him I had put his advice on a pedestal, looking up to him for answers to life's hard questions. He had projected an air of authority. Perhaps I had given too much of my personal power away. His presence in my life was not for my benefit, but our being together was extremely helpful to him. My presence alone was enough to help him not take his plan so seriously. The Builder can become obsessed with his tasks and lose sight of what's really important.

Another example was my mother. In contrast to her slim appearance in human form, her soul appeared quite rotund, emanating a very jovial quality. Her soul's four-hundred-pound shape resembled that of the Happy Buddha – who is depicted as fat, a symbol of lacking nothing, and laughing – completely content, beautiful and silent. My mother was called Wise Woman. She had been in that role for a couple of lifetimes, but I saw that she had become complacent, hence her contented silence. She didn't seem to be aware that the bridge between that contentment and the universe was broken and needed mending. Her condition wasn't an especially bad thing, just stagnant.

Then I turned to see who was next and was extremely surprised. Taken aback, I almost didn't recognize that I was seeing myself. I was gigantic, but not in the sense of being jovially overweight. In fact I was exactly of my normal proportions, only five hundred times the size of my mother. This was my higher self. Before this moment I only ever had the faint awareness that she existed, but seeing her now before me brought tears to my eyes. She was the definition of beauty and perfection, at least to me. Perhaps my higher self was reflecting to me my best possible self. That perfect image revealed much longer, darker, wavier hair and a glowing complexion that seemed to sparkle just like Sanat's. At first, just her face was displayed, but I thought I could fit hundreds, if not thousands, of planets within her form. Then, as my awareness of her expanded, it revealed that she – I – was dressed all in white and radiated power, like Yogananda. Maybe Uncle Robert's guide and I did have something in common after all.

It was very to strange to see myself from the outside, able to interact with myself. It was also strange to see myself that powerful. The attraction I had to her was so strong that I had a hard time recognizing that I was already her. For a moment it was like two mirrors reflecting each other. I could see and interpret stimuli and information from both sides of the mirror: the all-powerful side, who was larger than life and so beautiful, an observer, and the everyday self, who had yet to step into her greatness. An intuition instantly arose. "Oh, now I get it. I'm formless – *I am the Witness.*"

"You can see, Sarazen, that being the Witness is not lesser than being the Travelling Man, the Builder or Wise Woman. In fact you've already sampled all possible roles. The Witness is the final archetype and includes all the others. You should be grateful. Your 'job' is to relax. *Just be.*"

12.

Timeline Jumping

I FOUND MYSELF back in my parked car with Sanat, in a state of confusion as to how I could exist in multiple dimensions at once. It seemed to me that my soul had a predisposition to a somewhat fragmented dimensional state. I felt it was a natural tendency that could become a valuable gift if it was directed properly, different parts of myself multitasking in other planes simultaneously. It might be very efficient nonetheless.

The version of me in the car, however, was experiencing information overload. It seemed we must have been sitting there for a very long time. I couldn't quite remember who or what we were waiting for. We seemed to be at a point previous to "Mikey's" full transition into the blue being, because he still retained some of Mikey's shape and form. To become more grounded and to pass the time, I asked him about which movies he'd seen recently. We discussed the current movie releases, including the more obscure ones. "What else do you like to do for fun, Mikey?"

"Mmm, I like playing video games."

"Which is your favourite?" I asked, seeking distraction.

He didn't mention the title, but made me close my eyes and pretend to be one of its characters. "Now, Sarazen, you're on another planet and there's an infectious disease running rampant."

"Okay, so who are some of the other characters?" I asked.

"Well, there are little girls and there's Mr. B – Mr. Bubbles," he explained. "He protects the little girls."

"Hmm. That's pretty cool. Who else?"

"Nurses gone bad, scientists, people like that."

"That sounds kinda scary," I prompted. I was indeed quite frightened for some reason and didn't think I had the stomach to continue playing, let alone watch someone else play.

"Yeah, I guess."

"What kind of music is there in the game?"

In response, Sanat/Mikey sang eerie songs about insane asylums, run-down dental clinics and technicians in white lab coats spattered with blood.

I wasn't really sure I wanted to play a game like that. Until then everything he had shared with me seemed so uplifting that this new direction was very confusing.

"Come on, Sarazen, this is my favourite game. It's really fun."

"Okay… if you say so. So what do I do?"

"You keep mutating. In one hand, you have a wrench. Pick it up off the floor," he explained. "Hold it in your right hand and tap your open left palm with it."

I wondered why he liked the game so much and if it was somehow a metaphor for life on Earth. If so, it was lost on me.

A crazy lady ran towards me.

"What do I do now?!"

"Now you press 'B' and you hit her with the wrench."

"I – I don't want hit anybody!" I protested.

"If you don't, she'll die," he explained. "And you have to mutate yourself. In fact, do it now."

Reluctantly, I gave myself a shot of who-knows-what with a syringe that appeared out of nowhere.

"Now your hand is a claw," Sanat/Mikey said.

"All right, but I don't want to keep my hand in this claw shape, because it might stay that way," I fussed.

"Don't worry about it. Now you can just press 'A' and electrocute people. Then you only need to hit them once."

"Huh?" I realized I still felt somewhat inebriated, slow to understand what he was saying. A zombie would run towards me – and I'd hit A-A-A, zap! – but nothing happened.

"Sarazen, it's like the old one-two punch, you gotta remember the right combination. Get the rhythm of it."

We played the game for a while, then I watched "Mikey" play a couple of levels alone, but finally lost interest in the whole thing. Without warning, I was back in the passenger seat. Until then, I hadn't realized I'd been in the driver's seat for some time, so concluded that I must still be OOB, only a wee bit closer to so-called "normal" reality.

In fact I felt a lot more "down to earth." I had just spent much time in higher realms, but it was strange how I didn't notice the more drastic transition back to the car. It seemed as though my attention had simply flickered because I wondered how she was doing, the version of me in the car, that is. In the blink of an eye my attention toggled to the part of my soul that was still fixed in its starting position.

That of itself was not so alarming, possibly even a mild relief to see my body was still here in some shape or form. Yet the scene in the car with Mikey seemed quite phantasmagorical, existing simultaneously with many other experiences – somewhere else. I knew we were not done with our travels yet.

Maybe we were in a buffer zone, somewhere between worlds, a means of adjusting to information overload. I got an idea: *While I'm still in psychic mode, I might as well snoop around to see what's in store for the future.* I closed my eyes. The process of looking into the future came very naturally. I was able to understand two different mechanisms by which I was able to use this form of sight. They both seemed strange and quite unexpected, not that I had any preconceptions.

The first method was to close my eyes and put my faith into a receptacle, like a birdbath or some other pool of water. When I opened them again, I was transported in a moment to the Active Memory of another person's past or future, feeling all their feelings. At first I was randomly taken to places. It was like I was a living being inserted into the memory. I was not, however, affecting or changing the outcome in any way by my presence. I noticed the more constantly I focused my thoughts leading to the question, and maintained the intention to know a person's future, the clearer and quicker my sight seemed to work. That method of seeing was quite enjoyable and seemed to rely heavily on both faith – confidence that I could see – and the concentrated thought prior to questioning.

Another method was to close my eyes and think of another person. My mind would energetically carve out a wormhole above my head, sometimes with a diameter as small as a drinking straw, and at other times larger, about an inch-and-a-half. The wormhole was translucent, multicoloured and rotating very rapidly. It was as if it were a stalk with an eye at the end projecting into the future, a kind of periscope. Vision would speed towards its target, and when it arrived, I'd be there too, again walking around in a body within the living memory that was very real and ostensibly taking place in real time somewhere.

As I looked into each person's timeline, I was projected to their current location. If they were sleeping, I would end up in their bedroom. Sometimes they would be floating around, then notice me, shocked to find someone else floating in their room with them!

Looking into Alexander's future, I saw the two of us at a gala awards dinner four years in the future. He was heading for the stage to receive a Grammy. I had always felt this was in his plan so it came as no surprise.

My friend Katie's future showed difficult times ahead. She and her boyfriend seemed fated to break up, followed by years of challenging lessons of the heart.

Uncle Orbit's future could go two ways too, depending on his choice. He could release my book as fiction based on my experience, under my name with permission, and it would be adapted for movies with a wide influence in the world, like the next *Star Wars* franchise. I was even shown the producer, which was pretty cool to consider. I saw myself relinquishing the entire book experience to him in that timeline, unable to step into my power and own my truth. It seemed much easier to pass it on to someone else. I had a deep fear that my family would disown me if I told my story. A large portion of its members are religious. I was almost certain it would not be well-received. I had always wanted to be closer to them, but our differing beliefs seemed to have limited that. I was very concerned that if something like this was thrown into the mix, it would challenge too many of their beliefs instead of making them curious about my remarkable account with the Divine. The little me desperately wanted to hold on to the love and acceptance that I had in my life, even at the cost of disclosing the truth.

Uncle Orbit's tranquil life would change drastically as a result. If he chose to publish this work, I saw him being friends with people such as famous Hollywood directors, living a life of luxury, but not of excess, because he would use his influence to be of service to others. The movie adaptation would require a massive budget for the amount of CGI needed to give it life, the location being in outer space and all. Given the content, that version of the book would appeal to a broad demographic, avid readers from children to seniors.

My mother's future was less certain, only because she was unclear herself. In her case, it was like being inside a computer that was crashing a lot, with mixed signals and incomprehensible data. Each of her options seemed to be in conflict. She didn't know where she wanted to live or even whether to move. She didn't know if she should quit her job or keep it. She didn't know whether she wanted money or not. Indecision. I tried to shake her up by grabbing her arms, but the more I did the more incoherent she became.

When I was younger, my mother was very much on the spiritual path. She has a vast understanding of the universe and the curiosity to keep building her wisdom. I loved learning from her and valued her wealth of information. In recent years, however, the stresses of daily life had become a priority and her connection to her true Self less important. In the state she was in now, there was no getting through to her. She was like an automaton. I started to get upset because, of all the people whose future I looked into, she seemed most in need of help. I desperately wanted to help her in return for all the support she had given me over the years. I consulted her nearby guides. I pleaded, "What can I do?"

They said, "You've already done it by superseding any challenge we could have given her in this lifetime, just by showing up as her child. The rest is up to her and to us."

I accepted that and moved on to preview other family members' futures. My cousin Steven is artistically inclined. I saw him performing, fronting a rock band. I saw its name in a logo. He became a fairly well-known artist in other media as well. I saw an image of a spider that became a hand. That turned out to be a drawing by Steven's brother Trevor, likewise an extremely talented visual artist. Trevor's future showed a lot of good things as he grew into more of a free spirit.

When I focused on my grandparents, I saw a square car tire, which seemed quite odd. The whole wheel it was on fell off my grandpa's car. No one was hurt, so I wasn't that concerned. In fact it didn't even seem out of place, because my grandfather had become quite erratic in recent years. He had many unusual incidents with automobiles, such as his old Cadillac catching on fire in traffic, and backing into parked cars. Another time he almost burned the entire house down while experimenting in the attached garage with a battery charger and some exotic fuel additive.

I had been perplexed after looking forward along my mother's path, but nothing was more confusing than looking at my own, because I saw a flood of images in multiple streams. I began to look through my timelines, and seemed to be transported into the real-life waking events that were in store for me, living them first-hand. That proved to be both enlightening and horrifying.

In one timeline, life returned to exactly the point at which I'd left it before travelling OOB. Several weeks into the future of it, I had left Alexander's neighbourhood, moving along Lougheed Highway late at night in a downpour, driving a silver sedan. Despite the late hour, traffic was fairly heavy. The rain increased. Just then my attention was distracted for a mere second when my phone rang. The future seemed to split into different options at that point. In one of them, a car drove head-on into mine. In another, I hydroplaned into a tree. In a third, an oncoming eighteen-wheeler jack-knifed. I could not avoid driving straight into it.

They differed slightly, but all three branches bore the same fruit. I saw myself thrown from the car, landing on the wet pavement, which felt cold in contrast to the rain. Only semi-conscious, I felt no pain due to the extent of the injuries. I was in shock. Then the paramedics arrived, transitioning to the next stage of the vision that showed a choice of outcomes. It would take several out-of-body journeys in order to receive the next communication. How much got through to me would depend on how badly injured I was. One scenario showed such brain damage that it would take years to recover. Another showed that either my limbs had been amputated or that I was paralyzed from the neck down so that I would be forced to travel out-of-body to achieve my divine plan.

I continued to cycle through many time tracks, feeling an inherent responsibility to myself to examine all I could.

Along another, there was no feeling in my face. In another, I saw myself as a homeless person, almost unrecognizable because although I wasn't that much older, my appearance showed decay from the inside out. I was filthy and living in a makeshift cardboard shelter, sleeping under old newspapers. This impression would haunt me for years to come, afraid to fulfil what I had seen.

In yet another timeline, I saw my best possible outcome for my current lifespan. I travelled all over the world and became a successful artist with the ability to manifest my circumstances at will. I even looked almost exactly like the vision of myself as the Witness, radiating youth, power, joy and freedom. This vibration alone radically influenced others. I was teaching them too, but in an indirect manner, through being. Instead of practising philanthropy overtly in support of good causes, I helped each person as the need arose.

I asked about giving birth to my first child, if Alexander and I stayed together. Previewing that proved to be absolutely wonderful, the most breathtaking event I had seen. I was filled with much emotion.

In another one, I would participate in an art exhibition organized by a woman named Monique, and was even able to speak to her directly while still suspended in the connected state. I very much liked her and hoped we really would meet in the Earth plane. Perhaps we could become friends.

I began wondering about how to make my Earthly life better. I circled my attention back to my art and chose to paint many pictures while still in the astral plane. Here everything was so effortless. I had unlimited space and resources, the ultimate artist's studio, never running out of supplies. On a huge translucent canvas with the starry blackness as backdrop, I began to search a seemingly limitless stream of galaxies and nebulae, taking mental screenshots of my favourite sights. I began to paint them, feeling the textures, refining the colour palettes. After this, painting them when in the physical plane would be that much easier.

I saw myself writing a book about my experiences while out-of-body. There were ramifications, depending on how it was written. I had to be careful. There would be no point in attracting the wrong kind of attention. To make the process easier, I sat down and wrote the entire book from beginning to end in the air with my forefinger. An added benefit of doing this would be to embed the memories that much more deeply.

I saw many, many possible futures for myself, which I interpreted as the future being fluid, unfixed. The most vivid and disturbing possibility, however, was the highway accident in any of its forms.

"Okay, Mikey, I'm going to make predictions for the world now," I proclaimed. "There's going to be an earthquake in Chile of extremely high magnitude, with a huge number of casualties. I see devastating storms in the Southern U.S., a bunch of hurricanes and typhoons. Now I'm seeing numbers – get a pen and paper!"

Sanat/Mikey said, "I don't have one. And there's nothing in the glove box, not even gloves."

In the exalted state I was in, even though I was sitting in the car, it was as if peering down, looking into the world from above. I had an astronaut's point of view and could behold the Earth in all her majestic glory. I saw storms and upheaval unfold as the planet ceaselessly worked to rebalance herself. In fact upon closer inspection I could see her breathing. Gaia began to send out a series of rippling earthquakes to shake off the discord we humans have caused her. Those earthquakes were precursors to bigger events, and only signalled the beginning of her changes. I saw volcanic activity and a series of small storms, some so very large they would wipe out entire cities. I saw several incredibly strong hurricanes. One was set to head first for the Southern United States. It has since been named Katrina. The other series of storms were not yet mandated as absolutely compulsory. Need for further storms would depend on the reaction of the people affected and what they would manifest in the meantime.

These in fact were karmic storms. Gaia has done a terrific job of tolerating our toxic waste, our destruction of her wildlife, our abuse of natural resources. She has been storing vast amounts human negative emotional energy as well. I saw she cannot hold that energy indefinitely. While I could feel that she did not enjoy hurting the people she cares for, by cosmic law she has to make herself a priority. The power of those great karmic storms would be very much dependent on human ability to advance towards kindness to one another and the planet we share; for example, whether we transition from burning fossil fuels and fracking, which is weakening her crust, to cleaner, sustainable energy practices and modes of transportation.

I was also shown the Pacific Plate subducting some 100 metres into the planet's crust, giving way to a new coastline all the way down to California. This agrees with what numerous prophets have for decades claimed to see as the future West Coast. For the time being it seems fairly stable, yet by scientific calculations we know we are overdue for a shake-up. Reason now tells me the Divine is waiting for the precise moment for this change. An event as substantial as that needs to occur in such a way that the outcome is in accordance with the Divine Plan.

It is the downside of karma, which has been so long delayed that most people cannot easily connect the dots. I had never considered that a storm could be Mother Nature's way of dealing with discord, by releasing negative collective planetary karma. What we don't see readily is that by fracking in Canada storms are triggered along its east coast, travelling all the way down to the United States, often in the form of devastating hurricanes. Yet the patterns and her responses to every event that has ever been inflicted on her are still there. They are obvious and perfectly aligned, given the ability to look closely enough, although to many her reactions will appear random and not caused by human action.

I could not tell how far in the future these events would unfold, as to me it seemed like I was watching them in fast-forward mode, months of activity taking place in seconds. It was a similar sensation to flipping through the pages of the book of my life: everything was so readily available.

Having neither pen nor paper, I used my finger to trace numerals in the air. I didn't know if they were lottery numbers or referred to something else, but they seemed important and appeared over and over again in the same pattern and sequence. I wondered whether I was just making them up and tried in vain to remember my bank account number, but could not even recall my phone number. But the numbers kept coming, including dates.

Before that night, I had been highly sceptical about anyone's ability to predict the future. But then my view shifted to my own life again. The next seven days were quite clear in every detail.

"Mikey, this is crazy. If my predictions turn out to be true, then whatever's been going on tonight is even more likely to be real. You have to be my witness. You're my proof."

I wanted to warn the people. I felt afraid and highly concerned. At the same time, I felt powerless. Who would ever believe me? Was I supposed to be a whistle-blower and call the leaders of nations to tell them catastrophes were coming if they did not change their ways? I felt deeply sad at the lives that were yet to be lost, but understood it was not my place to intervene, nor had I the power to do so.

In the view of the next week of my life, I saw every element and event in minute detail. I saw that Alexander and I were going to get caught in a fire drill in his apartment building and for some reason have trouble accessing his suite via the stairwell, needlessly climbing twenty-six floors. There were also familiar sequences of numbers mounted in the stairwells that stayed with me. Then I saw us going to dinner at an unfamiliar restaurant, the Rocky Point Cafe. He was going to order the spicy seafood soup and I was going to get spaghetti and meatballs. All the events I saw seemed quite ordinary. I was able to restrain my typical doubt because in a way I felt those incidents had already happened and I was just reliving them, even though at the time of seeing them they had not happened yet.

Bottomless sadness arose for a while, as looking into my future did not give me the clarity I desired. Then I became aware of something wonderful happening to me somewhere in another dimension. That was enough to cause a shift. I flickered into a different version of myself.

An earthquake of magnitude 8.8 on the Richter Scale hit Chile on February 27, 2010, making it the largest earthquake to strike the country ever. That earthquake was so large it also caused a major tsunami, with more than 500 fatalities.

13.

Spherical Time

FEELING HEAVY AND sombre, I regretted tempting fate by peering into my own and so many others' futures. What impact would that have? I wondered if I had influenced my own and other people's destinies just by observing them, by what is known as the observer effect in physics. Sanat Kumara tried to reassure me that everything would be fine, but I wasn't let off the hook that easily. Like a schoolteacher, his attitude seemed to indicate that I should have known better in spite of his having done nothing to stop me. I had assumed that if it wasn't supposed to have happened, then something would have blocked me. The temptation to look ahead had just been too great.

In hindsight, there had been no preventive measures in place to stop me from getting marooned on desolate planet Hell, so it was logical to assume there would be nothing preventing me from making other mistakes. This logic, however, had not been applied. It was like driving a car with a manual transmission for the first time, with no instructor. But I did have an instructor. He just seemed very liberal about allowing me to experiment by trial and error – and the logical consequences of grinding of gears and stalling, so to speak.

Without trying, I left my body again and returned to the astral plane, where I appeared in a roomful of people awaiting my arrival. I was surprised to find a celebration held in my honour! Apparently, my breakthrough to the out-of-body state was an achievement to be recognized, although I wasn't entirely sure what the celebration was for, to be honest.

There was a new and noticeable change in my state after returning to the higher vibrational planes. Previously, it had seemed to take a lot of energy to communicate and to remain alert. My mind would wander and my vision would periodically blur, similar to earlier in the night when in the process of leaving my body and going through periods of feeling inebriated from time to time. It was a struggle to maintain the stamina to stay on the same wavelength. Just then I felt a crystal-clear fluid energy moving through me. I no longer had problems with interpretation or communicating with the guests at this lavish party.

The venue was a grand room, but not like the ordinary everyday rooms we know, however grand. Like the other out-of-body environments I'd visited, there weren't really any tangible walls, floors or ceilings. The "walls," however, were more prominently symbolized and less translucent. In fact the walls themselves were made of light and energy. If I looked closely, I could sense an energetic thought-current running through them holding them in place. Seemingly contrary to what I have described, the room and house felt very concrete, of tangible substance. It was a permanent venue created for frequent gatherings. I tried to take my bearings and figure out where I was in proximity to Earth. The message I received from my soul was that I was not that far away, somewhere still in our solar system, situated on a nearby neighbouring planet, although which one I could not say.

Whoever created the space had a very beautiful imagination indeed. It felt delightfully Venusian, imbued with beauty and opulence. It was like I had walked into the grand parlour of a fine old house. The room radiated luxury, with ornately decorated carpets, leather sofas and chairs, hardwood panelling and alabaster ornamentation. There was a large crescent staircase that started at one end of the room and descended at the other, showcasing some of the many books on the premises. A large chandelier hung from above, casting an enchanting glow on the numerous guests in attendance. Hand-made leaded-glass lamps, oil paintings, marble sculptures, walnut cabinetry, tables and bookcases rounded out the impression. Yet there was no upper limit, no ceiling, only stars visible above. The "floor" was apparently reliably solid, yet had no visible surface in spite of the support it gave. That was fine, as many of us were floating, having a very noticeably prominent upper body and torso, the lower body more or less a softer, wispy form, as legs were not essential.

There were about one hundred souls present. Although they were all equally glad to see me, acknowledgement came from some more than others, as if I was meant to interact with them specifically.

I knew some of the people in attendance to be deceased, but others were still among the living. I assumed the latter were either enlightened or else had passed the same threshold I did, being able to participate in work in higher realms as the physical body lived on down below. Some of them were famous movie actors, some former American presidents, some legendary spiritual leaders of the past, one of whom was Paramahansa Yogananda. I spoke with him first, relieved to see a familiar face, but the topic of our conversation was memorable more for its energy than its content.

It was so much fun making the kind of small talk that says nothing but implies everything. Small talk was not something I was fond of on Earth, but I also seemed to act a lot younger up here. I felt that I was somehow the most out of the loop among this beautiful group of people, feeling like everyone knew exactly what was going on and exactly what we were doing here. I nevertheless tried my best to be sociable and follow subtle cues so as not to appear completely ignorant at my own party.

Many people kept coming up to me in groups, each waiting to get a word in edgeways. They felt like aunts and uncles I had not seen in a while, who were all so eager to share in the excitement of reunion. Each seemed to get one to two sentences in before being interrupted by someone else. It seemed I knew all these people intimately, perhaps because of the massive amount of information I perceived emanating from them with each greeting. We were all so uniquely different but shared something special. Just being in their company was greatly uplifting, especially compared to some of the other experiences I'd had. It was just what I needed.

As I became more comfortable in the elaborately decorated palace, I felt closer to this assembly of great souls than I'd ever felt to anyone. It occurred to me that perhaps attachment to anyone or anything is not good. It may be better to leave yourself open to new and beautiful experiences like the one I was having – so I left – or maybe it's more accurate to say I just ceased being in that beautiful room.

I appeared outside now and continued to peer through a small stained glass window at the celebration continuing inside. I was ecstatic. Now I knew that I had a lot more control than I'd imagined and wasn't such a neophyte after all. In the beginning, I thought I needed an instruction manual, but found I already knew how to do everything necessary. In fact I believed anyone could do what I was doing and actually does frequently, perhaps every single night of their lives. I seemed to have no problem with memory, and knew retaining my memories of this event was something special permitted by the Divine.

Having left the celebration, I found myself back on some version of Earth in my car with my friend the blue being, and asked, "Will I ever return to my physical body?"

"You already have, Sarazen."

95

"I have?"

"Yes. Time doesn't work the way you've been used to thinking it does, that is, in a linear fashion. It's not an arrow. It's round."

"Round? What do you mean? Is it a circle or a sphere?"

He showed me an orb whose surface, of course, has no beginning or end. I saw that time is not segmented into past, present and future. All these divisions were happening simultaneously, eternally existent. I peered closer into the glowing sphere in Sanat's hand. Greater understanding arose. It was like a self-luminous ball of yarn that had within it billions of intersecting points of contact. Events were stored in this highly organized bundle. If you knew what to look for, you could dive in and access one immediately. Because it was in one gigantic loop, it was impossible to position one event before another. They were all intimately connected and interdependent. This fact allowed me to perceive what I considered the past and the future in greatly illuminated detail, and to experience multiple time periods simultaneously.

Time is a mental construct. We have created it as part of our need to measure happenings. We have become attached to the belief that time is necessary, but its value is only in coordinating events, such as getting to work at a specific hour or catching the last bus home at night. In fact clock time, calendar time and psychological time are the biggest hindrances to finding true understanding of life and our place in the universe.

What may have at first been created as a useful tool, as with many inventions, has taken on a life of its own. Time has now become a noose around our neck in the game, something that governs us, not something we freely employ. We chronically feel late, like we do not have enough time. This has created dangerous manifestations in our lives, such as neglect of the personal self, insecure that without working constantly we will not be able to afford to remain alive, let alone happily alive, habitually checking the clock to immediately race to the next activity in an already full day.

This has done several things. Number one, the feeling of shortage of time creates exactly that, since we are operating in a realm in which whatever you can conceive of you create. Through your God-given power as a creator, you are responsible for your creation. Secondly, the illusion of scarcity of time has effectively disconnected us from intuition. When your day and entire week has already been tightly planned out, when is there opportunity for spontaneity? Perhaps there are more important things to do and places to go. How will you ever know if you never tune in? This lifestyle definitely does not allow for reflection on the oldest question: *Why am I here?*

As humans, we are so caught in the rat race we have created that our energies are enslaved to time. We are soul-depleted as a result. There is no amount of chasing the clock that will result in recharging it. How satisfying is it to a dog to catch its own tail? As mentioned, this prevents natural insight and intuition from guiding our attention in the present moment. For example, a person may be inspired to go on a hike one beautiful Sunday afternoon. They feel they have the energy and are excited, then they look at the clock and their human programming chimes in. Their internal agenda attempts to protect them by convincing them there is simply not enough time: *But we have work tomorrow!* Or, *But we still haven't made our lunches for the week!* That is the key: this limited programming revolves around making plans that exist in the future and not in the now. They revolve around a time that does not exist yet and may never exist, tarnishing the power of now and suppressing the soul. This also applies to being stuck mentally in the past. What we don't get to see from our habitual limited perspective is perhaps that same individual was *supposed* to have a powerful realization during that simple hike, something so big it could change their life for the better, finally solving a difficult ongoing technical problem at work or perhaps something greater yet, such as at last gaining the resolve needed to leave a relationship they have really outgrown, staying only because they have told themselves it is the kinder thing.

Another example: your higher self is well aware that you need to prepare your lunches for the week. However, your knee-jerk response insinuates that you know better how to live your life than God does. Overriding any intuitive suggestions, you decide to skip the hike and pack your lunches instead.

These spontaneous suggestions come through for a reason. It's okay to trust them. On another level, the hike could have been highly restorative to their body, creating better rest, equipping them to cope with stress more effectively, thereby tipping the scales on the possibility of disease manifesting. Intuition often provides warnings and clues to states of health. It should not be ignored. Intuition wants to protect and guide you. The belief that *there isn't enough time* has the potential to rush the out-of-tune soul from calamity to calamity.

In the above example, because of the person's perception of time, the hike never ended up happening. Whatever potential realization that may have happened was lost, reserved for a future date when the higher self may still intervene.

Most scientists have long based their work and calculations according to the current concept of time. If the fundamental theory they are working with is incorrect, then all other work they base on that will have errors. People often become attached to certain widely accepted theories because they've been around so long they are taken for granted as irreducible truths. This lack of flexibility and creative thinking is what allows us to remain largely ignorant of many truths hiding in plain sight.

If we were to raise a group of children without imposing upon them the hard and fast rules that comprise our rigid belief systems, they could far supersede all our scientific advancement in their generation's lifetime because their minds would be free of the limitations that inhibit creativity, the signature quality of top-tier scientists.

Beings such a Sir Isaac Newton knew this. He did not adhere to the general consensus. All his great work was done in extreme seclusion, allowing a stronger connection to his own divinity. Newton predicted that light would be bent by gravity, which would not be proven for another three hundred years with Albert Einstein's work. Newton himself said transcendental ideas poured down upon him from a divine fountain. Great minds like his are not often considered spiritual, although he is known to have been religious, like most people of his time, even an insightful and scholarly theologian. History shows that Newton, Galileo, Copernicus, Heinrich Cornelius Agrippa, Leonardo da Vinci, Pythagoras and Plato shared something in common: they were all brilliant, creative thinkers who listened to their inner guides, even when the whole world insisted they think and behave differently.

These men were outsiders by society's standards, nor did they care to fit in, because they were connected to the greatest source of knowledge. They upheld their beliefs at any cost. Sadly, their radical discoveries of truth often went unpublished until after death for fear of repercussions.

All these great souls believed in something greater than was known in their time. They did not see science as separate from spirituality. In fact they saw the two methodologies as absolutely interdependent. In those times, beliefs that contradicted organized religion were treasonous and grounds for execution as a heretic or a witch. How fortunate we are to live in a time when the human voice is allowed enough freedom of speech to continue to speculate. While science is still progressing slowly, at least you won't be hanged as a revolutionary or burnt at the stake for discovering something outside the box.

My guide and I had dived deep into the sphere of time. He showed me that space-time is like flexible fabric, which allowed us to slingshot ourselves across thousands of light years as galaxies and nebulae flew by at terrific speeds. The fantastic thing about it was that it did not seem frightening or even so unusual. Instead, it was as comfortable as a Sunday drive. Once we even grabbed a handful of that mathematical space-fabric enclosed in our fists and shot ourselves forward in a very playful, comical way.

I also saw that space-time was spherical, the same way our whole universe exists within another sphere, which at each moment was both visible and accessible. While I was not used to using such a method of accessing information, I was able to interact with that concept enough to grasp it. It was as though all of time was suspended in a bead of water. I could swim into the water and travel to a specific point in time because all points existed simultaneously. There were hundreds, possibly thousands, of possibilities in every moment. As we advanced we would "jump" into a version of our own reality. Everything I was being shown put a very different spin on, for example, string theory, which prior to this experience was strongly what my belief system was leaning towards as currently the most accurate description of reality. This is not to say it is entirely incorrect. It touches on some truths, yet I saw fundamental incongruences with scientistic belief systems that prevent understanding the universe as a whole. The existence of higher dimensional beings is one example. The bead of water was also a beautiful metaphor for how time is fluid. As an event occurred, a ripple would pass through the vibratory fabric of space-time, revealing a new course had been set.

I saw that I was not at the mercy of powers beyond my control and could manipulate space-time at will. In fact *will* had more to do with it than anything. The adage "where there's a will there's a way" acquired new meaning. I saw that the times when I felt like I was getting submerged by life circumstances were when my will was very weak, unable to be imposed and aligned with the greater will of the Whole, putting me at the mercy of whatever interference came my way. Likewise, I saw that during the times when my will was very strong, when I had an unbending vision of what I wanted to happen, more often than not I achieved exactly that. That was because of another universal law, the law of attraction. The universe has to match your desire because you are *creating your own reality*. Your thought, backed by emotion, is broadcast into the universe like a beacon. Great universal processing systems hone in on the beacon and match it exactly with its manifestation in form. You may put out requests unknowingly, asking for more of the same in the form of unwanted feedback. Its manifestation then seeks out friends and circles back home to the source that created it: you. This is an absolutely flawless fulfilment service for each and every cosmic request. Unfortunately, the precise mirroring effect of manifestation is enforced regardless of picturing something beautiful or something horrendous, which is why so many of us have learned many valuable but often painful lessons while on Earth as entry-level gods in training.

*

Especially at first during this experience and whenever I got tired of intense concentration, my guide would often adjust my state by "hitting" or tapping on specific points on my "body," making me toggle between dimensions to refocus. The effect of that was instantaneous relief, like a cosmic chiropractic treatment. Or ears unplugging after being underwater: suddenly you can hear clearly. Or lucidity in a dream, when you can see after fumbling in the dark trying to navigate unfamiliar ground.

Even though the OOB environments were crystal-clear, my main mistake was out of habit straining to see with my physical eyes, which would begin to cloud and distort my vision. When I again saw properly, that is, via consciousness alone, the sensation was more centred in the middle of my chest or stomach, sometimes in the centre of my head, depending on the mode of being. If I had a partially formed upper torso, then "sight"seemed to originate in my head area. But if I was closer to a formless state, existing more as a collection of energies, then my vision would be from my core. I would at times become aware of how strange it was to "see" from the centre of my umbilical region. This in turn would immediately warp my perspective, hence require another adjustment.

Specifically, there were times when I experienced myself as a mere dimensionless point, such a simple form of condensed, undiluted energy that no form was needed. The point was enough. In this state I absorbed information from every direction at once. The sense of "I" was centred in what I would normally associate with the heart. I understand the paradox because in this state – while I did not have a physical heart or even a body, for that matter – there was the essence of "heart" as in the expression "the heart of the matter." To speculate, probably in most beings' souls there are structures that are able to retain their roles regardless of changes of state.

My "heart" always seemed to be fully operational, from which love emanates. There was an instantaneous connection to it at any moment. It was never not present. In retrospect, my "mind," although a pale version of what I call my mind now, was always present as well, meaning there was never a moment when I lost consciousness, nor did I not feel connected to the native awareness that is me. Many times there was an expansion of mind as I transitioned through different states of being. But never did I feel like the speck that is my individuality had disappeared. It was always there, sometimes more in the background, but that was quite okay.

There were also times when I experienced something quite different. I was allowed to passively observe other worlds and planets, getting to see what life is like for other beings and what types of learning situations they had created for themselves. The feeling then was in the middle of my head extending to my forehead, like the "third eye" of yogic tradition. Hindsight can sometimes lead to the most powerful realizations. Deeper memories are still surfacing years later, the more I study and am able to find references in texts to things I have experienced. Perhaps this method of seeing was a device that was loaned to me from the First Creation, Metatron, who is widely believed to be the first creation ever made by the I AM Presence of our universe because he is so ancient there is nothing that can exist without his presence being woven into it. In sacred geometry, the structure of any object in the Earth or throughout the universe can fit within Metatron's Cube. He is a part of everything we can see, touch and feel, and even everything we can't. It is also speculated that in some ways he works as a "lens" for the I AM, possibly even serving as a filter through which to project our entire holographic experience here. At the time, however, I knew nothing consciously of Metatron's existence, nor his capacity to function as a viewing device. No wonder it had such greater accuracy and detail than my own vision.

I reflected on some of my past attempts at journeys out-of-body. I wondered how many times I'd been successful. Four instances stood out immediately.

14.

DreamTime Training

1. A Lucid Dream at Age Seven

THE FIRST JOURNEY was what I'd thought was a lucid dream at around the age of seven. It opened in a market town in a vast Arabian desert plain, where I thought I was marooned. What was once a magnificently beautiful empire had left only scattered remains. Scared and lonely, I wandered, floating along the gritty streets of a sand-coloured world. Then I stumbled into a dusty market lined with streets of shops. One in particular caught my eye and invited me inside. Its keeper was an old man with an incredibly long white beard and a turban covering his head. He seemed to recognize me. From beneath a counter he retrieved an object hidden under an old scarf. Pulling it away, he revealed a large, glowing glass ball.

The old gentleman handed it to me, making it clear it was a gift. He spoke to me telepathically, but before handing it over demonstrated that the orb could be controlled by consciousness to transform it into anything I envisioned. Holding it in the palm of my hand, I attempted to do as he had done, making its mass and size vary from being as light as a feather to heavier and larger than a bowling ball. The amazing thing about this dream was that it did not seem like any normal dream, more like a waking-state experience, but even more vivid. There were strong sensations, such as the weight of the ball in my hands and the warm, dry caress of the desert breeze, never mind a conscious control I had never before experienced as the ball changed its state.

I remember wondering where my sleeping body was stored as I dreamt and a slight agitation at being very far away from it. I then was awakened by my mother to go to school. I begged for ten more minutes of rest, although it did not permit return to the dream. For months afterwards I pondered the experience and told no one of how convinced I was that I had really met an ancient wizard in my dream, as I didn't believe anyone I knew would have anything of value to add. In fact speaking of it at all would only diminish its power and the magical effect it had on me. I was, however, very curious as to why he had come to me, a seemingly ordinary seven-year-old.

I now know the name of the sorcerer in that dream, who was indeed more ancient than I could have known. His name is Melchizedek, mentioned in the Old Testament as a priest-king of Salem (usually synonymous with Jerusalem). He is one of the oldest known souls still participating in and lending a helping hand in this universe.

2. A Lucid Dream at Age Nine

The second lucid dream happened a couple of years later. It was both beautiful and disturbing, not because of its content, but because of what it suggested. It made me question the nature of identity.

In the dream, I was about nineteen years old, but more pure, more knowledgeable and luminous. I entered my first-grade classroom, where I saw my six-year-old self colouring a drawing at my desk, as I so often did then. There were one or two other children present, but the teacher was not. It seemed like school had just been dismissed. Most of the kids had left, but the little girl was waiting for her mother to pick her up.

"Hi. What are you drawing?" I asked her.

She explained.

Then I continued, "You know, you're really talented. You should never stop drawing, because you're *really* good at it."

The little girl seemed pleased.

I could empathically feel the warm fuzzy feelings that arose within her.

My nine-year-old self awoke from the dream crying, touched by the memory of the young woman walking into my first classroom. This triggered confusing feelings and memories highly incongruous with what I believed was possible. The dream had been superimposed on an actual childhood memory, and from both perspectives, that of the child and the adult commenting on her artwork.

Whether it was a dream or by some magical twist some version of my future self was allowed to go back in time to deliver a message, it didn't matter. The words she had implanted influenced me nevertheless. Though I would forget about this dream and my plan to become an artist, as well as take a few years' hiatus to see if the pursuit of a medical career was for me, I would eventually return to my true path. I have been a visual artist now for more than ten years at the time of this writing. I was given this dream a second time as a reminder much later in life, when I was twenty-nine, after I had already been an artist for many years. The dream was a powerful reminder of how the universe works through all of us in ways that are far beyond our understanding. It showed me life is so much more interesting than I could have ever imagined.

3. An Etheric Projection at Age Fourteen

It would be many years before my next incredible dream, yet throughout childhood I would often have difficulties falling asleep, as I'd feel and see threatening dark entities hanging around my bed. I know now that was actual paranormal interference. I gave my mother a hard time, constantly waking her up to console me.

By around the age of fourteen I had become very curious about the idea of astral projection in light of my experiences so far. I knew about the astral plane, and Uncle Orbit had given me a book on it that I flipped through but didn't really have the patience to read. This was also the time in my life when my mother was still quite spiritual and gave me Tarot readings. I had also begun to learn how to give myself readings, using cards and other methods. Astral projection, however, was what fascinated me the most. I thought for sure I could do it. I tried to introduce some basic techniques before bed each night, but with no luck. Intuition led me to the strange practice of visualizing my entire next day in advance before bed, which initiated some minor but interesting dream sequences in which I often experienced events that would occur the following day.

One night I'd gone to bed as usual. I don't think I had done any particular dreamtime preparation, but became aware that I'd fallen asleep in a funny position, curled up in a ball with my arms wrapped around my legs and close to my chest, and of course eyes closed. I felt my head hit something. Upon opening my eyes, I looked down from the ceiling of my room to see my body in bed! The room was dark. Confused and shocked, I could not believe it was possible that I had succeeded in leaving my body while in the waking state.

Not knowing what else to do, I decided to leave my room and explore the street outside. I remember the street lights as blindingly bright. Traffic flowed by. The street lamps were like giant starbursts and the light was streaked and blurred by the falling rain. I was frightened of being hit by a vehicle, although none seemed to affect me. I floated through the night sky to my high school, which was about a mile from my house. I banged on the locked front doors. The building was mostly dark and had a few dimly lit security lights to deter vandalism. Then I simply decided to pass right through the locked doors. As a typically rebellious teenager, I thought it was cool that I was breaking the rules, and went in search of fun. After wandering the upstairs halls and some of the dark classrooms, I turned a corner and bumped into a menacing giant black shadow, which ferociously began to chase me. Blindingly terrified, I believed I was about to be swallowed alive or mowed down by the spectre. I raced all the way back to my bedroom, taking no detours. I dived head-first back into my body and woke up shaking, sure that it had followed me. Eyes wide open, I dared not go to sleep. I tried to verbally command it to leave me alone, not because it was anything I had learned, but because it was all I could think of.

I've heard that one should confront their fears in dreams, but to this day part of me is sure that tactic would have been fatal, or at the very least harmful to my soul. Perhaps confrontation is only true for typical nocturnal dreams, not astral projections (more commonly known now as OBEs), because now that I have more knowledge, it seems what I'd encountered was some dark sinister force, an aspect of the collective unconscious rather than the personal subconscious, not some gratuitous fear that needed to be faced.

To speculate further, perhaps one could learn to face these dark forces in the OOB state and learn to heal them by bringing them into the light, but that was far too advanced a concept for my younger self.

4. An Etheric Projection at Age Twenty-Two

The fourth brief but significant foreshadowing happened when I was twenty-two, a month prior to the journey with Sanat. I woke standing at the foot of my bed, where I watched myself asleep in the darkened room. After a few minutes, I dived back into my body. It was very brief, but it had been years since I'd had any projection dreams, etheric or otherwise.

Regarding projection and the accuracy thereof, it is said that if you can project somewhere and it is the same time of day as your starting point, that is a good sign it's really happening. Also, if you can project to a place where you see key objects and details in that environment that you could not have known were there otherwise or even visit a friend and see them doing something specific that you can then later recall and verify, that confirms you have successfully travelled in your etheric body.

There are two common types of projections. One is etheric projection, in which you are in the Earth plane. Another is astral projection, in which you leave the sphere that is our planet and are out in space. The latter is usually associated with higher work with your guides. You may also have enough control to direct your own experience, the location to which you consciously wish to go, for example. There are no limitations with this type of OBE. You can travel to other planets and star systems, but those with great control have been known to access any moment in time in the future or the past.

With those qualifications in mind, I could say with confidence that I had left my physical body and transitioned to my etheric body twice, staying in the Earth plane. Perhaps I had successfully transitioned into my astral body and gone on cosmic voyages many more times than that. If I had, however, it was not something that I either remembered or had made much sense.

What was frustrating about those amazing experiences was that although I went through long periods when I was outwardly practising to improve the frequency and quality of them, there didn't seem to be any specific triggers. There seemed to be little to no correlation between concerted efforts and success. Sometimes years would go by and I forgot that leaving my body was even a possibility before another experience would remind me otherwise.

In addition, while I had read reports that many people have succeeded and learned techniques to "project" at will while still consciously awake, this was not a gift I seemed to be blessed with. Most of my OBEs happened while I was asleep.

In later years I came to develop a very close relationship with my guides, and the tone of the OBEs changed dramatically. Going "to sleep" then became my work, or my second job, if you will. I have come to name this type of dreaming DreamTime Training (DTT), which invokes very different qualities than normal dreams. DTT dreams have a very specific purpose, one that is designed to both move you forward and to heal different aspects of yourself. This can be varied for a vast array of experiences, such as soul retrieval, travelling back in time to help a version of yourself that's stuck, unable to move of its own volition. Or to work in higher realms with your higher self to assist the current version of the personality to move ahead. For example, that dream I had in which a version of my future self travelled back in time to implant a suggestion in my child self was this type of training.

What is interesting to note about this type of training is that, in the testing environment, your guides seem to be able to block out large portions of memory to allow increased focus. One example of this is, in the efforts to heal from a past long-term relationship, I underwent countless dreams in which I had no memories permitted of my current relationship status. This flawless type of testing allows you to see how healed you really are, by showing how authentically you react in a situation with your ex. It has not always been ideal. The ability to respond always with love, to see that you do not need anything more from that person, such as closure, and to remember that you have found "the one" and are married is what enables the passing of such a test. In my case, this is often greatly dependent on how much awareness I have going into the DreamTime experiences.

Another example of this type of DTT concerns attachments. It is said that the less you need from this plane – including but not limited to possessions, accolades and even relationships – the more powerful you become. During tests that concerned my mother, starting roughly two years ago, I have been placed in many DTT scenarios in which she had recently died or is dying. My reactions to this type of test have not always been wise. At first, I was too overwhelmed with loss and despair to even focus on any clear thoughts. I was shown that this event was powerful enough to potentially derail my life and my plan. While the training was infrequent, this type of test surfacing every three months or so, it was enough to show me that it was an ongoing block that was in the process of resolving.

I have only just now at the time of writing passed this test for the first time. In the dream, I was in a very large house, hers. I had known that she had been very ill and time was short. Just prior to my arrival, we had spoken on the phone. She sounded weak. But I managed to sneak in a joke to make light of the situation. This caused her to laugh. Feeling better about it all, I raced over to spend some last moments with her. To my surprise, when I arrived I was informed by her guides, who acted more like her handlers, that she had already passed. I was shocked and confused. *But we had just spoken,* my mind complained. Speaking to a female guide directly, I insisted again to confirm that she had indeed died. The guide consoled me, touched my arm and said that my mother's suffering was over, she was free now. Just as our conversation was ending, I saw two men coming down the staircase carrying a gurney. It was partially uncovered. A powerful wave of alarm passed through me.

I asked them to stop so that I could have a moment. I carefully examined the details of her face. It was absolutely her. With the level of detail that comes with an OBE, I was able to sense and feel the weight, texture and other tactile qualities associated with her already decomposing remains, all the way into the insides. She was pale. Redness and bruising around her eyes had begun to set in. As I drew out the moment a little longer, I concluded that this was indeed her. She had moved on. With that I turned to the two men holding the gurney and thanked them profusely because there was no way I could imagine handling her myself. With that the dream ended, completing the training in its entirety.

More interesting yet is that I have now met many people who have also experienced this type of dreaming. We have even shared dreaming, undergoing the same training at the same time, including one person who is a mathematician and a physicist. It has been both grounding and validating to be able to remember through shared experience.

✳

Sanat Kumara then broke my concentration and brought me back to the present moment, suggesting that I now return to my physical body and my life in the Earth plane. I was highly reluctant. I fought him all the way, tooth and nail, wild and rebellious at the suggestion of going back into my body, defiant even. *What a horrible thing to even insinuate!* I was afraid that I would never be able to feel this free again. There was also no guarantee that I would be allowed to remember all the experiences or the planets and places I'd seen. He could decide to wipe my memory upon re-entry. What if erasure was common practice every night and I was merely lucid for a moment, as in the movie *Groundhog Day*?

"I assure you, Sarazen, you know how to leave your body any time you want. You've done it hundreds of times already. It's as easy as breathing, for everyone as a matter of fact."

I was still unsure, so I toggled between the astral plane and my car twenty or more times until I felt comfortable that I indeed had the significant control he said I did, partly to test the strength of the connection between the spirit and its physical expression. I was aware of five or six of my "selves" then, all operating independently, but the one I was most present "in" was especially strong. I wasn't sure if every person had the same gift, ability or soul structure. I seemed to demonstrate a remarkable ability to control space and time. This was something that seemed more specific to me, and perhaps was a gift, but I couldn't be sure. The strongest version of myself at the time was the one the majority of my attention was focused on. At that moment, it happened to be the "dimension" or aspect of my soul that was the most grounded in the Earth. I call her Dimension One. She is very simple, very childlike, the type that gets confused easily and is prone to frustration and silliness, my less evolved self. Her main soul function is to keep me physically well-balanced and sensible, so naturally she had been gifted with a strong survival instinct, with similar qualities to the root chakra, anchoring me in place. As I moved up the strata of my soul, the dimensions ascended as well, becoming more advanced, more intelligent, more beautiful and more godly. The higher dimensions have always been there, independent of my awareness of them, yet at this time they seemed more accessible than in normal waking life.

The tether to the physical body was like a well-made rope. I hoped the more I exercised it the more easily I could travel. It was hard to say if Dimension One was actually coextensive with my physical, tangible body. I guess in some respects she would have to be in order for me to still be alive. She was in fact conscious. I continued the practice of phasing between the two bodies, which got easier each time. In some ways she did not seem to be fully in the three-dimensional realm of "normal waking life." I still felt less solid than usual. I could still move through objects with ease. Perhaps the disunity of my incarnation had been put on pause until some unknown decision about my fate would be made.

I sat on the hood of my car for a while deep in reflection, wondering if I really should stay in physical form. My guide's advice had not indicated that I must.

15.

The School

"SARAZEN, I'VE ALREADY spent more time with you than I was supposed to. I have another appointment. I need to go now."

"What? How could you?" I cajoled. "You mean I have to make appointments?"

"It took you a long time to prepare for your journey, but as it turned out, you were late and I had to reschedule a lot in order to tag along. I must insist. I won't be able to come back for a while."

Almost childishly, I continued to plead: "But – but can I come with you? I won't get in the way!" I nearly got down on my knees and begged because I just did not want to go back to the prison of my physical body. Eventually I was persuaded to return to Earth and wait. Before completely returning, however, I looked in on Uncle Orbit and a few other people, then decided that, if I really must be patient, I would rather wait peacefully in an abyss of nothingness. I dived back into the night sky and rested among the stars, sitting in silence, not a thought in my head. Eventually the time came when my guide reappeared. I was so blissfully at peace by then that I was completely unfazed by the passage of time.

"So, how did it go?" I asked him.

Instead of replying, he just grinned.

I loved his smile. It filled me with great warmth. My curiosity about the whole "appointment" thing was overwhelming. He now was familiar enough to be given a name, but what I really wanted was his real name. Who was he? What was his role exactly? Why were appointments necessary in a universe where time is an illusion? Who were the others he was seeing?

Not all my questions were answered. As usual, he was well-versed in the art of deflection. I was given the understanding that, although there is no rigid predetermination for what a soul is to accomplish in their lifetime, most lives are loosely scripted. Important markers and checkpoints are required, however, in order for the life to be reviewed as successful or not. Certain sequences of events are necessary for growth.

My own experience had shown there are multiple alternate futures, implying a wide range of choice. I concluded that new trails could be blazed in the wilderness of infinite possibilities. Just as the goal was to strive towards fulfilling one's highest plan, I saw that it was possible for a person to supersede it if they had successfully accomplished goals or advanced beyond the lessons that were slated for them, skipping a grade, so to speak. If so, something very interesting would happen, a new highest plan would be forged in the Great Central Sun, created in part by their God Presence. A person's God Presence, or higher self, works within the Great Central Sun to create a new plan that holds even greater promise, a plan that could impact the world in a more substantial way, since now they could also apply all the attainment they'd just earned from accomplishing their prior completed plan.

The God Presence would work with a team of advisers to do this, keeping close counsel. Ultimately the new plan would be passed on to the Creator to approve, ensuring it would align with everything already set in motion. With this level of meticulous planning, nothing could be overlooked and no detail is insignificant. That is why a gestation period that seems like aeons would pass before the new plan becomes firm.

Nevertheless, I could also see that when it came to the topic of learning, some aspects needed a certain level of commitment for them to acquire meaning, and more time required focusing on each lesson, processing it authentically without skipping steps. For evolution to occur, certain relationships and events needed to completely fulfil their potential. Even natural disasters and so-called acts of God could not be avoided if certain lessons were to be learned or complacency shaken.

It reminded me of someone Uncle Orbit had told me about, a man he'd known who slept so soundly that he was forced to install an industrial fire alarm directly over the headboard of his bed just so that he wouldn't be late for work. Pleasure induces sleep, but there is great pain in awakening. This statement alone explains the complacency of worldly people and why a great number do not more readily accept the consequences of their actions or value self-awareness.

Still, I always returned to the unanswered question of my guide's identity. So far, I've referred to him sometimes as "Mikey," but that is only because the human Mikey had acted as a kind of doorway or conduit to help facilitate the out-of-body experience. I presumed Mikey's soul must have given permission to allow an ascended master to take over his body, in which case he would have also received some karmic credit. I wondered if my friend Mikey had indeed died in the original timeline, along with myself, in a collision with that huge truck. Calling him Mikey only served as a temporary label so that I might feel comfortable, and in fact only what my mind would allow.

Though I had stared directly at his face for what seemed like centuries, I could not visualize him well enough to sketch his portrait on paper, although he did have a vague shape most of the time. Perhaps this was his preference, not wanting me to see that degree of detail and become attached to an image. Sometimes, while in the OBE state, he appeared like a much younger boy, glowing blue and with black hair. Yet he seemed to be able to present himself in many shapes and forms, the commonality being the instantly recognizable energy that radiated from him.

He had an aura and an energy signature that was absolutely unique. That's how I unfailingly recognized him, time and again regardless of appearance. He was someone I knew extremely well, yet could not describe, an interesting contradiction and a true enigma.

"So where do you work, Sky Man?" I asked facetiously, while testing a nickname. "I mean, if I want to contact you, where can I send an email or a letter?"

He completely surprised me by offering to take me to his workplace, where he said necessity had created a position that only he could fill. Complete astonishment was now becoming a common reaction to each answered question.

We arrived at a kind of school with a serious demeanour. It was vast, an extremely large structure in space, which is saying something because in that setting everything has so much room around each object that there is little contrasting background to provide scale. It looked very much like an advanced industrial warehouse, something you would see in a movie in which a billionaire or president uses hand-held devices and retinal scanners to enter, although its technology put ours to shame, making me feel like we are still living in the Stone Age. Its exquisitely crafted architecture was reminiscent of the room where I had been invited to celebrate my last milestone. This environment too had no "solid" floors or ceilings, yet there was the energetic impression of air vents and ducts, doors, lofts, mezzanines and staircases. The interior was dimly lit, although there were many self-luminous objects. The high "ceiling" had some sort of glowing LED-like lighting that wrapped around the entire area in a minimalistic pattern. The floor, desks, chairs, tables and signage too had a similar glow and pattern quite pleasing to the eye, yet the place's gravitas made it seem like the American president's emergency command room, with brightly illuminated, complex graphs spanning one grand wall representing the fate of the world. I intuited that all the many beings present were the most advanced in the building. They were not students, but great teachers in constant oversight of the developing timelines of the Earth, monitoring and taking action when necessary.

They looked very happy, some even quite excited. As I walked with Sanat, all the fifty or so who were directly in my line of sight turned and faced us. I had the feeling some of them had been here a very long time. Most had elected to come from Earth, having completed their ascension, fortunate souls because they had transcended their conditioning enough to explore beyond their physical planet's plane. A being in incarnation is not eligible to sign up for new adventures and projects until their experience on the Earth is complete. This is not to say that one cannot have the occasional experience out-of-body in which something specific is shown, even project to Venus, for example. But the soul is not allowed to begin a new soul assignment until all the plans for their incarnations have been completed and all lessons assimilated. There are advanced souls on the Earth who remember life before Earth. Some have recalled previous missions prior to incarnating here.

After graduation comes post-graduate studies with beings of different levels of mastery, who fill the need of beings still stuck in the game who need assistance to reach the final level of freedom. From that higher vantage point, they have great freedom to do that effectively, no longer bound to the duality of the Earth simulation. Comparatively advanced, accordingly greatly imbued with Divine Love, it is their great joy to help others reach the same level of freedom.

Sanat Kumara used the expression "last level" several times while we were there, although he never defined it further. He had such a delightful sense of humour, which often expressed itself by withholding such definitions, instead making funny cryptic references until understanding dawned on me. He was one for the dramatic and loved to create suspense and surprise.

"I am the owner-operator, CEO and head honcho," he stated. "I am the leader and these are my followers. I am the shepherd and these are my sheep – wait, maybe that one's already taken – or you could say I am a teacher and these are my students." The last metaphor appealed to me the most because I'd spent most of my life so far as a student in one school or another. It also implied the possibility of graduation.

The students seemed elated to see me. I was surprised they had all heard of me, possibly through my guide. Recognition lit their eyes when greeting me, as if a short break had intervened since they'd seen me last and had missed their dear friend. The lack of conscious memory of our relationship was not embarrassing, as I was getting used to it, and because the love they had for me was so great. Each one greeted me as I passed along the hallway on a guided tour of the facilities, a sparkle in their eyes in the warmest acknowledgement, some clasping my hands momentarily before resuming their tasks. I was told it was possible to become a student in the school while still alive in a physical body, but only rarely. In fact I met none who fit that description, although Sanat told me there was one, who was not present. Was I that student or was it someone else? After all, people seemed to recognize me.

There were other teachers present throughout the school, in classrooms that were more like laboratories. The goal for all students was to reach "oneness," or to realize Wholeness again, united with their Higher Selves through experiential research. I was shown that not all students had achieved their ascension, in fact many had not. Perhaps it was a school that students went to between embodiments, maybe also serving as a final classroom setting after completing their last life. I wondered, yet many questions remained unanswered.

Each student's curriculum was tailored to their specific hang-ups, to whatever was blocking their progress. Fear in all its forms was always at the root of it: fear of heights; drowning; disfigurement; fire; enemies; insanity; disease; abandonment; entrapment; poverty; death, by misadventure, illness, murder, wild animals, war and so on; letting others down; inadequacy; loss of control; supernatural forces; failure and even success. In some cases, greed, grief or attachment to material things and people were the major hindrances.

As I walked through the corridors, I saw each student had their own dedicated room designed for their particular learning curve. Most students had a desk and often a bed. Each of them seemed completely engrossed in the task at hand, many times not noticing our presence.

Like any institution, it had its dissidents. Simply being free of the physical body did not guarantee increased intelligence. There seemed to be different sets or classes of students, depending on their level of attainment. Some who had released their Earthly bonds felt no need of further education, sometimes out of a spirit of rebellion, sometimes out of doubt as to its value, perhaps because of a limiting belief that achieving ascension was beyond their ability. Some even believed it was only a myth.

114

There are accounts of beings who in their last life were very close to completing all their lessons, thus the notion of another embodiment was deemed unnecessary. In that situation, it is said they are carried up to Shambhala, where they are able to complete the last of their lessons in a place of less density, hence less interference. Was this school such a place? Many of the students did not seem like they were studying their final Earth lesson, however.

That said, the process of ascension has not been completed in droves as the beings in higher planes hoped for us. The ones who have fully completed it serve the school as educators. From what I could estimate, approximately two hundred beings total, at the time of my visit, had completed it at all. Some were present at the school. The others, it seemed, were somewhere else. That leaves a greatly disproportionate number of souls below, still in the process of completion. This information is not meant to discourage, only to illustrate how difficult it has become to let go of one's favourite game.

I wondered how this could be, as these students, like me, existed in their light bodies, a far superior state to being in a physical embodiment. In the short time that I was out of my body I had seen so much and had so many realizations crystallize. I wondered how it was possible that I seemed more advanced than these students, as from my perspective they were at a huge advantage attending this school full-time. As I viewed these souls, who seemed so much like Earthlings, very stuck in their ways, I thought perhaps I had been shown something special and had even heavier veils lifted.

While in the OOB state, truth is the universe's most ubiquitous and obvious feature. Freedom is also intimately associated with truth. One can choose to be ignorant, free to ignore reality, to only see what one wilfully wants to see. I could see this now reflected in the various attitudes of the students. That is the power and the gift of free will.

My guide led me from an atrium towards an upper floor as we scaled an illuminated wrought-iron staircase. The second floor had glass windows and floors, allowing us to view the busy workings below. Before me I saw a long and narrow corridor, with numerous doors on each side. The scene looked like something Dr. Seuss might have imagined, but even he may not have been able to capture its curvilinear surreality.

My visit thus far had convinced me that, if to become whole is the ultimate goal of all the students here, I did not want to be stalled some-where along the learning curve. My incandescent and only desire was to push through every obstacle as fast as possible, now that I knew there was a way. As I stepped forward, I opened a door to the left, the first of many in that hallway. I could not have imagined how that decision would unfold experiences orders of magnitude worse than the nightmare of planet Hell.

16.

Trials

THE DOOR CLOSED behind me. Very quickly the room began to dissolve as I was projected into the life of someone on Earth, just as I'd been placed on the Cosmic Divine Web while in nirvana after having escaped hell, only this time I was not pulled out quickly by an unknown force. I was on my own. There was no one who would come to grab me out of this body. I had been inserted as a witness, and at the mercy of that host person's actions. I did not quite understand what my goal was at first. It took some time to understand what was going on.

Each door I opened, one after another, transported me into someone's life. Each person was at a critical juncture: a decision had to be made that would shape their future or even their past. Imprisoned inside their body, I essentially just had vision and only sometimes was given the gift of slight control, similar to an ordinary dream, but even more restrictive. I was forced to go through their experience and feel what they were feeling, and to surrender, as there was nothing I could do, a spectator of their situation only. It was my job to take from it what I could.

In spite of the corridor only apparently having a small number of doors, perhaps eight on each side, I had to perform that act hundreds of times. Somehow the rooms themselves facilitated the jump into the other people's lives. They must have been reset in some way, as each door repeatedly opened onto a new experience.

The first body I stepped into was that of an older man, perhaps sixty or seventy years of age. He was a very busy, very wealthy Wall Street tycoon living in New York City. We were in his office building facing Central Park, close to the top of a luxury commercial skyscraper, near the end of closing time that day. He received a telephone call at his opulent desk, informing him that his only son had died after being hospitalized for some time. The tycoon had not visited his son even once during his illness. There was no excuse for the neglect, and he knew it. Yet the news of the death came as a shock, as in many ways he had taken his son's life for granted. His entire being flooded with remorse, not only because of this most recent failure, but because of any and all such lost opportunities that his long life and powerful position

117

had afforded him. It was as if a long overdue bill had been presented, with compound interest. Without warning, all that had accumulated caught up.

The choice presented was either to continue on the unhealthy path of love for money above all else or to begin to form meaningful relationships with others while there was still time. Even if he failed to create such a big change, it would serve him so much better to have a strong relationship with anything other than money: nature, art, sports, science, philosophy, even just reading for pleasure. It was his undivided fixation on money that was decaying his soul. For a moment, he seriously contemplated taking his own life. I begged and pleaded for him not to. He had no idea of the consequences, that he would be sent to a completely new kind of hell worse than his present existence. To take your own life is one of the greatest acts of ingratitude you can ever make to the universe that created you. This would have wide-ranging implications for your next embodiment and perhaps time spent in specific realms to process the gravity of your decision. Learning still takes place in order to *qualify for permission* to go through the incarnation process again, of course carrying the load of the additional karma attached.

The Creator does not desire people to take their lives. He wants us to learn to embrace love through the process of living. In that respect, a little time-out is often required so that hopefully that soul will learn not to take their life again. After that, you are reborn in a new incarnation inferior to whatever bad situation you started with, creating great delays in your incarnation cycle. A single suicidal act can take lifetimes upon lifetimes to pay off.

Fortunately for him, events took a turn for the positive. He joined his daughter-in-law's family, and so got to know his grandchildren and they him. He was able to form lasting bonds built on love and trust that began to soften even the hardest parts of his soul. Best of all, he was able to evolve at last.

Ejected from that test, I found myself sitting in the empty room, the level completed. I opened the door and exited into the hallway where I was welcomed by a small group of my teachers, including Sanat Kumara, politely ushering me towards the next door. This time I chose the one on my right. Again, only a second after the door had closed behind me, the white room began to dissolve and I felt myself being forcefully crammed into another human's physical body.

This time I was in far worse circumstances than before. The first room had only served as a warm-up exercise. I opened my eyes to find that everything was cold and dark. I could hear the echoes of beading water drip-drip-dripping on what sounded like a stone floor. As my eyes adjusted,

I saw I was locked away in a terrible dungeon, condemned to a life sentence. There seemed no possible escape from this abysmal trap. At first I panicked, afraid of being tortured. As time dragged on, my thoughts settled. I began to move through the stages of acceptance, letting go of all fears of being trapped, imprisoned, starved, abused, powerless and stripped of rights. I learned to figure out what was expected of me. Once I accepted the situation, I found freedom again.

Beyond another door, I was transported into the body of a driver who had accidentally killed a pedestrian. Although he could not have avoided doing so, the challenge was to deal with guilt and grief, to overcome knowing that he had inadvertently caused immense pain to others, and to try to see the bigger picture. I learned that it was highly desirable that a soul move past a major life trauma without picking up bad habits along the way, such as drinking or other destructive behaviour as a means of coping. The goal was to move past it and heal. Ironically, the lifetimes with the most adversity stood to have the most potential for learning and growth.

At one stage, I found myself trapped in a rapist's body. This was extremely alarming and unwanted. The moment I realized what the situation was, I thrashed about in panic – as I knew what scenes were sure to come – and I would have to *feel* them. I thought, *The universe sure has some interesting ways of teaching.* I looked deeply into the perpetrator's motives and innermost feelings. This was highly revealing. I was surprised to find myself very interested in understanding this character. As with all the others, I was given full access to all of his memories. I could flash back through them to find the causes of his behaviour and the seeds of his downfall.

In another sequence, I was trapped inside a murderer's body, a serial killer. Just when I thought the rapist was at my personal maximum limit, I was proven wrong. My teachers wanted me to experience the full spectrum of humanity, to gain a very elevated perspective on what constituted suffering and the opportunities each person is given through choice as appropriate response, perhaps so that when placed back into my own body I would be able to apply the graphic lessons to my own life, to see options as they arise instead of feeling caged in by circumstances. Little did I know how incredibly valuable the training would become.

Witnessing the murderer's life was a really terrible experience, probably the worst of all of them. I was not permitted to leave until I learned what I needed to. My initial fear and upset caused me to linger in the lesson a lot longer than necessary. If only I had been able to allow enough presence of mind to learn! That, however, required a certain level of mastery I did not have quite yet, so I stayed in his form for some time, watching him plan and commit numerous killings. I found myself hoping he would get caught. He too was toying with that idea. It turned him on. That disgusted me. Eventually I had to find a way to just watch the situation unfold in a very unbiased way to understand what was really going on. I was starting to see how my guides must be able to view our situations if they're to be of assistance.

After a while I was able to absorb enough information to form an understanding of what created such monsters. I was able to go through his life and see intervals that were absolutely traumatic, dark periods of family and societal abuse that led him to continue the cycle. In fact it was a miracle he was still alive after suffering so intensely. My heart finally found compassion and a deep desire to heal and console, as if he were a child who had gone very astray, a tremendous turnaround from when I first entered his life.

The better question now is, whose lives were they? Were they carefully hand-selected experiences of complete strangers or were they my lives at some point in time? It has taken me almost ten years to even consider that possibility because what I experienced in those rooms was so far out. I wouldn't have been able to accept it as a possibility then if it had been suggested, at least not in a constructive way. Knowing what I know now about how the Divine teaches, it seems highly improbable that they were not mine. It is much more likely they were creating a deeper healing in this life as well as my past ones. As the masters have often said to me, we have all walked the path of darkness so we can understand it and appreciate the light.

Then the experiences seemed to shift. I was no longer opening doors and being transported into other people's bodies in the quest to learn. I was now walking through doors and confronted with all my deepest and darkest fears. I discovered that one of my biggest fears was of being murdered myself, especially by being stabbed or disemboweled. Great.

Again and again, I was gored to death in every possible way! I could not help but be panic-stricken, even though I knew full well I would soon see my teachers and that no harm could come to me. My logical mind just couldn't help but keep interpreting everything that was happening as so *real*. Each attack felt so fatal. I saw myself unable to let go of the fear of losing my body. I was afraid of the pain. I was afraid of what would happen to me after I died. I did not trust that everything would be okay, so I clung on instinctively and repeatedly attempted to fight for my life.

I eventually learned that I could go within, that there was a hidden sanctuary beyond life and death. I could ignore the pain. This hidden sanctuary is available to us all, no matter the life circumstance. We all have the right to the inner peace within. That is something no one can ever take away. Once I was able to cease hating my killers, each situation would be over in a flash, not such an obvious realization when you are absolutely scared out of your mind and coming to grips with your life ending.

I was murdered hundreds of times in various different ways. Every time I successfully completed a new "hell simulation" a deep blackness would be extracted from my being and then disappear. This was progress for my soul. I began to see that I was advancing by subjecting myself to those cruel and unusual punishments. With each darkness expunged I began to feel ever so slightly lighter.

The darkness represented qualities such as greed, self-pity, vanity, desire and malice. Some students became stuck in one or another of these obstacle courses, as one might expect, because to overcome any one of them was daunting to say the least. Complacence and melancholy were usually the emotions that dampened the burning desire to move forward. The ego was largely responsible for it and constructed a barrage of compelling excuses for why one shouldn't do something that is in their best interest, such as, *You could never achieve that. We are comfortable where we are, aren't we?* Or the classic, *But what will people think?*

The study of those lives was by increments from relatively easy to most challenging. I had considered the notion of past lives so little that I hadn't done any exploration, but hoped they were not mine.

Each student had to learn to totally accept any experience in order to overcome the corresponding fear. The universe was showing me how skilled it was at creating experiences to evoke hidden fears and bring them to light. Despite how it may sound, this was done with the highest love and best intentions for all, as God doesn't want the lives he has given to be devoted to ignorant slumber, hiding in delusion or treading water in stagnant complacency. Yet many people eke out an existence here in which they live like an ostrich with its head in the sand. One can always try that method, but the Divine will always prod you forward. And yet I saw it was what many people chose, losing themselves in the distractions of the material world in order to prevent the necessary work on their inner being, essentially delaying the inevitable. This seemed like a funny contradiction to the eagerness the soul displayed just prior to embodiment. Now in human form, most just wanted to sleep.

While undergoing the testing in the different rooms, I experienced their worlds as totally real, but there was always the knowledge that I was actually in one of the rooms off that hyperspatial corridor, observed the whole time by the powers that had put me there. I could feel their eyes watching me through something like the mirrored windows of a booth in a police interrogation room. They were there to monitor my progress in case I came to an obstacle that was just too difficult or painful. Periodically, when I was stuck in a test that was particularly difficult and was screaming, I heard Sanat's powerful voice project from a loudspeaker: "*Let go!*" It would snap me back to the task at hand, reminding me that this was a test in many ways just like ordinary life. I thought, *Why couldn't this voice be with me all the time?*

My determination to succeed was great and, especially after I understood that nothing irremediable would happen to me, it became easier to subject myself to those horrors. I took solace in knowing there was a good reason for having to endure all the painful scenarios. Each was a test of faith. Sometimes it took a very long time to grasp what the lesson was. Yet what was consistently being taught was compassion for the *suffering individual,* whether victim or perpetrator, and above all to let go of hate.

As I completed the course, everyone seemed sad to see me go, although I was quite happy at leaving to experience something new. I had stayed in the hall of doors a lot longer than anyone had planned, but my desire to move forward had been very strong. I didn't imagine I would get another chance quite like it anytime soon. Having been given the information from my guide that I was behind on the plan for my life, I hoped this experience helped me to catch up. The opportunity to purge so much accumulated darkness from my soul in this type of guided environment had been a tremendous privilege. I'd wanted to release as much resistance as possible. I was very happy that I'd come and thanked myself for the courage to beg to stay disembodied a little longer or else this never would have happened.

I also was beginning to understand why my guide was so busy and had so many roles to play. The concept of "appointments" was also starting to make sense as I reflected on the beings I met at the beginning of the tour of the school, who were monitoring the plans for the Earth. My guide seemed to be very important. There were many students he was training, never mind his role of looking after the Earth. I now appreciated how valuable his time was and contemplated his comment about me being more powerful than him. He seemed extremely powerful indeed.

"I now want to introduce some important beings who want to meet you," Sanat Kumara said.

17.

Examination

IN THE ASTRAL plane, Higher Dimensional Communication (HDC) was often conveyed through images I was familiar with: scenes from movies, dramatic characters, cartoons, commercials, photographs or segments of songs, often with a humorous twist. For example, the last time Sanat said goodbye to me, he switched on an old radio as he was floating away, and the chorus from The Carpenters' song *It's Only Just Begun* came crackling through its loudspeaker.

We left the school Sanat presides over. He encouraged me with a very brief and direct pep talk – "You can do it, kid" – followed by a soft yet firm punch on my upper arm.

I didn't understand where he was directing me to so fast. Even he seemed hesitant about how I would fare. I still had questions for him regarding everything I was still processing from going through the doors, but it didn't appear there would be time for that.

I was now being introduced to a new group of beings, who employed the same methods of telepathic Lumaelian communication: presenting pictures, little movies and sounds containing the texture of words and phrases. I was not as proficient in the art. They gracefully demonstrated a profound ability, while I was concerned that I came across as a "telepathy as a second language" student. They appeared to be a kind of panel or committee whose members numbered from anywhere between four and seven. The memory of that detail is indistinct now. Maybe it's because they were of such bright whiteness that they were hard to look at, creating the illusion of their forms blending together. Everything suddenly went very dark. I sensed there were perhaps more beings participating as onlookers from further rows behind. I was right at centre stage. There was a bright spotlight overhead, further impeding my view of my surroundings. The situation seemed similar to an interrogation, only not quite that dramatic.

They were very friendly, but in an impersonal way and, I felt, not judgmental. Whoever those beings were, they seemed so advanced that no specific form was needed anymore. I sensed they were lowering their vibratory rate so that I would be able to perceive them at all. I wondered avidly what they really looked like and how they perceived each other. Their true form, whatever it was, must have been extremely beautiful in higher dimensions because even just standing close to them flooded my entire system with a rebalancing euphoria, as though lifetimes of being slightly off-key were tuned up as I was rebooted to my original factory settings.

Sanat introduced us, but then departed, leaving me unsure of what the meeting was about. It was clear his presence was no longer needed for this part of the journey, like a parent dropping their child off for an exam. Was it some kind of interview? Would I be expected to make some kind of pitch? If so, I was unprepared.

I moved into a place reminiscent of a colosseum with them, where they formed a semicircle of sorts around me and began to ask questions.

One of the members of the tribunal addressed me: "Please tell us why you should be allowed to advance."

I felt completely flustered because I was off guard. It seemed like a really important question. Until that night, I hadn't realized that soul advancement was something to be desired or under my conscious control. I hadn't considered my spiritual progress with this degree of seriousness – let alone ever given thought to what I could possibly say to make my case should a panel of advanced light beings offer the opportunity.

Many nervous thoughts ran through my head, all of which I wished I had been able to shield them from. I thought if they were as omniscient as they seemed to be, they must already know *all* about me and know I didn't have an answer. I wondered, were they just curious about how I would react?

I don't remember what I said then in response, but it must have struck the right chord as some strange force came through and answered for me. I am not sure exactly what I did or said, but I know my soul performed something. I can say it was some type of action that is unfamiliar in life on Earth, but the impression it gave was something reminiscent of singing. Whatever it was, my conscious self wasn't able to interpret it in a way that made sense – it was as if the higher portion of my soul took over at that point, the part that had the answer. It seemed to be filtered from ordinary perception, yet I felt a small relief that at least I had demonstrated *something*.

Certainly the little me, the portion that lived an ordinary life, did not believe I had anything of value that could persuade them to permit my soul to advance. I felt undeserving and had no idea of what was at stake. I knew there was no reason to feel so down on myself and recognized that I still needed to learn how to step into my power.

I spent a long time with the committee in HDC, during which they answered some of my questions about past lives and presented further teachings and suggestions for my life upon returning to the physical domain. They added that, out of all my lives, it was interesting that the current one was the first one in which I had decided to become an artist. It was a new role for me. I was told I was often a writer or a teacher in previous existences.

In a very recent life, I'd been an astronaut who had died in an accident on her first space flight assignment. She was to be the first teacher in space. Her name was Christa McAuliffe. That launch would go down in history as the space shuttle *Challenger* explosion. I found this very interesting. The information aligned well with many early childhood memories and desires.

I loved space. From the moment I learned of it, I just wanted to hear more. When I was in kindergarten, astronauts visited our class, and we got to eat dehydrated strawberry space ice cream. I was hooked. Immediately I told my mother that I was going to be an astronaut. She was not thrilled by the idea and told me it was too far from home. But I had fragmented memories, that seemed like only yesterday, of being aboard a spacecraft. I could feel the G-forces on my face while strapped into a reclined seat looking at a brightly illuminated complex dashboard. But the vision always ended abruptly right after take-off. I shifted my deep desire for space exploration to painting outer-space subjects.

I contemplated their comment about being an artist for the first time, in my current life. Was that really true? I thought for sure I had been an artist in some distant life as well, perhaps during the Renaissance. I wondered if perhaps it had never been considered my full-time occupation before.

Looking around at my present surroundings, it would appear that I had accomplished an even greater feat. Many previous lives had been difficult and exhausting, but this time around I had more freedom to do whatever I pleased. In past lives, it seemed I had a lot to prove, both academically and intellectually. My current lifetime does not carry the same burden. Indeed the task at hand is to simply *just be.*

I loved to read, but had only recently acquired the surprising impulse to write. Yet I didn't consider myself any good at it. No one had ever encouraged me to be a writer. In fact I'm pretty sure every English teacher I had would have advised to pursue another path. English was the one class, especially as I got older, that seemed harder and harder to excel at. Comprehension was effortless, but when it came to writing, formulating and constructing my well thought out ideas on paper, it seemed communication in words was not my friend. I took far too long at exposition and wrote too many words to get to the point. I struggled to earn a C grade. I naturally excelled at science and the visual arts, compensating to raise my grade point average. To learn I had often been a writer was interesting, as I had never considered it a talent, nor had I had any desire to become a teacher. That news seemed even more foreign. I had attached a stigma to the role of teacher as an old, outdated woman, trying to lecture her students perhaps.

Yet a far more important question came to mind. I sensed that I needed to word it very wisely: "What should I tell people of my experiences?"

"It does not matter really whether you say anything or not. You will be a different person now, which will manifest in ways you cannot yet see."

"Should I write a book about my experiences?"

"It is entirely up to you what you want to do now."

Like Sanat Kumara, the tribunal often didn't answer my questions. I got the impression that I was being overly inquisitive. But really I was just looking for some kind of direction. How can I resume a normal life after something like this, how could I relate to anyone, having such a powerfully moving experience that transforms all parts of your person, and feeling like you never really have someone to share it with or who could truly understand? Do I keep it sacred and secret or is it my responsibility to share it with everyone? The questions weighed on me greatly. The fact that they could not direct me signalled that these imponderables were going to take some time to process.

I had just been shown the Holy Grail of existence, privy to direct teachings about why we exist, the true meaning of life. Yet who was I to be the voice that spoke these truths? Surely there were people more qualified, better equipped to share those things. And yet I couldn't deny that I was the one present. For some beautiful reason it was my experience and mine to share if I should so choose.

Very few questions were answered directly, including ones about who they were. They seemed so non-attached, much more so than Sanat. If they had been human, it was so long ago that humanity's concerns had nearly been forgotten. Rather than individuals, they seemed more of a collective entity. They also tested me in ways that didn't make sense. For that, I was given a small hand-held device about five inches square. It displayed many different characters and had spinning portions that needed to be matched up in some sort of sequence. I worked with it for some time, reminded of early primary school tests with matching images and fitting the correct blocks into their respective holes.

I then sat down on a bench that appeared, which had a very large projection screen in front, almost the whole length of a side of the stadium. I was glad to sit, as I was longing to take a mental break, although not wanting to leave their presence entirely. The panel showed an image of planet Earth, only without the human population. I assumed it must be either far in the future, when its natural untrammelled beauty could flourish without inhibition, or in the very ancient past. In addition to lush tropical flora, I could see colourful airborne birds and pristine tranquil beaches. This world seemed to be a living, sentient entity, like an animal, aware of its environment in space. Such a being must have felt extreme pain and anguish when the human species infested it. It seemed like I sat there for hours, peacefully watching the sequence of sublime images on the screen.

The presence of the committee imposed a state of harmony that is the standard for alignment with the highest aims of the cosmos. This state brought with it the obviousness of the nature of manifestation, how mind creates personal realities. All people without exception participate in this creative activity. I wondered how divinely perfect *the committee's* powers of manifestation must be. Since I was not given a name to call them, I have named them the Elders, as that is how I interpreted them to be, although I am sure there is a more divinely inspired name they go by that better expresses the serenity they provide the universe.

By extension, everything in my own life was there because I made it happen, on every level. Because of me, existence is. Because of existence, I am. The two are inseparable. I had, as explained, heard about the law of attraction and techniques of manifestation. But I couldn't see how meditations and visualizations could have any practical application when it doesn't matter whether your creation comes in an instant or thousands of lifetimes later.

We are creators. Our creations are absolutely dependent on the signals we broadcast. The correspondence is exact, like an image in a mirror. But, you know, making faces in a mirror is fun sometimes. Just don't get sucked into believing that face you see is who you are. My earthbound aspect kept making that mistake, reverting to the belief that I was just this smaller version of myself, who did not understand fully the impact of each decision I made.

I had studied much, trying to understand my higher self and how to create the circumstances I wanted, yet I couldn't say I was having any luck in changing my life. I ate healthy and worked out at the gym often, yet I weighed and looked the same. I tried to find new friends and change my living situation, yet my outer world stayed the same as well. I gave in to periods of stagnation because to continue to try for change and to see none was exhausting. This led me to discredit a lot of the information I had gathered, not being able to validate it through experience.

Even so, dreaming was one of the gifts I seemed to have some intermittent success with. But even that I was not able to perform on command.

I had not understood there were many reasons why my manifestations were blocked. It was not due to not trying hard enough. I was able to see there were some things that my God Presence did not want me to have. In fact she was the one doing the blocking. She had demagnetized me from getting certain jobs and even meeting new people. It was not part of my path to go on to a medical career. In fact the progress of my highest plan was overdue, so she had to use any means necessary to propel me in the right direction, even if that included accidents. I have come to know her as Zeta – that is the name she goes by – and she is highly adventurous, all about high-risk plans. Not everyone's higher self is like this. I saw that we each have truly different higher personalities caring for us.

I first discovered her name three years ago. Hers would be the first divine name to intuit. I have now helped many people do the same. I had travelled to Arizona to take care of my girlfriend's cat while she took a vacation, at the same time preparing for an art exhibition there. Her tiny kitten was so magical. She had the ability to absolutely vanish from the apartment for hours, which caused concern. Not being able to find her, I would eventually get absorbed in another task only for her to spontaneously appear in the blankets on the couch beside me. She had not yet been named, only labelled as "kitten." I believed this little cat greatly desired a better name. I quite abruptly heard a voice whisper in my ear – "*Zeta*" – and was shown an image of the beautiful actress Catherine Zeta Jones. *What an absolutely beautiful name,* I thought. Enamoured of it, I took to calling her Zeta during my time there. While it didn't appeal to her owners, after I returned to Canada the name stuck with me.

While driving my car one day, my mind still seemed very stuck on thinking about that kitten and the name I had given her. I acknowledged that some part of me was thinking, *Why couldn't that be my name?* I had been trying to intuit the name of my God Presence for months to no avail. A surprising thought process began: *Why was I so attached to that silly name I gave a kitten? Why did I want it so badly?* It seemed a strange desire. I decided to explore it. My given name is very unique. I have felt it was perfect for me my whole life, at least until now. Sarazen is a beautiful name, and many would say it suits me just fine. Then it hit me. Zeta *is* my name.

Months passed by. I decided to let the idea of the name settle. If it was right, then I would know, allowing myself time to get comfortable with it. One day I passed by a shop I'd never noticed before, only a few blocks down the street from where I lived. Its signage read "Zeta Cafe." This was news to me. It's a very uncommon name. I was sure I would have noticed something like that before. It piqued my interest enough to research the symbolic meaning of the name Zeta.

To my surprise, there was a definition listed in *The Urban Dictionary*: "1. A concept (heretics refer to it as a 'function') in mathematics. 2. The meaning of life, the universe and all. *Zeta will show the limits of the human mind.* 3. God."

What a strange and elaborate game I seemed to have created for myself! Amazed at the magic of the universe, exhaling slowly I thought, *I have some rather large shoes to fill.* Whatever did *that* mean?

18.

Parallels

SITTING IN THE car waiting for such a long time was making me – or Zeta Zero, as my husband likes to call her – restless. I have officially named her Dimension One, as it seemed more dignified to promote the lowest part of myself to at least number one. But I admit that "Zeta Zero" has a ring to it, and often in conversation with others that is her name.

My guide said, "Do you want to play another video game?"

"Sure, but only as long as it's not as gory as the last one," I insisted.

"Well, what do you want to play then?" he asked.

"A long time ago I had a computer game called *Lara Croft: Tomb Raider* which was pretty fun. I guess I could play that."

In possession of the power of enhanced imagination as before, we became immersed in the stunning picturesque landscapes that were larger than life. This time I was able to play for quite a while, now that the scary epidemic of crazed nurses had gone away. I found this new game quite intriguing. It had beautiful graphics with lots of semi-tropical foliage and interesting ancient ruins to explore. I was having fun. But then my attention started to wander. The same distant restlessness returned strongly.

A signal demanded my attention. Now agitated, I wondered what I was doing still waiting for an eternity in the car. I was also feeling two very distinctly uncomfortable events happening simultaneously. In one, it was as if I were bombarded with information, hundreds of thousands of images and other stimuli channelled into my consciousness from above. Zeta Zero was not intelligent enough to determine what was going on, but my higher dimensional self did and showed each piece of information to her with precision. Concurrently I felt the intense pressure of a powerful unknown force trying to cram itself in. It was causing panic. I could no longer concentrate on playing the game. Was I just being babysat? What was its purpose?

On top of all that activity, I began to feel the heavy weight of all my personal possessions. I didn't know what compelled me to collect so many things over the course my life. I wanted to rid myself of them. Every sweater, even every sock was like an anchor sinking my attention into a dark, dank depth I wanted no part of. I could also see how much more powerful I was without their limiting weight and desired to stay in the space of instantaneous creation as long as I could.

I wanted to travel so light that everything I owned could fit into a backpack, including all my emotions. My desk, my bed, my new computer, my car: all those things were unwanted burdens. Freedom seemed to demand shedding almost everything I owned. Truly, I was acutely aware that all I needed was my soul, the only constant I'd had while travelling on such a long journey, and I'd done just fine. Nevertheless, I was operating under the assumption I literally had to defy gravity to continue to travel. Logic implied that if I didn't get rid of all my belongings, I would not be able to easily re-enter the exalted state again, because attachment to them would weigh me down.

I wanted to start the unloading process immediately. I looked down and began the countdown to lift-off by ransacking my purse. I found my earrings, stood up and threw them into the woods beside the parking lot. Walking further away from the car, I threw lip glosses next.

Sanat stopped me by saying, "You may not remember doing this in the morning. What'll it be like to wake up and see that all those things are gone? You might blame someone else for stealing them. Think about it."

"I'm not concerned. Drunk people lose stuff all the time. Besides, I have my ways of remembering everything I want to." I got into the back seat of the car and pulled out the ashtray at the end of the console between the front seats. Ripping its lid off, I threw it out too. It felt so good to be destructive.

"Stop it, Sarazen, this is childish. You'll be upset at yourself in the morning. I repeat: even worse, you might blame someone else."

I couldn't argue with his logic, but I was in no mood to be agreeable or act reasonably. Whatever emergence was happening, I wanted no part of it. The trip had taken a toll on my emotions. I wanted to escape my physical body and its world by sheer indiscriminate will power alone, just like at the beginning when trapped in the coffin before being feasted on by crocodiles.

The version of me in the car, the physical person, was just one aspect of what was happening simultaneously elsewhere. On separate planes, other sides of me were having many, many other adventures. Meanwhile, the girl in the car was flooded with images as she downloaded the thousands of lessons her soul was learning. She wanted to freak out and run away. She was beside herself with impatience too because it seemed like at least six hours had passed waiting for "Mikey's" ride to show up. Worried that Alexander, who was bound to arrive soon, would find her in a flustered state only made matters worse. He had often insinuated that she lacked self-control. Ironically, he did not see that mistrust, suspicion and accusation only created more of the very behaviour he rejected.

"Mikey, call your ride. Hurry him up."

"You can go inside while I wait out here if you want."

"No! I don't want you to wait out here alone after going to all the trouble of driving me home."

19.

Becoming One

THE PANEL OF Elders expressed their pleasure at my progress and the understanding I had gained from the trials, deaths and sacrifices. My reward would be to go to a state of "singularity." This is my term, which after my research is the closest I can find to what the Elders simply expressed in a "ball" or bundle of thought that I absorbed and immediately understood.

Sanat Kumara was brought back in. He also seemed very pleased. "Come with me," he motioned. My guide took me to several places but, as before, the events in each version of myself happened simultaneously. I reasoned that if all were accompanied by my guide, then all of them must be one and the same. In one iteration, we flew through space for a very long time and eventually arrived at the centre of the universe.

"If this is the centre, is there an end, a boundary?" I asked.

"Like time, space is spherical, but not in the geometric way you're used to thinking of the meaning of that word. Your curious mind is not allowing you to discover it yet. Be still. Let understanding arise."

Our destination was a vast, almost immeasurable blue orb, the Source of Creation where all information is coordinated. We hovered there. I stared at the orb for what seemed centuries. Its hypnotic surface was a kind of jelly-blue plasma, incessantly shifting its hues, tints and patterns, the face of a super intelligent entity. It's impossible to describe how a blue ball could be so magnificent, which had more to do with the invisible energy radiating from it than its visual image, incredible as that was.

On a higher level, the version of myself that had just passed all the testing had gone to the state of singularity. There was no moment in which it took place, which sounds strange because we're so used to labelling moments either "before" or "after" due to our concept of linear time. The feeling was somewhat similar to what I'd experienced during my trip to Source, that huge web of comfort, only now I actually *became a part of* the universal web of existence instead of being an outside observer.

I was now alone and could feel my soul being positioned effortlessly into the proper alignment. I was not scared. Any part of me that could object switched off. I then began to feel an expanding sensation that started slowly at first, like all the molecules, atoms and particles that comprised my body were being gradually spaced out. Things began to speed up. Every single atom in my "body" collided and exploded in an infinity of directions. This process repeated again and again until it seemed I had no atoms left to smash, eventually leaving me with the feeling of being an immense multi-dimensional blanket. I enveloped everything. There was nothing in the universe that escaped my gentle touch. My intelligence penetrated every nook and cranny known and unknown, seen and unseen.

Everything was accessible in the infinite database. I knew everything all at once without exerting any outward effort. Unlike the nirvanic visit to Source, I never wanted to leave the state of singularity. Perhaps "singularity" is not even the best word for this state. It might be more appropriate to say I merged with the Creator. To call it a state of singularity diminishes it by tacking a vague technical label on such a powerful state of being. This state embodied the full feeling of the Power of Creation and Universal Intelligence simultaneously expanded to infinity. In short, I was God.

If I honed my attention, I could interpret a large number of scenes playing themselves out around the universe, which felt like I had created them because our will was one. I could see the light and the dark battling it out, as they often do, and indeed found it supremely interesting to observe that dynamic. I no longer found sorrow in the sadness of a small few. I could see everything that was to come to them in the future and everything that had ever happened to them in the past. It truly was all good, and apparently all for my personal enjoyment. I drew much pleasure from watching everything in Creation unfold before my very eyes.

I could not have cared less if I ever went back to my physical body, my life or even if I might be missed. I felt so much bigger than that because I literally was everything. My life on Earth subsequently seemed like an ancient dream that happened to somebody else because in this state I was emotionally non-attached. It might sound like indifference or a lack of love, but such was not the case.

Love was not an emotion, although it didn't preclude emotions. Love was simply *everywhere* and permeated *everything*. Love was what the entire universe was made of. There was no place where Love was not. For the darkness to exist, even in the deepest reaches between the galaxies, there had to be some light. After all, it was my Creation. All was an imperturbable, perfect, beautiful and loving tranquility. An ever-present, absolute stillness and peace pervaded the dynamism of Creation. It was as if I had died and gone back to my true natural state, which was absolutely blissful, totally fulfilled. There was nothing I needed or wanted, because I knew there was nothing that I couldn't create and it was all me anyway. I knew that a part of me had been here forever and had never left. That realization filled me with deep warmth and contentment. It had just been forgotten because part of my consciousness had split off to do its own thing, something I could never justify again. *How could I ever want to break away from this transcendent state?* The thought seemed ludicrous. Why would I not want to be God?

After aeons merged with the Great Divine, an unknown force pulled me back to Earth. Perhaps a signal had come from my physical form, because I felt a strong need to return to it. Reluctantly, I decided to go back to live out my last Earthly life. The calmed waters of emotions stilled by my trip to singularity had been replaced with turbulence. I now became depressed to the point of aching bitterness. Despite the decades of astral experiences under my belt, in which I held no attachment to Earthly life nor identified with any form or role, my consciousness seemed in jeopardy.

I didn't just snap out of one state into another – the state of singularity lingered for some time. It was a slow transition. After being so free, it was hard at first to take the tragicomedy of human life seriously again. Maybe it was for the best that darkness was part of it. After all, it was *just a game*.

20.

Meeting *the* I AM

IN ANOTHER ITERATION, my consciousness branched off, ushered to somewhere very special. I don't know exactly how I arrived there, but it was to be arguably my most significant meeting yet. I recognized this was a sacred space, very bright and permeated with gold. There were passing scenes all around in what looked like some sort of shielded environment so that no one could access our private meeting, creating an illumined fishbowl effect.

Dozens of golden angels came to my side to escort me, the most glorious ones I had seen yet, fit for a prestigious heavenly queen. They were draped in luxurious textiles, also golden. They had many musical instruments, such as trumpets and harps. I suspected they might be seraphim angels who, according to Christian angelology, belong to the highest order of the ninefold celestial hierarchy. They are associated with light, ardour and purity. What I was witnessing was very close to what many artists through the ages have tried to capture. They were the most spectacular display of the heavenly messengers I had ever hoped to see.

I was ushered into the middle of a giant, swirling, golden vortex of light. It was about fifty feet in diameter and rose higher than I could see. The whirlwind seemed to have objects in it, mixed scintilla that served as shielding. The particles too were golden in colour, moving at such a fast rate of speed that I was unable to determine what they were made of. I felt my hair swept back. Floating silently, I did not know what to expect next. It was then that I was graced by a most powerful presence. An unknown majestic force came to me and spoke. His voice boomed. While there was no visible face, what I felt was a greater connection than to any being I had ever encountered before.

Very clearly, He questioned: *"Has it been so long that even you do not remember me?"*

As he spoke, I was engulfed in the passing tornado, consumed with emotion trying to interpret what was going on. This was unlike any meeting I had ever had before. I felt myself raised up to a more convenient height. He seemed patient, giving me time to think. I tried to look within to find recognition of the question that He had asked. His voice was very deep and bold, thunderous even as it shook me to the core. I was very alert and clear-headed, although unable to think fast enough to come up with an intelligent response. We paused in a long silence.

An insight came. A deep familiarity began to rise to the surface. It was not something that I could put into a clear verbal thought. Indeed, I absolutely recognized this being, but from where? He seemed so ancient and powerful – even mighty, a word I do not use often – but He was that too. I continued to float in silence, allowing more remembrance to arise naturally. The less worried I became about remembering the easier it was. He seemed like someone I had known forever, yet somehow had completely forgotten. How could this be? How could I ever forget this relationship, this deep a connection? The magnitude of power radiating from the tornado all around was sweeping me away and my attention along with it as I tried to contemplate His strength. I didn't know exactly what I was experiencing, because I was so overtaken by the power of the moment, but that bond seemed of utmost importance, a friendship vital to my personal existence.

He then spoke again powerfully, booming: "*I AM THAT I AM.*"

I did not understand what He was saying. I had never consciously heard of that name before. How could anyone's name be I AM? That was an introductory phrase, I thought, and believed what I was hearing must be incorrect. I waited for Him to complete the sentence. After a long moment passed and no further information seemed forthcoming, I sought clarity. "What? I – I don't understand!" I yelled loudly through the thundering windy torrent encircling us.

He repeated: "*I AM THAT I AM.*"

There was no mistake nor any room for misinterpretation. As confused as before, I accepted the words He spoke with such unquestionable directness.

What happened next was a blur preceding becoming trapped in the folds of the sands of time. I stayed suspended in mid-air and was lifted up higher to view Him face to face, so to speak. My arms were raised to my shoulder level. I stayed there for some time amidst that unspeakably fantastic and chaotic display of power. There was a long time spent in communication, but that was where memory was permitted no longer and direct witnessing cut off. Perhaps that is something only my individualized God Presence Zeta was privilege to.

Then there was a shift in perception. A deeper explication of my plan was being communicated, what I was to do now united with intense soul work I gratefully received. The shimmering golden vortex began to transform. While it still held its outer rigid shape to shield any other being from accessing it, part of its interior began to dissolve into a golden waterfall. The I AM sent His helpers to me: I was surrounded by the most beautiful golden birds, slightly resembling toucans, except maybe even more exotic and prehistoric-looking. They had very round bodies and much rounder, fuller beaks. And they were unbelievably friendly, surrounding me, nuzzling into my neck and caressing me with their boundless joy.

Accompanying those exotic birds were the seraphim, who served two roles. Some were stationed as protectors. I could see them guarding the perimeter of the whirlwind, keeping an eye both on me and the surroundings. Others not on guard aided in the transformation process. These two roles were interchangeable, however, and some switched back to guarding, then swooped back down again and resumed working on me, a fully synchronized and seamless acrobatic display of the greatest finesse. It was as though the I AM was the choreographer of this scintillating ensemble, and they his consorts. There were beings other than birds in that sacred space as well, possibly resembling fairies, but it all happened far too fast for my mind to apprehend their movements. *This is the most thrilling experience of my life,* I thought.

It was the most sublime immersion I had ever undergone, a baptism of sorts, such a state of hypnotic euphoria that nothing else existed in that moment. I prayed to fully let go, allowing myself to receive it all. No words could express my gratitude as the Creator Himself showed His great care for me.

21.

Life Before Earth

I WAS CURIOUS about what the other fragments of my soul were up to and tried to tune in to the various frequencies they were operating on to see if I could receive some information. Just then I became aware of a part of my soul that was on a slightly lower plane, flying at great speed. Intuition was activated. I toggled my awareness there.

Flying at Mach speeds with my guide, we seemed to be headed to a planet that was very nearby, so close in fact that it was Venus. It looked very different in higher planes, however, just like Earth had been almost unrecognizable in this dimension. It was beautifully blue with touches of pink, with sweeping clouds lightly breezing across the upper stratosphere, tinted by a soft magenta hue. We travelled effortlessly though the lower levels of the atmosphere and landed at what seemed the planet's capital point of interest.

There I saw an enormous palace in the style of ornate baroque architecture. The entrance was graced by an immaculate promenade, which was lined by trees with broad full leaves and continued towards a lake to its left. Beautiful young people, who all appeared to be close to their mid-thirties, walked the paths, some with babes in prams, enjoying a beautiful mild summer day. The sky had a yellow glow, and the sun was partially obscured by light cloud cover.

This place was very familiar, although I could not say why. I felt very much at home. Something about it was reminiscent of the dream state as well. Maybe it was because everything seemed so perfect.

Sanat guided me into an Active Memory from the not-so-distant past. We landed on the palace grounds on the soft grass of a wide field between the main entrance and the lake. All was effortless and bright. No discord or interference of any kind was evident. I felt truly at ease. The memory moved forward. He held me as we rolled in the grass. Sparkles enveloped us, like the drops of dew themselves were actually magical liquid light that burst at our touch. I had never seen anything like it before and was dazzled, although the version of me connected to the Active Memory just laughed. My soul touched his and I felt so close to him that I never wanted to be separated, nor for the moment to ever end.

I looked at him as we laughed and rolled down the gentle grassy hillside. His skin began to sparkle with a glorious intensity, just like when he first showed me his true form while sitting in my car. I picked out notes of many different colours, but primarily his overall hue had become a deep gold, sprinkled with lighter, more luminous specularity. From the bottom of the hill, I cast my gaze up to the forest and saw the trees were performing the same scintillating light show. Everything here was so alive.

I looked at my hands and arms. *I was glowing too.* I now had control and was an active participant in the scene. He was right: we were the same, and I did indeed glow. My heart felt very much at peace as he began to talk.

"Sarazen, this is your home and you know this place very well. You are a part of my family, and in fact I am your father."

There was a pause as I took a moment to internalize what he had just said. It resonated immediately, the only explanation for the familiar feelings about this place and the depth of my feelings for him. My mind, however, began to hang up on the Earthly hurt feelings emerging. I became upset. "But, I don't understand," I interjected as tears started to well.

"It has taken us a very long time to forge our plans. You are starting to come into full remembrance now of everything that you really are. The days are going to increase in difficulty. You will be tempted to turn your back on your plan and even me. You are my daughter, and I have made an oath to you to get you home safely, something I take very seriously. This is goodbye for now, but not forever, and I will return for you, in time."

My mind was now completely consumed with racing thoughts. On the one hand, I was deeply touched. He clearly loved me so much. I could feel it with every fibre of my being. I also could sense that every word he spoke was truth, yet my heart started to break. I had been raised without ever knowing my father. He had chosen to have another family, which was very difficult for me to accept as I grew up. In recent years I had begun searching for him. In the midst of that I learned that he had just died of colon cancer. I did not take the news well and felt I had lost a part of myself I would never get to know. Yet there was some wiser part of my soul that never gave up the desire for the fatherly bond, something I felt was lacking but knew must be somewhere. That desire seemed irrational. It hadn't made any sense. Perhaps I was never allowed to know my biological father so that I would keep looking for the bond with my real one, even if he did live in higher planes.

I tried to push him away, feeling hurt and abandoned already at his mention of leaving me again. His words had revived a deep pain. How was

I supposed to know if this was real or not? How convenient was it that I had now met my father? My mind could be completely making this up to fill a void. Yet, looking around, I could not deny that I was distinctly on another planet, something I had not thought up nor could control, an external environment I did not have the power to create. Still, I did not want to believe his words were true. At the same time, I could not deny that it now made sense why this powerful being had gone to such lengths to guide and protect me on my journey. Looking into his soul, I saw that not only was he incapable of lying, he would have nothing to gain by it.

I tried to speak several times, but could not find the words. My deepest emotions were tangled as I continued to try to restore my previous concept of reality on Earth. Neither of us spoke. He held me firmly in a deep embrace as if he saw I needed it. Truly, it was going to be the last one for a very long time, which only made me weep all the more. The part of me that readily accepted this information thought, *But I've only just found you, and now you're leaving me again?*

He then resumed the Active Memory that showed my original departure from Venus, rendering me an observer again. It began to superimpose on our experience until gradually I no longer had any control over my actions. Then too we rolled on the sweet effervescent grass sparkling in the sun. We were so close, two peas in a pod. We lay there for some time and spoke inaudible goodbyes to each other.

We rose from the grass and walked to a nearby gazebo. There I saw more family members waiting, all young, apparently in their thirties, two females and one male. They were some of my siblings, my sisters and my brother. We sat with them, and it truly was a pleasant visit. I wondered why I would ever want to leave a paradise as blissful as ours.

Teary-eyed but filled with immense joy, we each gave one another our personal style of goodbye filled with blessings as they wished me unfailing success. I felt very confident, fearless. I thought the goodbyes were a bit over the top and unnecessary, as I believed I would see them again in no time at all. Perhaps they were cognizant of something I was not. I did seem somewhat overzealous and naive. I stood up and began to walk towards a large vortex that appeared not far from where we were sitting. For the first time I began reviewing the cycle of my reincarnations.

22.

Lifetime Pre-Planning

AFTER BEING SHOWN Venus and the memories of who I have come to know as my spiritual father, Sanat Kumara, I was upset. The lower parts of my soul were reeling in agony, so fond of him and missing him so much, wondering how it could be real, even though I had just lived the experience through viewing the "akashic records." My lowest dimensions were doubtful. The middle parts felt abandoned and betrayed. The higher, more advanced parts easily accepted parting, while rejoicing that they'd been blessed with a reunion, already prepared to move ahead.

The *akasha,* or akashic records, a vast database, is the perfect catalogue of every event, word and thought-form ever created, on Earth and elsewhere. Imagine the most massive computer server in the universe for that purpose.

Sanat directed my attention back to Earth. We circled back there. It was funny how Earth felt so little like home anymore. The place I had been so terrified to leave no longer resonated with my heart. I truly felt like an outsider looking down at a self-destructive world I no longer wanted to participate in.

We hovered high above the planet. I could see the beautiful glinting halo of its atmosphere and immediately became immersed in a part of another Active Memory unfolding. While it occurred a long time in the past, it seemed like it was in the present as I relived it in the same fashion I had on Venus, in a way experiencing it as if for the first time.

I was with a large group of souls, most of whom I knew extremely well, some from before my very first incarnation and others I had grown to know through many, many lifetimes together, somewhere between thirty to forty individuals plus a small handful I wasn't intimately connected with. We were engaged in a very in-depth conversation that required a high level of attention to detail, Earth floating below us, the focus of our attention.

Four or five of us in particular had incredibly complex interconnected plans. Together we orchestrated our last embodiments. We collectively chose Vancouver, Canada, as the host city where we could focus most of our work. There was a huge advantage to this location. As we orbited the globe, touching it lightly with our consciousness, we zoomed in on Vancouver as if it were on a self-illuminated, interactive map. It nevertheless was the natural planet Earth, not a hologram or product of advanced technology. The seaport city shone with bright light, a beacon, with many important structures buried off its coast yet to be rediscovered. I saw emerald pyramids buried among the fault lines in the seabed, and other hidden treasures partially shielded, not yet ready to be unveiled.

Not every soul who was a part of this advanced team chose Vancouver. A small handful chose cities elsewhere in the world in harmony with what they needed to accomplish. But we ensured it was inevitable that our paths would cross, as there were important occurrences to come during each of these encounters, gifts we would give one another, memories we would help unlock, powers we would bestow on each other. We created fail-safe after fail-safe, just in case things did not go as planned.

The extreme complexity of the plans were, firstly, limited by cosmic law in what we could create. Secondly, our desires were to be aligned fully with the Divine's plan for humanity and the awakening of the planet. Thirdly, we needed to ensure that each personal plan included everything necessary for a person to advance on the Earth plane to complete each individual ascension.

The process of ascension is a process of remembering who you are, reconnecting to what created you and mastering every lesson posed by living in duality. Many souls spend lifetime after lifetime repeating the same lessons, hell-bent on preserving broken manifestation loops they have grown attached to. To overcome the world by seeing through all the illusions facing us as only stepping stones we have created is a very challenging and arduous process. One has to be fearless. One has to be brave, brave enough to face and take responsibility for all of one's self-created darkness. One also has to come to accept that one truly knows nothing of how life came into existence or why we are here. It is only in the depths of openness that the Divine will be able to provide answers.

The game has become extremely complex as it has morphed and been subjected to countless modifications because of outside interference, effectively making the code nearly impossible to crack.

To master every lesson is something that takes a remarkable degree of tenacity, the reason that far fewer than 1,000 people have ever transcended the Earth plane so far. Many do not desire to become a master of their life.

A person has to create a self-generated burning desire for truth, one that burns brighter than any desire for material comforts. Once one has gained enough wisdom, such comforts lose their appeal because they are known to be impermanent. It doesn't matter how strong a house you build or how much money you save, all can be lost in an instant. The only guaranteed security is in self-knowledge, freedom, the art of achieving the requisite escape velocity to leave the material plane.

Yet people are drawn to routines, the familiar comforts that can entrap them. They come in many forms, often wearing the clever disguise of stability and support. For example, having grown into a different person along the way, stagnant relationships with loved ones may now need to be released so that resentment, feeling smothered, unloved or unwanted, possibly misunderstood, can be prevented or resolved. If your Divine Companion has no longer continued to be so aligned, instead of prolonging the hurt, the sooner an amicable break-up happens the sooner even greater love can rush into both your lives. A Divine Companion is the person who is most perfectly suited to you at any given time. And that changes as you each progress. It takes great courage to end such relationships because in many cases they may be fairly harmonious, making such a radical change difficult. It is important to know that the Divine never takes anything away, only adds something even greater to replace the apparent loss. With that knowledge comes assurance that there can be no loss – the universe doesn't recognize loss – there is only Love.

Another promise of comfort comes from the concept of a career and what it means to be a successful person, including the expectation that young people should surpass their parents' accomplishments. From a very young age, we are told by our teachers and other authority figures what is an acceptable path and what is not. Some fortunate souls have such a strong constitution that they're able to still hear their inner voice above all the external chatter. Our inherent survival instincts also play a large role in this decision. In many instances, what our soul is calling us to pursue is not always something that is considered a financially rewarding profession. Most, however, internalize the voices strongly encouraging them to find something that will "pay the bills" instead of developing soul-satisfying occupations. This is absolutely not what you were born to do, so depression, lethargy, diabetes and numerous other health problems later in life will be the bill to pay for taking the *more comfortable* route. At least take the time to listen to what it is asking of you.

Parents, forgive your children for not living up to your standards. Children, be brave enough to be different.

These are only two examples of traps to avoid. Now that they have been pointed out, it's interesting to review one's life to examine what provides the most comfort from a new perspective. In what way could these perceived blessings actually be limiting factors to growth? Self-examination requires total honesty: only you have the power to deceive yourself.

Your soul invites you every day to the quickest path to freedom, which most continue to resist, desiring the familiar cocoon of creature comforts, hence the ever-present sombre mood of quiet desperation that possesses the minds, bodies and souls of so much of the world's population. What they can't see is the world of good that is waiting for them on the other side of change, just a few uncharted footsteps away.

Hand-held electronic devices that capture short attention spans only serve to distract from the real and only reason why we're here. A melancholy mood, free-floating anxiety and lack of self-confidence are the by-products of failure to realize your life's purpose. You – and only you – have the answer to your own happiness. Each soul has been offered the tremendously enjoyable task of discovering their personal plan. The few souls who have done this are easily recognizable because they radiate a powerful joy and inner contentment that is not frequently found here. People who meet these great souls often have an impression of them such that they wonder what on Earth they had done to become that type of person, not realizing it's something available to them too. Invest more time in this discovery process and you too will reap what you sow.

Whenever the call to freedom is ignored, the powerful feeling of creation at your command available at every moment is ignored as well. The instant power of manifestation directly and effortlessly in higher planes is extremely gratifying. If it was that effortless on Earth, people would be a lot more interested in the process of curating their lives, carefully selecting every item they create.

However, that type of unlimited creation must be earned. If it were granted at our current collective level of comprehension, we would instantaneously manifest spontaneous disasters. It takes a very pure, focused mind for unwavering intent. You can imagine the implications if this gift were granted overnight to those with only a short and intermittent attention span.

The more an individual adheres to their plan the greater the sense of alignment. If the sheer exhilaration that comes from executing your highest plan is not flooding your system, it's likely because you are slightly off your path or just very late, as in my case. Most people are off their path, but they do not recognize their unhappiness and dissatisfaction as feedback from their higher self. These emotions are there to serve you as a guide, not to weigh you down. They are there to motivate you towards change so that you are always drawn in the direction where your happiness is guiding. Just like we intuitively know when food is spoiled and not to eat it, *intuitions* are the quickest way to find your way home back to your soul.

Following this template, one will also naturally start obeying and living in harmony with cosmic laws by following the still, small voice within, resulting in an equally radiant and harmonious life. Lessons will lessen as harmony increases.

Embedded in our souls is ancient wisdom acquired over millennia, accessible if you have the ears to hear it by getting to know the true Self, not the self you present to the world, the persona, the mask. We each have a unique path. No one else can walk it for us.

Once a being has successfully assimilated all the lessons slated for them and remembered the true nature of their existence, their soul, and divine self, is set free, enabled to advance to greater realms. The Earth no longer poses the same challenges it once did. In that sense the being can look at their surroundings from a transformed perspective, seeing the perfection that exists in everything, watching all that is unfolding as a perfect balancing act of cosmic law. It is at this point that one is able to fully reconnect to their soul and reintegrate their higher self. During this reintegration process, no part of you that has been living consciously in this *human experience* is lost; you only recover more than what you think you are now. Everything that you have become through the condensed learning system that is Earth is added to the infinite part of your soul, demonstrating that the Divine never subtracts, only adds. The universe desires to grow and understand itself better through experience, all information gathered incorporated into the whole.

As you approach your last life, there is a wide variety of circumstances placed in your path, serving to heal all the emotional wounds incurred during your stay here. While it may not always feel like healing – the process of hidden pains being exposed can feel extremely intimidating and uncomfortable – it is even more painful to try to suppress them. Rest assured life will send you teachers one after another to instruct and heal. This is also why people often repeat the same lesson, not permitted new ones until current lessons are learned.

This process is designed to restore your natural divine state as close as possible to the you before your fall from grace, thus healing the apparent division between you and your higher self. Just like oil and water are difficult to suspend harmoniously in a mixture, a purification process allows you to transform into the Divine Being you were initially created to be. The original spark of life that allows you to function throughout the day expands until that light is all that pervades your existence. What is eliminated through this process is all ignorance, suffering, ego, jealously, envy, greed and pettiness, as Divine Love fills all those holes, leaving no room for anything lesser.

Divine Love and everything that is one could also call Source, the Creator, God, the Divinity, or the universe. Supreme Being, YHWH, Yahweh, Jehovah, Elohim, Shaddai – it does not matter what name you choose, the Divine's only desire is to connect to you. Any of these designations are equivalent, as the Divine does not think in restrictive terminology as we do. I have had many encounters with the I AM now. He has shared with me many names that He goes by, the Tetragrammaton one of them. It is a personal process for each of us to find what resonates with our soul.

While restoration may seem like a supernatural process, it is anything but. It's the most natural rebirthing, so to speak, allowing you to gain permission to use all your God-given gifts. A being that is connected back to the source of their creation is deemed most trustworthy by the Divine, so any notion of misuse of power is off the table, impossible now that they too can see the grand plan and are in turn following their guidance. At this point, a being has the opportunity to help as an ascended master like Sanat Kumara, a great honour and blessing. Or, depending on their soul structure and attainment, there are other more rare positions they may advance to. Ascended masters are all-powerful and just like angels in that they can do anything so long as it is married with the will of the Whole.

A soul having graduated from this journey gains an enormous degree of soul attainment because a free-will system such as Earth is an unusual opportunity for growth. In most places in the universe, cosmic law is inviolable, although the level of freedom and learning environments vary from place to place. Free will means humans grow up in a place where there are essentially few rules, at least acknowledged ones. Through titanic difficulty and great ingenuity they manage to succeed against all odds to go from a state of disharmony to complete balance, with very little overt guidance from the Divine. This is a miracle in itself because in their three-dimensional world humans are conditioned to believe that only what their senses tell them is real. The first to graduate from the Earth school did so with the highest honours because they were the first to *believe* and *know,* pioneering a much gentler and easier path for others to follow.

As with all great discoveries of truth, development will go through the three stages of acceptance. At first it will be ridiculed, then violently opposed, then at last accepted as obvious.

Cutting the cord to spirit initiated the process of losing our powers, our omniscience, all our prior memories, shutting us off from communication with the Divine, at least consciously. This created what one might call a "closed system," an effective way to test the experiment we created. It would not have been much of a test if we had remained in constant contact with our heavenly guides and family.

In a world in which we are consistently conditioned to accept that we apparently exist only in three dimensions God is not obvious, although hiding in plain sight. Neither are any of the beings that oversee us, nor their abilities and advanced technologies. We have forgotten that *we* used to possess these qualities ourselves, such as telepathy, advanced space-time travel methods and access to the Divine Mind, to name a few. How long will it take to remember that God exists and in fact never left us, that the universe and God are one and the same? The implication is that God is within each of us, and that we are living, breathing *God-beings,* just waiting to be awakened to our true nature so we can each step into our greater destinies.

Beings who have evolved on Earth lived in perfection for two million years, but they have been asleep for thirteen million, dozing through many resets in a simulation that was only intended to last for one million years, such a long slumber that they have become a mere shadow of their former greatness. This comprises almost the entirety of the population. Sadly, Earth natives are typically the most asleep of all, since they have been disconnected the longest. Ironically, those we call natives, or indigenous peoples, are actually visitors from distant star systems who have come to help show humans how to live more harmoniously in their own simulation. Sadly, their selfless act has not been as well-received as hoped.

Many, but not all, of the I AM race have little awareness of their plan, their purpose or who they are. This outworn way of being is changing as the plan for the planet continues to advance and we are all given the opportunity to evolve. Evolution exists and is very real, but not in the way we have been conditioned to believe. The human form has gone through many cycles of evolution and devolution over the ages. At its highest, humans had scintillating, self-luminous, golden skin. At its lowest, humans had forms which today are known as protohumans, which were actually devolutions. Our experiment has been prolonged, but thankfully we are no longer allowed to live in denial. We have begun to see a ripple of spiritual growth across the surface of the planet, with alternative energy methods and sustainable transportation solutions cropping up. All great things start small at first. This influx of light is increasing at the rate at which our souls permit.

During the last few years especially we have watched the planet outwardly fall into greater and greater disarray, both politically and environmentally. Yet divine help and support has always been available. It was foreseen during these particularly turbulent and unstable times that significant help from above is warranted, since a species is not allowed to destroy the planet it has been given. The Divine is then permitted to step in to help in ways that direct the plan more quickly towards global healing, such as the repeated deactivation of nuclear missiles during events that would have proven to be fatal for all. These instances are largely unknown to the public, but one being I know, the founder of a major spiritual organization, has had it confirmed by a high-level military official, who was completely mystified as to how such information could have leaked. The Divine, however, does not overtly intervene in our situations without consent. It waits until the point at which we have collectively raised our consciousness enough to understand the true nature of our reality and are open to such help.

I suspect part of this accelerated plan reflected itself in my own life with the occurrence of my very rare type of OOB experience, subsequent awakening and search for answers, which would last for years afterwards and still continues. It has been so profound that now my quest occupies all of my time. Either similar events of this magnitude have happened to others and they've chosen not to speak or write about them or it is truly something that requires a very unusual set of circumstances, perhaps both. In my ten-year search I have only found one other account on record I know of that is somewhat close in nature to what I experienced. That is by Guy Ballard, the author of *Unveiled Mysteries* in the 1930s. He too was taken out-of-body, by Saint Germain, and permitted to have fully detailed memories of his experiences. Still, it is not a perfect match, as his nightly guidance continued seemingly effortlessly and without a hitch – not contiguous experiences that seemed to span the entirety of time itself.

Saint Germain lived many significant lifetimes on this Earth, such as Merlin and Christopher Columbus. In his last life as William Shakespeare he completed his ascension. He returned to Earth to project a portion of his consciousness as Comte de Saint-Germain in the early eighteenth century. He quickly materialized great wealth and became close friends with important members of the English parliament, and most notably an adviser to King Louis XV of France. He impressed everyone with his seemingly limitless knowledge, even going so far as to attend two dinner parties on opposite sides of the globe at the same time. When word spread of that, people became quite confused. Saint Germain was photographed much later with Madame Blavatsky, founder of the Theosophical Society, some time before her death in 1891. Saint Germain continues to support and help the planet from ascended master realms and is still very accessible to us all.

Nevertheless, while Guy Ballard's out-of-body experiences with Saint Germain were very significant, they differed from mine in that they were of much shorter duration and there was no NDE involved, which would explain the more brief OOBs permitted, as the body is only able to sustain so much stress. Alas, this is only my speculation. My research indicates it is a commonly accepted truth that people who frequently travel OOB can become quite ill. Perhaps all the time away from the body does not allow for significant energizing of all the necessary physiological functions.

For a long time I spoke to no one of the knowledge I had gained and the things I'd seen. I simply could not find a concise, elegant explanatory model or vocabulary, nor anyone who had experienced what I had. Communicating it requires a high level of permission from the Divine, which must align with the plan for humanity. That is why we have so much help in creating our plans, especially for our last and final embodiment. There can be no room for error. In that connected state, we create our plans all too aware of the pitfalls of human consciousness, such as forgetfulness, so we weave in encounter after encounter in overlapping staggered moments in time, a complex web containing many contingencies, such as "if *this* happens, then execute *that*" and "if this *doesn't* happen, then activate Plan B," all the while giving our guides full permission and authority to help enforce our plans, of course in alignment with the highest love because we may not consciously know everything at stake.

We knew there would be a great desire, once in embodiment, to use the life we had been given to indulge our human impulses. It would be a great temptation, one that is a plague engulfing the planet: human selfishness. Hence we also had to create – in some cases absolutely compulsory – extreme plans, involving such interjections as accidents and illnesses in order to return an individual to a course in harmony with their plan for service.

✳

Sanat and I then finished the completion of all plans. I looked up at two of my closest companions, soul family members I would meet in embodiment soon. We affirmed it by nodding in agreement. Even though we had checked and rechecked the plans from every angle, there was still an air of apprehension, a nervousness. Or perhaps it was an eager hope that maybe this time everything would go according to plan, that this time the dice of chance would roll in our favour so we could help lead the world to its own great victory. Still, our souls knew all too well, as the poet said of mice and men, that nothing ever goes completely smoothly, even with the best-laid plans. I was then privy to one last scene in the memory.

We uploaded the plans we had created into the simulation for a test run of sorts to see how everything was set to play out. Just like that, the Earth and all the players were illumined on the spherical game board, juxtaposed on the live experiences. Our individual human avatars moved about the board and began enacting our plans. One by one they hit roadblocks, and kept rerouting until each one found their way back home.

I got to see the end of my lifetime. From that distant vantage point, however, I was not permitted to see every event in fine detail. It was more like watching a concert from the back row of a coliseum. You can see the musicians and hear their music, but cannot quite make out all their features nor subtle details of the sounds they're creating.

I saw that my art would play a crucial role, a tool to help set me free through mastering my creativity. An impression of a scene was created that looked as though I were performing on a very large stage in front of an enormous audience. Out of thin air I painted hyperrealistic splashes of paint that existed in many dimensions at the same time. As I painted the dynamic scene, more and more of my soul integrated into my body and I became brighter and brighter, so bright that I was fully self-luminous. I began to rise from the stage. In fact I became so light that I began to soar. The Earth suddenly did not have its former density. It could hold me no longer.

I had burned off the last specks of my human consciousness and soared facing the upper atmosphere with my arms open wide, fully ready to embrace the universe with my heart.

Whether that theatre scene was meant to be an actual event or a metaphor for what was to come, I did not know. But after everything I had seen, both were equally conceivable.

23.

I Volunteer

MY ATTENTION FLICKERED and I awakened in the warm abyss of the astral plane, delighted to see that my guide had returned from one of his appointments.

"Would you like to meet some of my friends?" Sanat asked playfully.

"What? Really? Is that *allowed*? You would let me? I would love nothing more!" A momentary flash of unworthiness arose. *They must have it all together,* I thought, imagining they really had "everything figured out," although I could not possibly envision what that could mean in this plane. I just knew I was not even close to understanding it all. They were in this state of connection all the time. I was not. I assumed they were vastly more intelligent. If, however, they were even half as kind as Sanat, it would be an honour I could not refuse. Another flash of momentary introspection revealed my habitual mode of operation to be of a much lower vibration than theirs, leaving me feeling like an unsorted mess in comparison.

"They already love you," he beamed, in a very matter of fact but loving tone. "Now, come on, we can't keep them waiting."

We travelled through beautiful magenta, violet, gold and green iridescent nebulae, brightly illumined and breathtakingly gorgeous. The dazzling backdrop reminded me of the Crab Nebula. I had been in this suspended state for long enough that it seemed natural, but whenever I took a moment to observe my surroundings I was consistently flooded with awe and total amazement.

After some time, we arrived at the location where I was to meet his three friends, Maitreya, Metatron and Victory. We floated up close to join them. Sanat and I were both quite bodiless, although I was vaguely aware I had a form of some kind, primarily of my head and upper torso.

"These are some of my best friends. They are also beloved members of your team, which I helped hand-pick to guide you through your final Earthly embodiment. Though you might not remember them, your soul has a very close relationship with them – in fact I made their guidance part of the deal while we were planning this last life together – only the best for my daughter. I wanted to ensure you were protected."

Instant recall emerged as he delivered this information. I remembered the bulletin board on the wall in my neighbourhood close to Venus. A notice had announced a casting call for applicants to join the plan to save the Earth. At first the board was concealed by a veil of secrecy, sealed off from nearly all beings for "weeks." One had to have an incredibly high level of attainment to be able to read what that important new project in town was. I was dying in anticipation of the big reveal. I knew my father had been the first to be accepted and would not break an oath by spilling details in advance, no matter how much begging ensued on my part, of which there was plenty.

Finally, the day came when the posting was to be revealed to the "general public," so to speak. It truly felt like Christmas, although I hadn't the faintest idea of what that meant yet. Still, I couldn't wait to find a project to which I could apply. I remembered that I had signed up immediately, almost without looking. The project was BIG, an undertaking of the grandest proportions, so challenging that most beings did not even consider applying. It involved risk of the highest and most serious kind because it was to help save a rare and heavily damaged free-will system. The reward for anyone who enrolled stood to be the highest attainment they could earn anywhere in the universe because there was no guarantee of finding their way home, like a deep-sea salvage mission. You might discover the mythical buried treasure in the Earth-game system or you might become lost for a *very* long time, stuck in an iteration that will not complete. Earth is like the Marianas Trench. Few would be crazy enough to consider diving to such depths, but the ones who take the risk stand to be rewarded with the greatest discoveries. Required was a service of such significance that souls may never be given another opportunity like it again, that service being carried out through the process of reincarnation.

Free-will systems are also considered highly unstable, due to the extremely lengthy delays in enforcement of cosmic law. To knowingly choose to participate in that learning platform meant that you were confidently ready for a significant challenge. But a soul can only speculate what the actual game play would be like. It was like walking into a live mine field to try to clean up the debris from a war – in the middle of a fierce battle. Prior to entry, much of the true nature of the experiment was shielded to preserve the learning environment. Just enough information was supplied so the beings would have a chance of making an unbiased decision. This was exactly what my soul burned for. Although I was young, I knew such an opportunity might never present itself again. My "go big or go home" attitude showed now.

Another part of me also wanted to participate in whatever Sanat was doing, almost without second thought. I loved working closely with him, enjoying his energy and absorbing his wisdom. If it was good enough for him, it must be good enough for me. The fact that he was going to be overseeing it only made it better.

Sanat had made me wait before allowing the official submission of my application to initiate the reincarnation and forgetting process. He insisted that I was a very young soul, so enthusiastic that I did not often think things through. He wanted me to understand the gravity of what I was applying for, that it was a serious game with no way to stop the process or abort the mission once it had begun. I had to be absolutely sure of what I was saying yes to or else to deal was off.

I was impatient, but so appreciated his fatherly guidance and genuine care for me that I conceded and took the time to process the information, but in fact had my incarnation contract on my desk in my bedroom on Venus drafted since day one, knowing it was only a matter of time before I formally submitted it, restless as the time passed before I could officially be enrolled. The gruelling pre-incarnation training would last for what seemed like hundreds of Earth years.

I remembered then that I needed to select a team. I wanted the very best guardians, or royal militia of guides, so to speak. I chose wisely, a group of strategically hand-picked beings whose skill sets would complement my strengths in the challenges and adversity to come, adversity that I myself had selected for my plan. I desired firm guides, ones that would not let me off the hook if it appeared I was going to rebel.

To survive and complete my dangerous mission, I would need assistance. I was still too inexperienced a soul to have what it would take to see my personal transformation through to the end on my own, not to say that was impossible, only rather unlikely. I chose reliable guides to get me through the hard times to come. I did not pick guides who would take it easy on me, however. In fact I had chosen some of the strictest ones I knew, beings that were results-driven like me, ones that had the power to correct me if I veered off course.

✳

I directed my sight towards the three familiar beings. This wasn't an introduction, it was a *reunion*. I realized they were in no way strangers, but were more like family, old-soul family. Overcome with emotion, what felt like hot tears began to run down my face. I emitted a pulse of light that emanated from my heart and shot out across the starry sky towards them.

They glowed brightly too, sharing my excitement at my remembering. They looked like three kings, of completely different sizes, colours and constitutions.

Maitreya looked very human in comparison to the others. He had a bright and powerful glow, one that radiated luminous golden-yellow rays far beyond the range of his form, dappled with a few green tints, with a warm rose-pink glow emanating from his midsection. His handshake was firm, his hands large and strong. There was a sense of great roundness to him, much like the Happy Buddha figure from China. I gazed into his eyes. His smile melted my heart, although I knew intuitively he was not one to be messed with. He was my lieutenant or first mate, so to speak, the being I could trust to help enforce all aspects of my life. He was the one I could rely on to get me out of any jam with his tremendous power. He had an air of great discipline, yet playful in subtle ways. I loved him deeply. Maitreya is also lesser known for his great service to the planet as Jesus' primary teacher, and had escorted him to train in a mystery school during his years in the desert.

I threw my arms around him and thanked him, gushing profusely and repeating my gratitude in many ways, apologizing for ever having forgotten him. He seemed like an uncle, and I knew that was not inaccurate.

Sanat pulled me away, gesturing that I should "reel it in." Maitreya protested, waving his hand dismissively, insisting it was quite alright. We stayed suspended in an embrace for another moment, feeling deep gratitude for one another. I was not one to withhold emotions, especially joy.

Next was Victory, powerful almost beyond comprehension. He is also an Avatar like Maitreya, which means they have advanced so far that they are allowed even greater freedom because of their service. They have earned the significant trust of the Divine, hence they've also earned the right to choose which projects to participate in that deserve their aid in a much more selective manner than the average soul. It is speculated they might even be granted permission to visit other universes. This is a freedom so great that quadrillions of souls dream of belonging to an elite group of rock star warrior crusaders, if you will, endowed with tremendous authority to help where they see fit. The use of the term "Avatar" here is not to be confused with the traditional meaning of the word *avatar*, as in the original Sanskrit definition, meaning a manifestation of the Divine in human form. The title of Avatar that Maitreya has merited refers to a specific level of advancement he has attained, a reflection of a particular level of transformation.

While Victory did give an impression of having had something closer to a human form at one time, it was only vaguely humanoid, emanating through the expansive light that poured from his immense presence. He was at least five times taller than Maitreya, who was more round and stout but equally impressive. Victory was not only of great stature but more rectilinear, in a shape that tapered to a point towards his upper body and head. He radiated intense white light that held suspended mathematical geometries of a powerful blue that outlined his face and armoured chest. He spoke with a booming roar that resonated most powerfully and pleasantly through my being, one that made me want to laugh along with him in the great confidence he possessed. It inferred tremendous feelings of accomplishment.

I had chosen very wisely. Or maybe it is more accurate to say he had chosen me. Victory acquired his name by virtue of having known only victory in all of his undertakings since he was created several million years ago. I thanked my past self for choosing such a well-structured team. I thanked Victory for considering me a protégée. Like Maitreya he too is an Avatar.

Last, but not least, I turned to Metatron, the oldest and wisest of all, a being so vast that he is the blueprint of all Creation. Some may recognize him better by his brief lifetime on Earth as Enoch, the eldest son of Cain and the father of Methuselah, when he earned his ascension with help from Archangel Sandalphon. In that lifetime, he also delivered a powerful book to the planet, *The Keys of Enoch*. That book has been less altered than most scripture because it is not so well-known, hence it has come under less scrutiny. The "keys" that he delivered have been connoted to be released over many years, serving their purpose to help uplift the planet and its inhabitants by activating new divine blueprints and sacred geometries. Metatron is the first creation of this universe by the Infinite I AM. The geometry that is his soul, which is the Flower of Life, makes up *everything* one can possibly conceive of. The smallest raindrop, the structures comprising the largest supernova, all the planets, as well as our hearts, minds and physical bodies all exist because of his mathematical geometries. He is like a genius programmer's original source code that all subsequent programs are based on. He is so advanced by virtue of being in existence the longest that he exists within us all. We cannot exist without him.

I became a playful child as he condensed himself into a shape I could more easily relate to. I could tell he was simplifying himself to communicate with me, but I did not care, because it was such a fantastic joy to be in his presence. He was made of mathematics, beautiful, highly complex forms and geometries that radiated out like illuminated hieroglyphs in concentric circles and squares. He asked if I wanted to play some games with him. I squealed in glee at the thought.

Metatron then morphed his face into one of my favourite childhood toys, one of the first hand-held electronic games, an illuminated, colour-coded device called *Simon*. The original gizmo had four panels lit in primary colours laid out in a circle. As you started the game, you had to match the order of lights the computer displayed. Each panel also had a corresponding sound. As the game progressed, the sequence became longer while also increasing in speed, always adding to the original sequence, becoming more and more challenging to remember with the addition of each new light.

I was looking at something far more advanced and complex than that version of *Simon*, however. I played with his multifaceted face as he illuminated different sections, emitting various vibrations, sounds, feelings and energies. Sometimes, when I did well, sparks would fly out in celebration, and we laughed together as though I were sitting on top of a big, friendly, docile lion I'd tamed just for me to enjoy. He had a deep laugh that seemed to radiate in a boom throughout the whole universe. I could see that he was intimately interconnected with everything in existence and every so often saw how his form continued on, illuminated arms and legs that extended out, forming the matrix that suspends the universe in place.

I knew one thing: I never wanted to leave these friends again. The risk of forgetting them was too great. I silently vowed never to go back into my body, if that was even something I had any say about.

"Okay, kids, I think it's time for old Sanat to interrupt. It's time to get you back in your body. It's way past your return time, and I must deliver you home. I made you a promise that you wouldn't be late, remember? And I intend to keep my promise." Sanat initiated farewells as I protested gently.

I understood all too well that my very important friends must have incredibly time-sensitive agendas they needed to adhere to, so I did not make as big a fuss as I wanted to. I understood it would be deeply wrong of me to attempt to hold them back, as it would only block them from doing their service, yet I was still unwilling to let Sanat take me home that easily.

While I was not aware of having been given names for them that I could understand or remember, impressions remained. It wouldn't be until seven years later, when I found the path and began learning all the names of the angels and ascended masters, that I would rediscover them. Their presence was still felt even though, to me, much time had passed since that trip around the universe.

24.

Visions *of* Shambhala

I WAS BACK, looking at the familiar faces of my soul family, soon to be in embodiment as we concluded the finishing touches on our plans and said our goodbyes, knowing we would all be interacting with one another soon.

After a momentary pause, I looked to Sanat for guidance about where to go next. I followed him towards the Earth. We headed to an etheric city just above the Earth plane. I could perceive two entrances, one over the Gobi Desert and another over the Sahara Desert, although I sensed that its exact location varied from time to time when the need occurred. This was a place many have come to know as Shambhala.

As we dived through the upper atmosphere, I began to feel more solid due to a heavy pressure that surrounded me.

We breezed past thick cumulus clouds, the fluffy kind dreams are made of. They surrounded us in every direction, reminiscent of Renaissance artists' cloudscapes. They were pillowy soft and lit from within. Everything was very bright, so much so it would have been very hard to see if I'd resisted it. Accepting the light into my system allowed for the powerful blurring effect to subside, enough that I could begin to make out tangible forms. My prior travels had acclimated me to unfamiliar environments. I adjusted myself accordingly. Awareness now seemed dim compared to the heightened state I had just come from. Testing my ability to interact with my surroundings, I had little control. Events happened in slow motion.

As we continued to descend deeper into the angelic cloud realms, a large structure came into view. It was another palace of grand proportions, similar to the palace I'd seen on Venus, fit for royalty. Sanat and I landed softly on the front steps, our feet barely touching the ground. Bodies had automatically been generated for us that were adapted to this new environment. Perhaps this was the source of feeling less free. He told me that this was his other "office," the one he resides in situated right above the Earth. It seemed like a guard post of sorts, a stronghold from which a scrupulous eye could be kept on the environment. I sensed numerous points of entry connecting it to the Himalayas, perhaps many other strategic locations as well.

The building and its grounds were immaculately kept. Looking off into the distance, I could see many other sets of smaller buildings and lesser mansions of similar design. Their rooftops peaked through the tops of the clouds. I wondered how many beautiful worlds like this existed throughout the universe.

The palace had archways inlaid with gold about twenty feet in height. The floors, equally opulent, were constructed of an unknown type of polished marble, the likes of which I had never seen, but what appeared to be exotic jade veined with gold. Numerous rooms, alcoves and enclosures overlooked the beautiful city in every direction. There were lavish banquet halls and tables laid with elegant fine dining ware, as if at a moment's notice ready to accommodate the most splendid dinner party. Many ever-burning candles glowed most pleasantly, accompanied by a lovely fragrance that seemed to travel everywhere.

Yet even with all the spaces dedicated to socializing, the tone of my surroundings very much felt like a place for concerted labour, balanced beautifully by a hint of celebration of achievement that pervaded the atmosphere. This is what seemed to make the serious nature of the work flourish: every accomplishment deserved its reward and was celebrated joyously, recharging the people. We stood on a terrace overlooking the city in the clouds. I enjoyed being in Sanat's presence immensely, even if I did not understand the purpose. Any time together was time well spent. Prior to that day, I had not been aware that I had a divine father – or divine parents, for that matter – but now that we had met, I could not imagine life without him. I envisioned bringing him around to my art shows with me and laughed.

It was then that Sanat spoke about how I needed to find an appropriate partner: "I wish only the best my child and it's only right that I have a say about who she should be with." There was only a slight seriousness in his voice as he winked at me while holding back a grin.

I was not sure if he was joking or not and found his behaviour and answers to my questions unpredictable. I adopted the tactic of allowing him to finish his train of thought before jumping to any conclusions as to what his aim might be. After everything I had just seen, finding a partner was the last thing on my mind. I was still lost in the majesty of it all and tried to get on the same wavelength, but a mate seemed what he had brought me here to talk about. I was mildly curious about where he was going with it. Surprisingly, all memory of my current life on Earth seemed to be blocked. I had no remembrance of my major relationship back home with Alexander, otherwise I would have been hurt and protested. "Oh really?" I chuckled. "Well, do you have anyone in mind?"

Even before I had finished my question, delighted I had asked, he said, "Funny you should ask, indeed I do!"

Another being appeared instantly at our side as if summoned by a cue in our conversation. He too felt like family. I later learned his name was Serapis Bey, also of the larger Kumara clan. I guessed that would make him one of my brothers.

Serapis was an excellent soldier, standing with perfectly poised control, decked in layered medals of honour pinned to his regal attire. In possession of total composure, he was built like an athlete, highly obedient and, I sensed, exceptionally disciplined. As he spoke, I could hear that he was also intellectually sharp.

Sanat dictated a set of instructions as to *exactly* the type of being he was looking for, a long list of detailed qualifications the ideal mate would have to embody. By the time he was done, I was absolutely flabbergasted. I could not have put together a better list myself. Sanat really did have such a detailed inventory of everything about me. At times I forgot he had such insight into my personality, and it continued to blow my mind in the most unexpected ways.

Even though his all-encompassing list left nothing to chance, it was only fair that I add a few qualifications of my own.

The stoical Serapis appeared to be listening to everything with an un-mitigated ear for detail. There was something so meticulous about him, almost mechanical. He did not ask any questions or make any remarks as he recorded each item at lightning speed in his golden notebook. When we were done, he asked to be excused and took off with a sonic boom. I knew that he was searching through all of space and time for the exact person we'd described. No one lesser would suffice.

I began to wonder if it was even possible that the candidate as we had described him existed. Maybe our qualifications were too strict and too many.

Sanat, however, did not seem the least bit concerned and comically reclined in a lounge chair on the veranda, emphasizing his point to sit back and allow the universe to fill the order. He made his belly inflate, as if he had been concealing a large burden the whole time, as though it were the most satisfying relief to sit back and unbutton the top of his trousers. I appreciated his candour, but knowing he could make himself take whatever form he wanted, the theatrics were obviously for entertainment.

No sooner had Serapis left than did he return in the most spectacular fashion. All of a sudden something caught my eye rising out of the cotton-candy-like clouds in front of us: it was a machine. The clouds gave way to reveal a golden flying contraption out of some inventor's wild imagination. It had devices that expelled or recycled air into another gas, and numerous instruments like weathervanes, perhaps used to navigate the universe, though I'm not sure of their actual purpose. Most exquisite of all, the entire mechanical structure seemed to be made of solid gold. Although money was no object here, it was still a sight to behold. Standing beside Serapis Bey was the man in question.

He must be my suitor, I thought.

They stepped off the levitating platform together. The introductions began. I thought he was very handsome. He did not stop smiling from the moment he saw me. There was a distinct familiarity about him that I could not quite place. Prior to meeting him I was unsure I even wanted Sanat to play universal matchmaker, but I had to admit he had done an incredible job. This man was tall, much taller than me, lean but muscular, his hair dark and short. His eyes seemed to connect directly to my soul. We had such a connection in fact that I suddenly realized that he *was* the other half of my soul.

Since then I have learned that not all souls are created with the same, let alone the exact same, soul structure. On Earth, we may call it genetics or physiology. In higher planes, our souls are organized in a somewhat comparable fashion. Many, however, are created as a "twin flame." Twin flames are comprised of two parts, feminine and masculine, or yin and yang. There is a birthing process for new souls created, the final touch carried out by the feminine archetype, which some have come to know as Mother Akasha, as she breathes life into each of us.

One half of a twin flame soul is primarily masculine, seventy per cent male and thirty per cent female. The other half is predominately feminine, seventy per cent female and thirty per cent male. When the two halves are joined, the two flames form one complete soul.

Many of us have been in embodiment for so long that our yin-yang ratios are out of alignment. Though a being's Individualized God Presence in essence does not identify with either gender – it is pure, unqualified, potential God Energy – it seems we each have a predilection, a slight tendency to embrace the qualities of one gender over the other. While we have all experienced embodiments as either sex as an important part of the immersive learning process, you will naturally gravitate to the form that your

God Presence prefers when approaching your last life, which in truth is also your personal preference, since your desires and your God Presence's desires are one and the same.

It is very rare that twin flames ever come together in a lifetime. Since they can be very volatile when in proximity, there has to be a need for it, otherwise they will behave like similar magnetic poles and repel each other. Often their paths will cross or they will be acquaintances, but seldom are they destined to be in a romantic relationship. This is because of the disruption that results from combining the two forces. The only time it is deemed appropriate to pair the two is if they have something very important to accomplish together. Because each half has the missing components of the other, there will be a powerful attraction and even repulsion present, mirroring certain aspects of the soul back to the self. This can be a most unflattering mirror. Their similarities should be a recipe for union, yet the differences are enough to create disasters of epic proportions, each pushing the other's deepest triggers in a way only a twin flame ever could, creating an intense friction even when seemingly there is not much basis for it in the outer world.

In addition, it is unlikely they would incarnate at the same time, be of the same age, live in the same part of the world and be of the appropriate gender suitable to form a bond. Furthermore, if the twin flames are visitors, one of them might have chosen a different environment than Earth, in which case they will be reunited again when both their learning cycles have completed.

Since both come from the same spiritual parents, they are part of the same spiritual family, similar to twins born on Earth. They are from the same flame, so they are siblings in a way, yet their bond is much stronger than the bond between even the closest husband and wife. Twin flames are inseparable. Families are different in higher planes: what may constitute brother and sister here forms a divine partnership up there.

Yet a divine union as perfect counterparts is possible, under the most ideal conditions. If a plan is created with a specification that the two must work together, the importance of their plan has the power to override any significant differences. The plan alone isn't enough to allow them to get along, however, and it takes significant understanding by both parties to harness the full potential for power that is the twin flame union.

Gazing at my suitor, I saw parts of myself, but not metaphorically speaking. The state we were in allowed us to mirror reflections to each other through our eyes, revealing past experiences. He looked very wise, yet a youthful burst of energy came from him that invigorated me. I could tell he was very kind, but also powerful, yet not revealing his true strength so as not to appear to dominate. I was attracted to him, and what I thought was going to be an awkward first encounter ended up as more of a face-to-face with someone very important to me but whom I had long forgotten, a part of myself. I embraced him fully and saw the golden dust that glittered on his face.

He was very similar to Serapis Bey in character, but there was a softness, a vulnerability about him that I adored and which felt like "home," a happy one. I was overjoyed that he'd been brought to meet me as we discussed further plans.

The planning underway, the scenery softened and our words got quieter, making it hard to decipher what those plans really were. I began to feel my awareness pushed up into the upper stratosphere. It seemed the rest of the meeting was not meant for me to hear. My attention began to drift as I left, accompanied by another form of Sanat. We gazed down on the scene where other versions of "us" were still deep in conversation.

Shambhala receding now, I wondered what would come of meeting my suitor and why I was permitted to meet someone so perfect for me when I had absolutely no awareness of him in ordinary reality. I searched my memory, but no one even bearing a slight resemblance to him came to mind. I had no idea how to find him. There was nostalgia upon leaving as I wondered if I would ever see him again.

25.

Re-Entry

LITTLE DID I know my re-entry into Earth's atmosphere would require protection equivalent to heat shielding. Without it, a crisp trip could be expected, like jumping into a red-hot frying pan. Things sure were heating up. In fact things were so hot it was all I could think about. I was unable to recall how I got here, where or who I was. The only image I was able to relate to was that of an astronaut re-entering the Earth's atmosphere, except I did not have the advantage of a shuttlecraft to protect my extremities. Confused and descending at high speed, I tried to brace for the eventual impact.

There was a momentary lapse in thought. I seemed to see nothing but blackness all around. This was followed by an absolutely tremendous bang as I felt worlds collide all around me.

✳

Recalibrating quickly, I looked around and saw Mikey's ride had finally decided to show up. After all the time spent impatiently waiting, I had to admit that I felt particularly melancholy at the thought of going our separate ways. Despite my current disorientation, I had the deep realization that I had never been drunk to begin with and that everything I had experienced was far greater than my imagination had the power to invent. The ordinary world was starting to become more solid bit by bit. In this new light arose a greater appreciation for everything that had just occurred. There was clarity despite the wreckage as my awareness tried to leap beyond what I ever thought possible. Each dimension and realm that had been revealed created an entire universe of questions in my mind and crumbled all the belief systems that had grounded me in daily life.

In fact I had been pretending so well that I was intoxicated at the start of the experience that I'd even convinced myself. I laughed at how sheepishly I had faced the Divine and tried to conceal my shame under something so mundane as inebriation, but I suppose we all wear masks. It was the perfect plausible deniability that the human part of me clung to as a backup plan. This was now confusing to me. What kind of power could make me deceive myself? I turned within and recognized that ego was to blame and knew I had a powerful one, which continually tried to logically shoot down the powerful experiences I had with the Divine. If something did not easily fit within her logical set of explanations, then she would ceaselessly work to erode the majesty of what was shown until it fit into her narrow and often simplistic parameters. This was a dangerous operating system, as she believed she held the simple answer to everything. She did not.

Our egos work in different ways. The stereotype of the narcissist is only a minor form ego uses in self-defence. My own ego values reductionistic logic, to its detriment, believing strongly in the physical, material world, things I can touch, see and have been taught to *believe,* so much so that I now recognized she had even completely blocked out past experiences with the Divine when they failed to fit into her logical belief system. I felt sad I had diminished myself that way and realized the gift of this experience was something of such proportions that I would never be able to fully rationalize or explain it without accepting the truth of the existence of a higher power. Perhaps this was something the Divine had seen that I needed. I had just been given the gift of interacting with the universe first-hand for what felt like lifetimes, in a more concrete way than my existence is now.

I felt unsure how events were going to play out to affect my tomorrow and became concerned with a need to retain the memory somehow. I kept reminding Mikey to remember our entire conversation, including all the numbers I'd dictated earlier. With the sobriety of re-entry, I was no longer certain I wanted to brush off the entire experience as merely drunken babble anymore, which seemed cowardly.

I kissed Mikey goodbye and began to walk towards my house a few doors down from where the car was parked. It was now raining. There were large puddles that had collected in the shallow dips in the pavement. Still not totally of this world, I tripped and fell hard into one of the puddles, landing on my side, which soaked my jeans. But really, I felt a faint pang at the realization the fall was somewhat intentional. The internal battle with my ego dragged on as it desperately struggled to create circumstances which it could reflect back on later as a scapegoat, villainizing me and diminishing my credibility. The thought process I was witnessing was along the lines of: *How could you possibly believe everything you were shown if you were clearly so intoxicated that you could not make it to your door?* It hurt to be a passive observer of this type of destruction of the self, witnessing my unhealed facets struggle to get the upper hand. The majority of me was still greatly in shock and awe at the amazement of everything I had experienced, and because of this shock it seemed to put my consciousness at a disadvantage.

Even though I was aware of the inner turmoil, at this moment my ego was stronger, winning the battle for control over my body. I reflected on the events of the night. On a more innocent level, I knew I was still completely out of sorts and had no way to explain my state of being to others easily other than a quick blanket statement that I had gone out drinking with friends. I could always elaborate later if I were ever to give a proper voice to the impact of what happened. Right now I just wanted to find a quiet place to hide from the outer world.

Being a little intoxicated was at least socially acceptable. Being pulled out-of-body and shown the existential nature of the universe first-hand was not. My greatest fear was of entering my home as a rambling lunatic speaking in partial sentences about time travelling and possibly being committed to an insane asylum, put on medications and never given the proper time and space to actualize my plan. This scared part of myself was very weak and felt extremely threatened. My ego too feared its extinction because its existence was incompatible with the truth. Its goal was to make everything appear more mundane and familiar, supplying excuses and creating alternative explanations, anything to preserve its familiar reality. Nothing was too below-the-belt. It would even resort to bending its own twisted logic if need be, ironically distorting that which it was attempting to preserve.

My body was completely insensitive. I didn't feel a thing as I hit the wet pavement, only a slight disorientation. I struggled to pull myself up, heavy and soaking wet. The weight of my body seemed insurmountable, yet invulnerable to the cold or discomfort. I wasn't sure if this was *really* happening, that is, in the physical. The nature of reality had become extremely skewed. On the one hand, everything I had experienced had been real, but I just wasn't sure I was in a state yet where people in embodiment could see me. Concurrently I understood that because reality is experienced radically differently by each individual, whatever I was experiencing subjectively in fact was reality for me, as real as it could get. I entered the front door to my house, attempting to be quiet as I prayed that my mother and aunt were fast asleep. I just wanted to be left alone to begin the daunting task of processing. The last thing I wanted was to make small talk or, even worse, a meaningful conversation trying to explain in words where I had just been. I was not ready for that and needed more time for meaning to crystallize. I believed my state of mind would not permit a lie or simplification of my story. At best I would come across as insane. I suspected I was not quite home and dry, literally, as parallel realities kept manifesting and branching off, even now as I presumed I was fully grounded back in the Earth plane.

I walked into the kitchen, feeling absolutely ravenous, as if it had been days since my last meal. Opening the fridge revealed a strange array of substances. Whipped cream seemed like a good start. After sampling a dollop I immediately put the can back, and decided the main priority was really *gallons* of water. I downed glass after glass, attempting to extinguish a fiery thirst, and struggled to find the patience to repeatedly wait for the Brita water pitcher to refill.

What seemed like only a moment later a different part of myself came through the front door. This "me" found that indeed my mother and Aunt Karen were still up, having some wine and late-night conversation. It was the weekend, and they'd stayed up a little later then usual, enjoying themselves watching TV and talking. I felt embarrassed as I stood there half soaking wet, and didn't want to engage in any explanation.

To my surprise, the kitchen clock showed the night was still a youthful 10:45 pm. Breathless, I brushed the hair out of my eyes, staring at the clock, willing it to change and show the *real* passage of time. It should display at least 5:00 in the morning and forty years later minimum! My mind struggled to process how even a small fragment of the night's *real* events could have taken place simultaneously in such a remarkably short period. I was truly amazed, but more so shocked, which only increased my confusion and agitation. It seemed impossible – or at the very least highly improbable.

"So where were you tonight?" my mother asked.

I tried to be vague: "Where haven't I been?"

It was difficult enough to remember to maintain my body's ostensibly autonomous functions, such as breathing, let alone talk, leaving me feeling exasperated. It seemed like I was learning to use my lungs again or else there was a shortage of oxygen in the air. My breathing was laboured and erratic. In fact I had to relearn to use all my bodily senses. It had been an effort to even read the clock, straining my eyes while commanding them to focus. Communication on this now foreign planet was difficult, much restricted by thoughts subject to interpretation, mediated by sonic vibrations through the air interacting with eardrums and brains. It now seemed like a very primitive way of getting one's point across. I was ill-equipped to operate the mechanisms required to be understood. I kept trying to communicate telepathically and was probably just seen as standing there motionless, as my family seemed unable to receive the messages I was trying to broadcast.

Emotions disturbed everything even more because I believed I had to dumb everything down to make myself understood, not to suggest that my family was unintelligent. On the contrary, I thought I had to oversimplify and condense such a vast amount of information and sensory detail into words, which then had to fit into reasonable *sentences* that they would accept and understand. The task proved challenging.

A decision had to be made whether I would tell anyone anything of my journey. I imagined I must appear mentally deranged or at least extremely intoxicated. A diagnosis of schizophrenia wouldn't even have surprised me had a shrink been present. For some reason I found myself hoping for that diagnosis. At least that would satisfy my desire for a simplistic explanation.

My mother had a faint look of concern, but Karen merely stood staring at me blankly. In fact she didn't seem to be able to speak. I wondered if she had simply consumed a bit too much wine or was enjoying being silent.

"You know," I explained, "A whole bunch of things happened to me tonight. Maybe I should just tell you."

"What happened?" my mother prodded.

I started to cry and burst out, "I got *raped*."

Her eyes went wide as she turned pale. "What do you mean you got raped?! At the restaurant? You got raped by your friends?"

I didn't know why I had blurted that out. I was trying to speak faster than my mind was able to process and my choice of words proved questionable at best, although I really did feel like I had been violated in some significant way and "rape" was the closest accessible word that had surfaced in my mind.

"No. I mean, I think I was drugged."

"Oh my God, we need to take you to the hospital!"

"No. Wait," I paused, feeling and recalling my multiple spiritual deaths. "I… was murdered, so I'm dead."

Again, this was a vast oversimplification. Technically, I had died in the traffic accident with the truck. I had also been devoured by the spiritual crocodiles, as well as murdered countless times in numberless ways, seemingly all those years ago, so which death was I referring to I did not know. It seemed easier just to deliver a blanket statement that was more to the point than quibbling over semantics. Being dead wasn't such an incorrect statement, even if it did appear that Zeta Zero was doing the talking.

"What are you talking about? You're standing right here! Were you assaulted? Sarazen, did someone *rape* you?"

"No – yes – but if you take me to a hospital, they won't find anything. A doctor will find that I'm actually in better health now than before."

I wasn't making any sense. I laughed inwardly at the humour of the situation, but also out of frustration that I could not properly communicate. I spat out pieces of information from events that *did happen* but were blurred between the lines of what my simplest self could explain, which, considering my shock at being back in the material world, were highly fragmented explanations at best. There was a lump in my throat that blocked the free flow of information from readily coming forward as I struggled to verbally broadcast, human-style.

Concerned I had done more harm than good in trying to explain my whereabouts, I saw my mother clearly becoming irritated. Forming any words at all was cumbersome. I felt their extra heavy weight and roundness as they took shape and fell off my tongue.

She demanded: "How much did you drink tonight?"

"Not much. I was with Mikey."

"*Who's Mikey?*"

"He's a new friend. I've known him for a while, but now he's a new person. He has a secret and he told me a lot of stuff," I explained, lamely.

"Where was this? At the restaurant?"

"No. It was in space." *Ha,* I thought, *I know how that sounds.* This wasn't going well.

"What do you mean?" she asked.

"I saw *everything*."

"What do you mean you saw everything?"

My mind was moving too fast for her to keep up or for me to explain. I skipped ahead and remembered the inaccurate version of my childhood that she'd given me, that I'd been so easy to raise, and became instantly angry. "*You lied to me!*" I said, taking an accusatory stance.

"What do you mean *I lied to you?*"

Frantically, I tried to make the words come out right, not even considering whether the topic was relevant. She denied that she had distorted the truth and failed to see the connections between any of my statements thus far.

I had a momentary spark of inspiration, then pleaded, "If you call Uncle Orbit, he can confirm it," I insisted. "Call him right now and ask what I was like as a baby. He will describe me in one word: angry. I was an *angry* baby."

She shook her head slowly, "*No.* He won't say that. It's not true."

"Then I'll call him," I insisted, though I couldn't imagine how to use the telephone. I had another idea. "If he calls in the next five minutes, is it okay if we talk with him about this?"

"Well, I guess so – but that would be unusual. He never calls this late and never calls without a reason anyway."

I focused all my intention on making the phone ring. It remained silent. Somehow it made me doubt whether the events of the evening had happened at all. I had made a bad bet, thinking magically that I could make him call simply by willing it. I did not at all feel as connected as before. Maybe I really had been hallucinating the whole time. Maybe I was schizophrenic after all. Maybe I had been drugged. I could feel myself spiralling in a downward plunge as my doubts continued to feed into a vortex, creating an inescapable negative feedback loop. I wished my guide had given me some preparatory advice before returning to my old world. *How to cope with being solid again?*

At the same time, I also believed it was a major mistake to have come back to Earth, because it was the most frustrating place imaginable. My agitation escalated with each passing moment. It was highly incongruent in contrast to higher realms, where everything was so effortless. Maybe I was lying and had made the whole thing up. But then again, how could I even know the difference between the two planes if it wasn't something I had experienced first-hand?

Being back home was like regressing to preschool, learning to communicate from scratch. Going through childhood once was quite enough. I wasn't at all prepared to relearn my environment. I just didn't get it. It was also very physically painful just to be in a body again. I ached all over. My nervous system burned like an electrical fire as it tried to recalibrate to the Earth's ecosystem.

Without provocation, I blurted, "Why are you being so stupid? You're the Wise Woman!" She looked supremely offended and mystified at the same time. It had not been my intention to hurt her feelings, in fact it had been the last thing on my mind, yet my mounting frustration prevented giving any statement a second thought. I had no filter. It was a big problem.

I noticed the empty wine bottles in the kitchen. "Oh great. This happens to me on a night when you happen to be drunk." Apparently self-importance created the idea that some sort of injustice had been done to me deliberately. "That's just perfect. You won't even remember *any* of this in the morning."

"What do you mean I won't remember? *Of course I'm going to remember this*," she insisted, still looking very concerned.

It did not occur to me that perhaps their not remembering was exactly what the Divine wanted. Shifting my attention, I tried to talk to Karen, who seemed to appear and disappear magically from directly in front of me, but when present never said a word. Her behaviour didn't seem as odd as it should have done. I continued to interpret the entire scene as typical, even though the dreamlike elements continued. She looked at me but didn't seem fully cognizant, only vaguely aware of what was going on and unable to speak. It was as though she was just wandering aimlessly.

Still very confused, I said, "Wait. I'll prove to you that I'm psychic now." Despite having failed to get Uncle Orbit to ring the phone, I still believed I had the power to influence my surroundings and bend it to my will. I ran to the TV in the living room, which was almost always on in the background. Channel surfing, I came across an image of Yogi Bear. Seeing the cartoon character reminded me of the guide I had just met, Yogananda. Instant recognition flooded me and I began to reminisce about my previous experience with him, so wowed by his power. I wondered silently: *What is a show that is so new that I could have no idea of its content? I could predict what we would see.*

"Perfect! The news. I'm going to predict what's going to happen in the world." I began dictation, starting with predicting storms, snow in areas the meteorologists had missed. Philadelphia suddenly came to mind, but I could not determine why. I predicted an earthquake in Chile, fires and volcanoes erupting that would affect the whole world. Still seeing dates, I could not tell if the numbers were directly associated with the revealed events or if they were for something else. My sense of time still askew, I was unable to tell if they were events already passed or still ahead. Whatever gifts I'd hoped I had been given seemed not that profound, with nothing predicted that I could yet prove.

"What year is this?" I wondered aloud, never anticipating saying anything so cliché. I had a vague idea of the year, but needed reassurance, given all the timelines I'd experienced while OOB had happened in parallel. Now that I was back in what I had been accustomed to call normal Earth-time, there was no accurate way to tell *where* I had been inserted back into the timeline without at least asking. Whether I was even back in my original timeline at all was a whole other question. I highly doubted it.

After the news channels, I turned to situation comedies, predicting the plots of new episodes and providing synopses of movies there was no way I had seen. After all that time in the car with Mikey discussing his favourite releases, perhaps his descriptions while OOB were accurate. Possibly this was my version of winding down after everything I had been through, even if I wasn't being fully accurate. For some reason it soothed me, and the act of watching TV was helping me return to reality as I'd known it.

My mother just looked at me as if she were thinking, *Wow, my daughter's really crazy.*

This made me upset because here was the perfect opportunity to prove my case and nobody was getting it. I tried to write down my forecasts. This proved difficult too, so I ripped up the sheet of paper and threw it away, not inside the house but into the garbage can in the garage. I didn't want to discover strange and illegible notes the following day that could be later deemed as evidence my experience had actually happened. With any luck I would go to sleep and wouldn't remember anything. Maybe that would be a blessing in itself. That would excuse me from any action required on my part or painful steps essential to initiating my plan. However, if I left a long trail of breadcrumbs, it may become a catalyst potentially triggering remembrance of everything. I wasn't sure I was ready for that. Next, I went to the computer in the family room.

My mother looked tired and said she was going to bed.

"Mama, can't you just sit with me a little longer?" I never called her that anymore. I radiated a little bit of desperation, wanting my mother to keep me company. As we sat together a little longer, I surfed the internet looking for weather reports, especially of natural disasters. It didn't surprise me that there were no reports yet. I knew for a fact I had indeed seen those storms. I also knew that the loose predictions could come true several years in the future, as I was not skilled enough to determine the timeframe.

I briefly looked into the accounts of others being out-of-body, but that proved too fresh a topic. It felt as though a large pressure was repulsing me from examining the subject further, at least for now. On a whim, I decided to look up Yogi Bear, and through a fantastically lucky internet search found a photo of Uncle Orbit's guide Paramahansa Yogananda, finally discovering who he had been in this world. His eyes were mesmerizing even on screen, which did not obscure as much of his power as I thought it would when viewing his photo in this plane. I paused for a moment, my gaze locked on his eyes. So – that was that – everything that happened had been real. Now I just had to convince *myself.*

The way I saw it was black and white. My best hope was to wake up in full acceptance or dismissal of the previous night's experiences. However, the more logical part of me knew it wasn't going to be that cut and dried as I continued to mentally contemplate the different outcomes I saw as likely candidates. Part of me hoped for the clarity to surrender, to accept the fantastic journey at face value lightheartedly and not blow it out of proportion trying to figure it all out. I could choose to accept the experience for what it was, a gift, as simple as that. Yet conflict arose within when I considered the instances I'd been shown things that were in opposition to my beliefs. Or things that had challenged the way my life was structured, including relationships.

There was the possibility I just wasn't ready for the implications. If I accepted everything as truth, what would the ramifications be? If action steps were required, I was not sure I was ready to take them. Should I disassociate from my friends as I had been shown? Was I required to break up with Alexander as had been strongly implied? Those would be serious losses. Both of those worlds comprised the majority of my happiness. I had seen that essentially none of my present most important relationships were serving me, nor were they part of my highest plan.

The Elders had said that having the experience alone would manifest in ways I could not see. I hoped that implied a positive outcome. Still, I would have to be prepared to lose everything, if that was the price of truth.

Even though it had been shared with me that I was behind on my plan, now back in my body I couldn't help but feel rushed. How could I ever prepare myself to let go of the life I'd created?

Sensing the enormity of the change required of me ahead, I felt I needed a backup plan, some alternative explanation in case I wasn't ready to face the truth in the morning. This seemed like the *reasonable thing to do,* the human parts of me said, an escape clause in case I chose to preserve my old life, to live in denial of the warnings I had been shown.

My computer skills unleashed, I began architecting my genius Plan B and honed in on studying a large amount of information regarding mental disorders. After what felt like two hours of research, the wind in my sails began to wane as surprisingly I could find not one that was a good fit. It had to be something that I could *believe,* something convincing enough to fool my entirety, which would prove a daunting task, considering the more awake parts would work ceaselessly trying to find an error. For starters, there was no history of mental illness in my family, perhaps some depression, but I have never met anyone who has not dealt with that in some form. Some search results described vaguely similar symptoms, but nothing that could explain a complete disintegration of reality paired with a newer, brighter, more realistic philosophy and knowingness that now took its place, accompanied by what felt like decades of memories to account for. There was no type of disorder with those attributes, I was frustrated to admit. It was an awakening. The term "awakening" had not yet been popularized or glamourized like it is today. The only experiences that vaguely fit the bill involved high dosages of hallucinogenic drugs. Their descriptions, however, were of a more ordinary high, nothing even close to the spectacular intimacy of witnessing the Divine up close and personal and for the duration I had. I thought myself in circles, failing to pass myself off as delusional. I am not sure why I felt frustration at this. I should have felt relief. Perhaps my frustration lay in a deep knowing that it was no longer possible for me to return to my life as it once was. As an ancient sage once said, you can't step in the same river twice.

My biggest fears started to rise to the surface. If I did by some miracle find the strength to own what happened to me and choose to tell people the truth of my experience, there was a very high risk I could be committed to a mental hospital. It might not matter how grounded in my truth I was, my story was just not one that others would easily accept. I feared the consequences. So my options were: (A) I could believe my truth, yet watch my life crumble because the people in my circle couldn't love and accept me anymore due to our now greatly differing belief systems or (B) I could accept my truth, but they *really* wouldn't believe me, and I'd end up being disposed of in an institution. I knew my family loved me, but perhaps this was beyond their ability to understand. It was not a great picture I was painting. Only five minutes back in the Earth plane and I had already lost sight of the fact that I could create whatever outcome I so desired. While there were options, my fear got the best of me, continuing to feed my disempowered state as I clung to the worst-case scenarios I could imagine.

Disappointed and believing I had no other choice, I continued to cover my tracks, abandoning the notion of framing myself with a mental disorder and hoping some other narrative might appear with any luck. I went the extra mile and cleared the browser's history. It was still possible I could wake up and remember nothing, a right I felt entitled to.

There was a third possibility I had not considered that would still allow me to keep the experience intact: (C) I could wake up with a deep inner awareness that everything really had happened, but instead of sharing, I could keep silent until such time I was ready. Maybe taking some time to process was not such a bad idea. Like a Buddhist philosopher might say, when you don't know what to do, do nothing at all.

Still not yet back in my normal "loving girlfriend" mode, I noticed that Alexander had repeatedly tried to call. But I had ignored my phone. I assumed he would show up eventually. That could be at any moment. For now, I needed to buy time. It would not do any good talking to him while still in this strange fragmented state.

My mother brought some ice cream to the sofa to share. It did wonders for my nerves. I knew I wasn't ready for bed. I couldn't get the anxiety to go away. Part of me also didn't want to go to sleep and break the continuity with everything that happened earlier. What if I did really forget everything? I had been so deeply touched by what I'd seen. Was I really prepared to lose the memory? I was experiencing cognitive dissonance, a state in which one holds a set of contradictory beliefs or ideas that prevents taking action because both paths seem equally undesirable. Furthermore, I had no idea whether I was back in my Earthly reality, still in another dimension or experiencing the longest-running vivid dream in history.

As a test, I held a Bic lighter under my forefinger for about ten seconds, but absolutely nothing happened: no pain, no burn. This was not a good sign. I had, however, successfully debunked the current reality.

My mother took the lighter from my hand and went upstairs to bed.

Even with the test results of the lighter in hand, I still couldn't accept and internalize that I just wasn't completely in my body yet. This was hard to consider because it would also imply that my mother was not in her body either. Was it possible that I had travelled back to the Earth plane but was animating my etheric body? And so was she? I had never heard of that before. But then again this experience had shown me that there was so very little I did know, feeling like Alice after she had her own journey down the rabbit hole.

I went downstairs to my bedroom and surfed the internet on my own computer while listening to music on my iPod, mostly at high volume, dancing at times, coping mechanisms to deal with the fact that it seemed like nothing was "real reality" anymore. The high volume seemed to re-verberate through my cells and nerves, and ironically settle them down.

They were in a high vibratory state of agitation and meeting them part way with a similar level of stimulation actually felt relaxing. Likewise with the dancing – I hesitate to call it that – which served to facilitate releasing of a large charge of energy still stored inside that was clambering to escape: part of me wanted to run but also felt the sheer exhaustion of being physical again. Yet if I didn't move, a pent-up anxiety would begin to percolate up my spinal cord and especially in my limbs. The most accessible way to discharge this surplus seemed to be to shake it out. The more intelligent, logical part of my soul found this behaviour highly unnerving and struggled to keep me preoccupied by getting lost in rummaging through old photographs nostalgically and calling people I hadn't talked to in years. I would find an image I could connect to and suddenly a caller would appear on the phone in my hand. I apologized for waking them up at such a late hour. Some were unreachable, but many friends answered right away.

When getting "grounded" back in my body had proven unsuccessful, the thought crossed my mind that perhaps I could just go OOB again. I attempted to do this by listening to music in case that was part of the triggering mechanism. There had been the loud jazz playing at the restaurant. While waiting in the car with Mikey the radio had been on quietly. Sitting upright, I tried to relax and focus on my crown, trying to determine if there was a magical alignment that could assist the shift. Leaving my body proved unsuccessful. My attempt only added unwanted stimulation, directing all the excess energy stored within towards my crown and increasing the sensations in my already frayed nervous system. Eventually, I fell asleep on my sofa with earbuds blasting, the television on and lights blazing, not a typical means of relaxation. Ordinarily, I needed total darkness and silence to get any sleep at all. I had become a sensitive sleeper over the years and the most I ever tolerated was the ambient white noise of a fan. In recent years, earplugs and sometimes an eye mask if travelling abroad are necessary. Blaring lights, music and television were most definitely out of the question.

The time was now approaching 4:00 a.m. How five hours could have gone by since I had arrived I could not explain. I was concerned that Alexander had still not shown up, but also greatly relieved. I hadn't been able to message him at all. What could I possibly say? If I told the truth, he would unquestionably think I was lying. Although he usually worked late and likely was still up, I did not feel compelled to call and needed to think of something to say the following day. It was not like me to just completely no-show, figuratively speaking. At the very least we'd usually message each other before bed. Maybe he was angry because I hadn't answered my phone. That would be a reasonable assumption. On second thought, I looked around my large basement suite, which I had now somewhat trashed in the process of becoming settled. I didn't want him to discover me sleeping with everything blaring at once, so I switched everything off, crawled into bed and prayed for one last mystical journey with my guide to worlds beyond.

26.

Bandana *and* Gnomeo

SANAT KUMARA TOOK me to some unknown part of the Earth where there were vast fields of tall sun-bleached grass under a clear blue sky. We flew over the grasslands at high velocity, our hands just touching the tips of the blades. We did the same with treetops, finally coming to the dunes of a desert where we drew large circular shapes and wrote words in the sand. I wondered then whether crop circles were formed in a similar fashion, by out-of-body graffiti artists flying through the sky.

I couldn't be sure whether we were actually affecting physical reality. I was just so happy to be in his presence again and relieved that he had appeared when asked. This made me feel more comfortable with everything that had happened, knowing that I could still see him and that he was real.

It appeared that only a part of my soul was now sleeping or, it might be more accurate to say, still travelling. My attention began to split. I wasn't able to fully maintain the flight with Sanat. There was something else commanding my attention.

I phased back to my bedroom aware of the persistent intuition that I was supposed to talk to a specific person or persons in the Earth plane. It seemed I had never actually succeeded in falling asleep as I had thought. Switching the television back on, I began to randomly call every number that appeared in commercials. Still in a very strange, lucid, receptive state, I assumed the numbers presented were meant for me to call. It didn't matter whether they were for multinational corporations or local carpet-cleaning services. I felt that if I just kept trying, eventually I would reach the people I needed to speak to. I became fascinated with the phenomenon of the telephone. I couldn't believe there was an actual human being at the other end of the line. Like a tiny child or a naive primitive, half the time I thought the instrument itself was talking. I didn't know what had been done to me, but I prayed I would snap back soon.

The last number I called was a chatline. The TV ad had promised: "To meet friends for talk and more." In my naive state, I didn't imagine what "more" implied, but thought it sounded perfect, a wide range of people to talk to and connect with.

181

At first it was funny because I met men who were lewd, rude and crude. Still, having no filter intact, it was hilarious to tell them off when they stepped out of line and asked me for inappropriate acts. Others had problems that needed a sympathetic ear. I thought maybe I could help, but it turned out they really were more interested in dating.

I wasn't making the progress I wanted, so took another approach and switched to the women's side. I didn't know whether it was a man or a woman I was supposed to speak with or both. The lesbians among them got angry when I said I wasn't one of them, but calmed down when I mentioned that I was confused. I didn't say about what, but I wasn't getting anywhere, so I changed platforms again and went to the gay men's side.

They seemed to assume I was a man with a high-pitched voice. I didn't talk them out of it, because it was comical, but eventually they too got angry with me, so I reluctantly went back to the women-seeking-straight-men's side. This time many of them were well-mannered and pleasant. I ended up talking to Dale, who said he was a motivational speaker and life coach. I told him about my search for the people I felt I must speak to.

"Why do you need their help?" he asked.

"If I told you, you would not believe me."

He kept prying because at some point I must have sounded quite distressed. "No, no, you found exactly the right person to talk to, even though I don't have experience with some of the things you mentioned. However, I do know a lady who knows exactly what you're talking about. Her name is Shanti. She's very experienced and very nice. Will you speak to her?"

I was very hesitant at first, but then agreed. For the first time since I had walked through the door of my house I felt like I was starting to make progress in finding answers. We jumped off the chatline, then he called me from his home where he set up a conference call to California. I was still very scattered, so I let Shanti do most of the talking. She told me about her life and her family, her beliefs and views on various topics. She asked me what kinds of books I liked to read. I told her I wasn't sure what I was interested in anymore. I had died and come back to the world and didn't have any preferences about such things. In fact – I didn't know anything for sure.

Looking through my bookshelf, I named random authors and finally came to the name Reinhart Toller on the spine of a book. Shanti said, "Oh, he's a good friend of mine. He lives not too far from you."

"Yeah, I know that," I responded.

"Would you like to talk to him too? I could call him."

Suddenly shy, I hesitated. "Oh, no. I do have a lot of respect for him but don't want to waste his time. It's very late, and besides, I'd just embarrass myself right now. I don't seem to have any self-editing skills. I'd just sound stupid." In truth I only vaguely knew who the author was, but my statement was true just the same. How she knew him was a baffling coincidence, though they were both well-established in the same profession. I'd lost the ability to distinguish between what might be offensive and what might be a normal comment. I'd proved *that* earlier in the evening while talking with my mom. I felt, because of how instantly changed I had become since returning to my body, nothing could offend me so how could I tell what might offend someone else? She eventually persuaded me to agree to a conference call with Reinhart. I found his German accent quite amusing. It was getting late for Dale, so he said goodnight.

My short-term memory was seemingly barely functional, I was so focused on each moment, so I gave them both nicknames which I hoped would help, mnemonic devices that seemingly had no connection to their actual names but I felt suited them more: Bandana Banana and Garden Gnomeo. I was not in the habit of nicknaming people, especially strangers, but my former self was considerably more serious and uptight. I felt free to do so now. Graciously, Reinhart just chuckled. I liked him, but found Shanti a lot easier to understand. We spent a long time on the phone discussing everything from their businesses to their life journeys. I was far more interested in their lives than talking about myself, especially since they were famous authors. They tried to draw me out, but it was like pulling teeth to get me to reveal anything. My personal history just seemed so irrelevant.

Reinhart told me that he'd just recently started learning to play drums, so we made music over the telephone, he tapping a beat while I sang. Shanti seemed very strongly compelled to help me and insisted that if I chose to reach out to her later she would be a supportive person to help me make sense of the experience I'd had. It now was getting very late, for all of us, and I was sad to say goodbye to my new friends, but did not want their contact information, for the same reasons I did not want any traces left behind. We all had Facebook accounts, so that would be our only point of further contact, if we were to connect again. In fact I went so far as to log on to my telephone and delete all my call history for the evening, although I couldn't help but have a pang in my stomach that perhaps I was going too far in creating plausible deniability and had just lost the contact information for some really good new friends. In fact I had found the people I was supposed to be guided to.

Exhausted, I was finally feeling ready for sleep. That's when Alexander finally showed up. I heard him come through the upstairs door, making his way downstairs to me.

27.

Am I Awake?

ALEXANDER WAS MILDLY concerned about why my car was in the visitors parking area and not parked in the garage.

I'd had the presence of mind to rehearse an answer to that question before I went to bed. I replied that I hadn't gone out, but Karen had moved it out of the garage. This was a flat-out lie, something that did not feel good, but the other option, telling the truth, seemed totally unwise.

While he did have a relatively spiritual outlook, sometimes even quite a sophisticated one, he was raised with a very strict religious upbringing. I knew he still held fundamentally different beliefs to mine, so accepting the tale of my night's adventure would be too big a stretch. He seemed more easily able to accept the experiences of others, but when it came to someone close to him, like me, he wanted them to fit into his parameters of what he believed was possible and no more. He believed there was a Creator and that there were really advanced spiritual people walking the Earth who had profound wisdom and could process life events at a much greater rate then the average person due to their philosophies, but he did not believe in invisible higher dimensional beings. He seemed to accept my statement.

I felt relieved knowing I had bought some time. Then I began to split off spontaneously and unintentionally. Why did this keep happening over and over, and now of all times? I hoped recurrences wouldn't be a permanent feature. It was like I was living the scenes near the end of *2001: A Space Odyssey,* in which each room David Bowman the astronaut appears in he experiences an older version of himself, which he then merges with upon sight of his future self. My current view began to surface. I became immersed in a new scene with Alexander, except in this version he did not take my ghosting him so well. We got into a big fight for more than an hour about every little thing that had been stressing our relationship.

I felt I was living a lie by not telling him everything that had happened immediately and I wished we had the type of relationship in which I felt I could share that. I had discovered something so beautiful, so pure. I had seen the reason for existence and had been shown my higher self, immediately changed as a result. That realization only became more apparent the longer

I stood talking to him. I felt there was a giant abyss between us. Mentally he seemed so far away that my heart could barely touch him.

Then arose a knowing from inside. Even though he was the closest person to me, after all the years we had spent together the fact remained that he didn't know me at all. He knew the version of me he wanted to see. This truth was painful. I had been suppressing it for years, trying to simulate closeness and create situations where I could be my more authentic self around him. Yet experience continued to prove that every time I tried to break out of my mould and be more true to myself I was laughed at or scolded for being inappropriate, and it was best to not draw attention. The fact was that I thought I was funny. Yet he wanted to see only a small portion of me. It made it impossible for our roles to evolve together.

I valued the part of myself that I had vanquished for years in order to remain loved by him. I no longer wanted to make any sacrifices, especially at the cost of self-knowledge. The intimate interactions with those various cosmic beings had shown me many things about myself. I made a silent vow to fulfil my destiny.

28.

Converging Realities

I AWOKE WELL-RESTED and filled with the deepest inner peace and contentment. My bed felt so comfortable, every part of my body felt nourished and absent of any pain or physical discomfort. This was a rare respite, given the chronic state of my injuries. I relished the moment and abstained from opening my eyes a little longer, trying to breathe in every last mote of happiness. A sunbeam hit my face as I lay there. *Such a beautiful day.* Often feeling the need to maximize the full potential of days when I could move with relative ease, when I felt able to get anything of significance done, painlessness was an infrequent blessing. I wondered how I should spend it. I cautioned myself to avoid burn-out. When a day this easygoing appeared, I often fell into another downward spell within a few hours of feeling I could take on the world. Still fuzzy-headed, I tried to tune in to which day of the week it was and if I had anything scheduled, yet the euphoria made it hard to care.

Bit by bit the world started becoming more solid, sharper, more ragged, jagged and harsh. As I opened my eyes and examined my surroundings, I was alerted immediately to something being not quite right. I sat up and looked around. The whole place had been trashed! As I had quite a large space, that much of a mess would have taken considerable effort. An orderly environment was very important to me. I felt I needed it to maintain a streamlined thought process, a prerequisite for doing my work well. Until I could afford a better situation, my open basement suite served not only as a bedroom but also a large painting studio. In addition to the disarray, my stereo was on at high volume, much too loud to fall asleep to. Any noise at all would have been too stimulating, but what was even more unsettling was that the receiver wasn't even accurately tuned to a radio station, but in between two stations so that both were coming through distorted. I cannot describe how perplexing this was, given my relatively sensitive constitution, which usually made falling asleep difficult in the first place. Confusion was further compounded by realizing that all the lights were on. It was not the sun I had felt, but the glare of about twenty recessed ceiling lamps, all at their brightest setting.

Rapidly trying to assess the situation, I thought of Alexander. He was not here. Where had we left off? I was not hungover, and happy about that, not feeling guilty because I had done something inconsiderate such as creating a big mess and forgetting about him, which surely would have been considered highly unusual behaviour. Still, I couldn't quite recall details from the previous night or the last time we had spoken. I found my phone hidden in the bedding and flipped it open to see that, yes, I had indeed neglected our plans. There were about eight missed calls and twenty text messages expressing his irritation, some bordering on concern for my well-being. The phone displayed 1:40 in the afternoon. How had I slept in so incredibly late?

I took a moment to collect myself because I was starting to feel quite rattled. On the one hand, I was relieved to see there was nothing immediately wrong. But on the other, upset that I had gone to great lengths to create such a strange disturbance just to annoy myself.

I got up to fetch some water from the bathroom. After only taking a few steps, something felt really unstable. My left leg gave out from underneath me as I collapsed near the door. Even more confused and now in a great deal of pain, I noticed I was still in the clothes I'd worn the night before, still quite damp. In a flash, the memory arose of disorientation after falling into the puddle out front, then falling again downstairs into the basement room. *So that had happened.* I really had fallen. Something was coming back to me. Heightened anxiety welled up, but I could not remember much more. It felt like alarm itself was a dam holding back my memories. Yet my state had to be dealt with. I needed to change my clothes as well as examine myself more closely. I saw that my left hip and knee sustained serious bruises from the falls. The bones even seemed bruised. I had always considered myself a clumsy person, but this was much more significant and unusual, even for me. So much for my morning euphoria. I felt glad that I had cherished those perfect moments while lying in bed, but knew I now needed to go around defusing bombs in my life – dealing with Alexander was near the top of that list.

After changing into pyjamas, I assessed my situation and began to think of what to say when I called him. What could explain where I'd been? I summoned the courage to reflect. A very confusing and overwhelming surge of data came up. I barely knew where to start.

I had gone to the Wag, that much was fact, but Ashley had not shown up. *Or had she come later? No, she definitely had not come. Then okay, let's see, I had some wine, then things seemed to get more tense.* I remembered the loud music had done something funny to me. There were some faded memories of a card game. Then I had opted to not drive myself home. But wait – there was more – I paused, breathless, as if all the air had been sucked out of the room. There were some inexplicable memories. I had been in a car accident, a serious one. In fact there was no possible way I could have survived, never mind walked away with only a banged-up leg. *How is Mikey doing? Oh my God! Was my car totalled? How am I not in the hospital right now?*

I needed another moment of silence. It was not the time to overreact. I was sure there was a reasonable explanation for where I had been and why I had neglected my phone. I started from the beginning and went through my memories again. They remained consistent, only this time I allowed myself to push farther before blocking them. Then for no reason I was filled with euphoria, such a sublime feeling of wellness at the memory of the being I'd met the previous night. Tears of joy welled up. How could I have almost forgotten him? All that I was left with was a feeling, a feeling of knowing him so well and having seen so much together. I remembered how deeply I loved him. Thoughts came slowly. *But that part was a – a dream, right? Where did the dream begin and the waking state end?* I felt more confused than ever. Yet as I contemplated further, I understood that the memories were real.

I surely couldn't tell Alexander that I had missed our plans because of a dream – that wouldn't make any sense to him. It barely made sense to me. I was certain that if I spent some time calling my work friends I would get the answers I was looking for, only I did not feel I had time for that. I had put off calling Alexander long enough and felt the urgency to let him know everything was okay.

Feeling stronger and relatively sane, I summoned the will to call. This time I would call for real, at least I hoped so. This was too familiar and I thought: *Hadn't we already got into a fight about all this last night? Hadn't we broken up or something?* I guessed now we had another chance. That thought filled me with the optimism needed to make the call.

"So what did you do last night?" Alexander asked, sounding perturbed.

"I went to the Wag for a drink, then caught a ride home because I wasn't sure I was feeling sober."

"You mean you lied to me?" He sounded pissed off.

"I don't know why I did that. I really did just stop in and came home pretty early."

Alexander was displeased, but seemed to let it go after a parting shot: "That's not good. Things need to change if you're telling lies."

We seemed to have settled things amicably enough. He was definitely not happy with me and sensed that I wasn't being fully forthcoming, but I felt I could only disclose the full truth *after* remembering where I'd been. I knew him well. He would press for a full explanation, a partial account would only serve as material for another ongoing dispute. So the better question was, where *had* I been? It seemed I had been far from home, really far, like outer space kind of far.

While I knew that he considered himself spiritual, he did not believe in OBEs, never mind otherworldly beings such as spirit guides. If I were to share that last night I had been visited by a god while still fully awake, and was then taken on a journey across the galaxy, that would be far more than his mind would accept. Frankly, while Alexander strove to be open to possibilities, he was programmed to accept things at face value. He had not personally experienced what I just had, so it would be a tremendous strain on his beliefs, leading to complete rejection of it. At best my story would be attributed to a highly overactive imagination. I knew that if I did get more information about what had happened, I would have to choose my words wisely if I wanted him to accept it. Was there any partial truth I could offer that would be honest enough? Yet there was dread in the pit of my stomach when I thought of him. Things felt different, something had changed. There was a gulf between us that had become very wide. I felt like we were speaking different languages. It seemed I could understand him well enough, but he had never learned the sophisticated dialect I wanted to try to articulate, nor was he likely to. He would not be interested, but it was the only language that could transmit my story. I felt strong in my decision to pass it off as having fallen asleep – for now. After all, maybe that's all there really was to it. However, the very acknowledgement that my profound experience was something perhaps I could never share only made the divide between us feel that much deeper.

At the gym that afternoon, I bumped into Ashley. I had completely forgotten about her being the very person I was supposed to meet the night before. She seemed blissfully unfazed and more or less unapologetic about standing me up. Our conversation was one-sided, about how she felt she worked so hard at her life and just really desired the fairy-tale relationship that hadn't appeared yet. Hearing this was very strange, as I had already heard the conversation word for word while in the OOB state with Sanat. Not only that, but while she was talking I saw that she also had exactly the same cut on her knee that I did, another strange, unexplainable point to add to the list of peculiarities. Our conversation and seeing the abrasion was enough to trigger a new onslaught of memories, releasing the dam and subsequent tidal wave.

I became increasingly upset and did not dare speak to anyone about what had happened, not without more information. I returned home and remained alone, in a semi-catatonic state, deep in reflection as I continued to cycle through my ever-expanding database of memories, which continued to be of the most beautiful but mysterious events one could ever imagine. The information the database contained was extremely dense and tactile. It seemed like they would never stop unfolding, much more real than regular memories. *How could it be possible? How could I be so fortunate?* I was given to long periods of sobbing tears of gratitude, yet there was truly no one, I believed, who could relate to me or my situation. I was alone on this one.

Once I had settled things with Alexander and cleared away anything urgent that could possibly demand attention by the outer world, I was able to lift the seal I had placed on the previous night, unearthing aeons of memories of my countless adventures exploring the universe. Surprisingly, everything was still very fresh, persevered with an unaccustomed crystal-clear level of detail down to the finest nuances. These were supermemories, larger than life. I could narrate and see everything that had happened, almost like replaying a movie – even all the dialogue was intact.

After gaining a considerable degree of insight and truth, I began to wonder how my jumping through the cosmic slit in time affected everyone I had interacted with. Presumably, I had died. I had no memory of any alternative, although I continued to search vigorously for one. And yet there was a part of me that had a deep internal knowing that the only reason I had been allowed to come back to a physical body was because I had agreed to something. It had happened after I had seen all the possible outcomes for my life, and when I met the Elders. I had agreed to choose my highest plan. That is what permitted return to the physical. Moreover, I had signed a binding agreement. There came a new memory: I was with my guide floating in a timeless space, and we had signed an exclusive contract. Although much, if not all, of the content was shielded from memory, I knew my soul was aware of it all. I wasn't sure if it was possible to sign contracts in outer space and how binding they would be, but somehow it seemed more airtight than a mortgage.

I considered the injuries to my leg. Surely, if I had fallen down the stairs of my house, that would have made a very loud noise. My mother and/

or my aunt would have woken up. In fact, hadn't we spoken for hours, at least I with my mom? But there had been some strange peculiarities I had overlooked, at least when trying to speak to Karen.

Then there were my work friends, who must have noticed some odd behaviour. At least one must have been a witness to what happened. I presumed that my friend Mikey was still breathing and completely fine. He *must* be, since I was also alive and intact. I calculated that we both would have died in such a serious crash. *Could he have been injured in the possible traffic accident and I not?* I ran outside to look at my car to make sure, which indeed proved to be completely undamaged.

As well, I remembered the late-night scrambled phone calls made when I had been too agitated to sleep. Were they real or was that something I had done while still in some state between a dream and a projection? The more I thought about everything I had been through, the more convinced I became that what happened was something personal, truly unique to me. I had the strong intuition that no amount of internet searching or even speaking to spiritual people would necessarily provide the answers I was seeking. Even though my spiritual IQ bordered on low, my intellect told me that what had happened to me was unheard of.

This thought was both a saving grace, filling me with a sense of purpose, and a very cold, lonely and isolated feeling, leaving me entirely unable to relate to people, preventing me from reaching out. I began to ponder more about what it means to live with purpose and for the first time ever began to feel unspeakably delayed in executing the plan for my life. If everything I'd been shown was true, then I had some sort of powerful divine plan and destiny that I was falling behind on, as my guide had so gently mentioned. I speculated that I must be years behind. *If so, how many? Six? When had my path deviated from the intended trajectory?* I tuned in and guessed it had probably been right around the point when I'd started college, which had never felt right. *So then where did that leave me?* I had just been kind of jammed back into my body with no instructions or how-to guide to readapt to life on Earth. I had even asked if I was to write a book, but did not find confirmation one way or the other. If I was supposed to indeed write one, it was something my braver, stronger, future self was going to have to do.

Feeling conflicted and afraid to face my own shadow, I decided to reach out to the one person I could think of who was (A) spiritual and (B) would not think I was crazy or at the very least would not commit me to an insane asylum: Uncle Robert. I cannot describe how terrified I was to be mentally examined. While I knew I had not lost my mind, I did not, however, have the reasonable explanation that I required and felt that doctors would be all too quick to make their diagnoses and prescriptions before I had a chance to process what could possibly be one of the most remarkable accounts of seeing "the other side" of all time. I felt protective of what I had been shown, knowing it was both meaningful and important.

What I loved so much about Robert was that not only was he spiritual but he possessed a highly methodical mind, very much a lifelong student, having examined a vast amount of information on many subjects. I felt that he of all people would have a critical ear and could either provide reassuring supporting evidence or else would gently and easily explain things some other way. After all, I had spent a significant part of my journey speaking to my uncle's soul. A part of me was intrigued to see if he remembered anything of that. I decided to invite him over. My story really needed to be shared face to face to be fully appreciated.

He came and listened to my full account of the experience from start to finish, showing little to no reaction and pausing to ask questions for clarification from time to time. This was a very welcome response, as I felt really vulnerable sharing such a personal and strange account, unsure of how it might be received. Narration of the tale began to invoke the out-of-body state, merely by recollection. I noticed that I had to keep pausing to take deep breaths to ground myself in my physical form. I was still very prone to easily take flight.

His opinion overall was that my experience was something highly unusual, indeed sacred, but had a very great significance which neither of us could fully appreciate just yet. He offered some stories of others who had some interesting and credible experiences of out-of-body travel, the term itself credited to Robert Monroe, a successful American businessman who spontaneously experienced leaving his body in the 1950s. Having no background in metaphysical matters and without knowledgable advisers, its import remained unexplained for many years. He at first believed he must have a brain tumour, but examination proved otherwise. In time he authored the classic *Journeys Out of the Body* and founded the famous Monroe Institute. Uncle Robert had given me something I was looking for, fact-based answers that could help explain what had happened. Hearing some of those accounts was very comforting, even if none matched what I had experienced exactly. Still, this was *some* corroborating evidence that I had not lost my mind.

He encouraged me to order a voice recorder as soon as possible and urged me to at the very least vocalize the experience in its entirety, preserving it whole. He explained that this could prove to become a very important book, just as I had seen. Whether I chose to publish it was irrelevant. There might be information in it that could help me later, and he thought a written account would be fascinating. Seeing my rather disheveled state, he offered to transcribe it. This resonated with me and I could appreciate the value of having everything written down, for my own sanity if nothing else. I felt that it would be cathartic, as I was deeply in need of some inner peace. His offer to help made it so easy for me that I could not refuse.

In some ways, my uncle did not even seem that surprised or impressed, as if my experience was still within the range of normal, as well as known throughout history worldwide, and that so-called "reality" was such a strange, funny thing anyway. This greatly helped to minimize what my mind continued to blow out of proportion.

29.

One Week *in* Advance

AFTER SPEAKING WITH Robert, it became clear that at some point I was going to have to talk to my friends and family to investigate what they remembered. A couple of things were clear to me: (1) I was not originally from the current timeline and (2) they would likely remember very different details, depending on their level of awareness and the structure of their plan. After all, it was my experience and probably subjective. It wasn't something that had been orchestrated to ruffle the feathers of my loved ones. It was a powerful, earth-shaking awakening that had been created for me alone.

I began with the easier calls, starting with the people I used to work with. That took some digging because, while we were close, it seemed there was never a need for many of us to exchange numbers, since we would see each other daily at work. I managed to get both Jordan's and Mikey's numbers by calling in. I was very careful in what I said, wanting their perceptions of the night before I shared mine. If they could validate any anomalies, that would be huge, although, I suspected, unlikely. Nevertheless, I was surprised that neither of them remembered anything unusual. They both stated that I had seemed completely normal at the restaurant, possibly slightly inebriated, but even that seemed a stretch in their estimation. Nothing was said about being out of control or falling down and having to be escorted off the premises. They could not recall anything we had talked about that night and only confirmed that I had won the card game.

I asked Mikey if he remembered my car stalling in the intersection. He did not. I pressed a bit further and asked if he could speculate as to how long we were parked outside my house before Jordan arrived. He seemed to think it was ten minutes at most. He did share one interesting piece of information. At one point during the drive, he said, a shift seemed to occur and I seemingly became more intoxicated, suddenly trusting him less, refusing to provide my address, which was exceedingly frustrating to him. I decided to open up with him, understanding that my call and form of questioning seemed a bit odd. I told him that I'd had some sort of fantastic otherworldly experience with one of my guides and had gone out-of-body. I explained that it was a longer story than I had time to explain and he probably wouldn't believe me if I did. He merely laughed in amazement and exclaimed that he wished something like that would happen to him. I decided to ask them separately one last question before I ended the calls. I asked if there had been any drugs that I'd consumed that they had witnessed or suspected. They each answered with an immediate no. However, they confirmed that indeed some friends had smoked weed after hours, but that I had opted out. The call was conclusive, validating some of my memories and suspicions as I had hoped.

This led me to the next set of questions for my mom and aunt. Several days had passed since the experience. I felt much more secure about it. If I had made a fool of myself, they had done a good job at laughing it off to save me the embarrassment. I casually asked them if they had remembered anything strange when I arrived home on the weekend, such as a loud noise as if I'd fallen down the stairs. Both their answers were in the negative. Slightly irritated, I felt sure my mother had to remember *something*. We'd had a long conversation, although after talking to my uncle, who had absolutely no remembrance of sharing a flight over the planet and ostensibly a much deeper level of interaction, I was beginning to feel they would recall nothing either. I prodded further and asked my mom if she remembered me coming home in a somewhat scattered state, needing to stay up and talk, requiring extensive consolation, watching television, and my attempt to predict world events with no real conclusion to prove their accuracy one way or the other. Again I was met with a blank stare and could see in her eyes there was not an iota of remembrance. I proceeded to tell them both a little about what had happened and explained that I'd had a miraculously strange night, greatly condensing the experience to make it short and sweet in a couple of sentences.

Although I didn't feel I would be met with resistance from either of them, the idea of going over the story again in fine detail was more than I could bear, considering its length. Once had already proven enough in the conversation with Robert. I knew I was going to have to repeat the process one more time into the voice recorder. To repeat myself was a strong pet peeve, causing irritation, which combined with the significance of the experience would demand an enormous amount of energy, as it was a narrative still in process. I decided to conserve for the recording session instead, knowing I would be able to share more later.

There proved to be many ways I would continue to test which timeline I was in. I remembered the embarrassing account of the game I'd invented,

Drunk Psychic, and recalled the unbelievable lengths I had gone to cover up any signs or notes that could possibly be considered evidence of my experience with the Divine. I was, however, missing many personal items from my purse and vehicle, which I remembered throwing forcefully out of my car when I had greatly desired to be free of possessions. At least now I had the ability to laugh a little about it. I searched the grounds several times, but the undergrowth proved too dense. Possibly I'd flung those things into another dimension. I again laughed at how much my mind had opened. The fact that I accepted *that* as a possibility, even the most likely, was quite funny.

I decided to try my luck with television, an unbiased and not easily manipulated source of information that could possibly help provide additional confirmation. Although I wasn't sure what exactly I was looking for, I felt the need to flip through the channels to at least find something to jog my memory. Had I planted something in there that I was supposed to see? I really wasn't sure of how being back in my body was supposed to work. I was making things up as I went. Supposedly there would be all-new episodes of television shows airing that I had already seen while in my transitional state. What I'd viewed could have been, however, only reruns I just hadn't seen before, thinking they were new and unconsciously creating the impression of prediction. I checked to see whether any were in fact reruns, but no, indeed they were all new programs, and yet they were familiar. This was indeed not the first time I had watched them. Ditto for the movies.

The research continued for many weeks, turning into months, but the most intense were the seven troubled days that followed immediately after returning to my body. Perhaps it was because I had made the mistake of looking into my future or perhaps because I still had some divine connection lingering. Of that I wasn't sure and had no real way to find out. That week was somewhat of a nightmare, although I imagine some people, perhaps of a stronger constitution, especially as regards the paranormal, may have found it enthralling – which I did too, a little. During this time every event was a déjà vu experience, but one that did not end, break or stagger. I had foreseen and continued to foresee everything before it happened, nearly to perfection, for the duration of the week.

At first this was easily dismissible. Any occurrences were filed away in a mental compartment labelled "there has to be a reasonable explanation for this." Yet as the days passed and the daily occurrences increased in duration and frequency, I concluded that this would have been incredibly difficult to predict. Something as fleeting as déjà vu can be interesting, mildly intriguing. However, one that was non-ending became quite uncomfortable and difficult to adjust to. I had only one conclusion, one I was very hesitant to make for some bizarre reason: I had become psychic. This was not something I dared voice out loud. I didn't understand how I could suddenly be gifted with something that profound after an entire lifetime with only small blips of psychic experiences that could be proven, validated by others, either seeing or knowing well in advance something I could not possibly have known of otherwise. But this – this was different – this was on a different spectrum of extraordinary. There was no possible way I could have prepared for it. Or was it that I had been here before while looking into my various probable timelines and only now was I remembering in detail? During those seven psychic days I had considered buying a lottery ticket because my accuracy with everything else was one hundred per cent, only there was one catch: I had not seen winning the lottery in my plan. That understood, I did not see it as important to waste time or money pursuing something I knew would not prove fruitful.

I walked through life in something like a daze as things seemed to be moving in divine orchestration all around me, all on cue – people crossing the street at specific moments, a server dropping items beside my table – it was a beautiful performance. There were brilliant moments of clarity as well.

At dinner one night with my mother and aunt, I thought I should mention some of the remaining future events I'd seen, just so I'd have some proof in case they came to pass. I began, "One thing I saw was that I was going to be awoken by fire alarms. I thought I was sleeping, but definitely saw myself getting trapped in a hallway in Alexander's building somehow. I got locked in and couldn't get out. Sirens were blaring and it was very hot. I could see smoke but no fire.

"I saw a plaque with several sets of numbers on it which showed a crossover to his floor in the stairwell, but for some reason we couldn't get to it. I suspected they were some of the numbers that I'd asked my guide to write down when he was looking for a pen in the glovebox. Either way, in the vision Alexander and I got stuck at a lower floor, in the amenities room, for hours. I saw three light fixtures in the room but only two of them had bulbs – square bulbs – which don't exist as far as I know." I paused before going on to ensure they were still following me.

"The vision continued, though not in a normal linear sequence as far as I could tell. I had seen a bag of groceries, and I told him I'd go shopping, specifically listing all the ingredients I would buy, including a banana, Jell-O and celery, not stuff I'd ordinarily buy, at least not in that combination. Remembering the grocery bag triggered a memory I didn't know I had, when my guide took me to his favourite restaurant, which he described in detail, the Rocky Point Cafe. I have never been there, though it's in Port Moody, not far from Alexander's place. I had vaguely heard of it before or maybe saw an ad. I saw that Alexander and I would soon go there. I would order the sweet and sour meatballs with organic pasta, and he would order a spicy seafood soup."

They seemed intrigued by my recollection and agreed that if indeed all those events were to follow, that would be something to consider a very psychic insight, and perhaps I could discover its purpose. There was something more to bear in mind: meatballs were not a normal meal for me to order, considering I had been a vegan for a year, and even prior to that seldom ate red meat. Yet if I was to follow my guide's advice, it sounded like I was supposed to surrender to including some animal protein in my diet again, at least temporarily, so it was *possible*.

After breakfast one Sunday at a local pancake house, Alexander and I stopped at a large drug store where we decided to buy a new Xbox game. One in particular jumped out at us that I hadn't heard of before, called *BioShock*. The packaging showed some intriguing imagery, and the game looked interesting, so we decided to take it home to his place to spend the afternoon.

I was shocked to remember that I'd already played the entire first level of the game while seated in the car with Sanat. This was the violent game: with the wrench in my hand, I had to inoculate myself against the bad nurses. How fascinating and bizarre! I struggled to find the meaning of it.

At the time, I remembered how out of character it had seemed for a divine being of his qualities to strongly encourage me to play something of that nature, so I had conceded against my better judgement. And now to see it had been inserted into my daytime plan kept my brain spinning its wheels trying to come to grips with it.

I had a similar occurrence when I later bought the Xbox release of *Tomb Raider: Underworld*. I had seen the ad for it come up on *Xbox Live* and wondered if I would find any familiarities. The previous version I had played was for my old desktop in high school. Graphics and gameplay had certainly come a long way since then. This new one was greatly improved in comparison and should have been a completely new experience to me. I ended up beating the entire game at lighting speed because of my super-concentrated practise while playing with Sanat that night. Certainly there had to be some higher purpose to all this than to come back from the dead with slightly improved abilities at playing video games. The idea that perhaps there was none made me laugh.

Earlier that same day, after purchasing *BioShock*, Alexander and I decided to go out for lunch because there was fire alarm testing in his high-rise building and the noise was annoying. It had been going on for hours as the tests progressed from floor by floor. There had been a notice posted for a few days in the elevator, but I had not been to his place for some time and was unaware of the scheduled testing. Suddenly my world began to slow as I had the same sinking feeling in the pit of my stomach all week when revelations became fact. It really was happening as I had predicted, but why? What was it supposed to prove? Was I being warned of some terrible danger? The answer continued to evade me. I remained a helpless observer as the scene unfolded.

As we left for lunch, we found the elevator had been shut down on account of the testing. In order to leave the building, we had to climb down all twenty-six flights of stairs, which did not sit well with me. We ended up driving around for quite a while because so many restaurants were closed on Sundays. We settled on the Rocky Point Cafe by default. It was a place neither of us had been to and it was conveniently open, becoming our only option. It didn't register until we were given menus that it was the very same restaurant Sanat had liked so much. I'd been so consumed with perplexion at the fire alarm testing that I hadn't a chance to take in my surroundings. I struggled to test my memories. The décor was eclectic to say the least, just as he'd described it. There were old china plates on the walls, tacky laminate tables and tiger-lily-themed wallpaper. One corner was dedicated to karaoke. Quickly remembering my vision fully, I expected to see my guide walk in at any time. At that very moment, someone parked in front of the window in a blue truck, just like his, but hope deflated when I saw my blue friend "Mikey" wasn't the driver.

Feeling a tad let down, I returned my attention to ordering, and – surprise – Alexander played his part and ordered the spicy seafood soup. Unsure of what to do in such an unusual situation, I thought I might as well play along, so I ordered the sweet and sour meatballs with pasta, fulfilling my own prophecy. In light of recent events, however, I wasn't really hungry, and greatly distracted by thoughts of the fire alarm testing and what would happen when we went back to Alexander's apartment. My memory at that point was not entirely clear. I did recall seeing us stuck in the hallway, but thought perhaps we had already fulfilled that part of the prophecy by having to climb down twenty-six storeys.

I decided to test the waters with my companion and felt this was the perfect moment to share some of what was troubling me, as he seemed completely unruffled by my distracted mood. Either he noticed and didn't care or didn't notice at all. Perhaps I was being too much of a woman.

I brought up the night that I had not answered his calls. At first he seemed slightly intrigued that he would hear the real reason for it. I'm sure he suspected I would confess that I had instead either stayed out late with colleagues or perhaps had confirmed one of his more flagrant suspicions by cheating on him. Neither was true to my nature, and yet those were the only two likely conclusions I felt he was silently considering jumping to. Wanting to both make an effort to be more open and to share the strangeness of the moment I was experiencing, I began my tale, right from the beginning. After he had heard my moderately detailed account of the spellbinding experience with a guide that had shaken me to my core, he tuned out, shutting me out completely. I could see and feel the disappointment radiating from him, as if to say, "*I thought you were finally going to be honest and tell me what happened.*"

When I finally got to the point in the story about being completely psychic and seeing this very fire drill in detail, he would not listen to another word. I wanted him to at least understand that if it was something I was adamant about, obviously I believed it truly happened to me. What motivation could I possibly have to lie? Yet the more I tried to speak, the more irritated he became.

He stated angrily, "Yeah, it sounds like you had a *cool dream*. Enough. *STOP IT!*"

I was hurt beyond words at being silenced so harshly. But what had I really expected to be met with after all? The more I tried to share the more irate he became. Any appetite I'd had now gone, I ended up getting most of my lunch wrapped up. We made our way back to his high-rise.

Once back at his building, we found many of the residents waiting in the lobby because the elevator was still out of service. We decided it would be good exercise to take the stairs. Finally, at the twenty-sixth floor, we discovered that every second floor's fire escape doors were locked from inside the corridor, including the one that had access to his floor. It appeared we needed a special key, not a regular staircase key. Theoretically, we could have entered through the floor below or above, but that would have required someone at hand who possessed a key to that floor. A stainless steel plaque displayed crossover floors. The numbers they displayed were eerily familiar. I started to feel trapped, anxiety arose and I was unable to steady my breathing enough to conceal my apprehension. I had tried to tell Alexander about my clairvoyance, but it seemed a bit late for that, as he would not have believed me anyway. In any case, I was dredging my mind to remember what came next. Banging on the door didn't help. No one heard us and we could still hear the fire alarm testing continuing on his floor and higher.

Left with no other option, we were forced to climb back down all the way to the second-floor exit, the designated fire escape. It opened into the building's amenities room. Having no other place to go, we decided to wait out the testing. He suggested we play a game of pool. I welcomed the idea, as playing pool with him was a far better alternative to sitting in silence enduring his cold shoulder after my attempt at honesty was refused.

As he switched the lights on over the pool table, I noticed that only two of the three sockets had bulbs in them. Never mind that, but the bulbs were square! I had never seen such a thing. I felt elated that some of my visions were coming to pass so clearly, yet it was mixed with frustration and sadness, as it seemed no one was to share in it with me. *At least I told my mom,* I thought. Part of the amenities room featured a small kitchenette, where I saw a grocery bag on the counter. "Look, Alexander, someone left a bag of groceries behind." Curious, I opened the bag, and was shocked to find a very eclectic assortment of items, including a banana, three packages of Jell-O, celery and a few other items, the list of which I had shared with my family a few days before. I dared not speak this out loud for fear of ridicule. I had been met with enough rejection for one day. I was, however, really surprised. Inner turmoil erupted upon seeing the contents of that bag. Whatever could it mean? Perhaps there really was no meaning. I had just accurately seen the complete next week of my timeline. It seemed the most likely explanation, as none of these details seemed to amount to anything of significance, at least not on their own.

There was another prophecy that came true, providing further insights later that day. We were to have a family dinner at my grandparents' house later that evening. I was reminded of the funny vision, seeing the tire fall off my grandpa's car, and on the way there described what was on the dinner menu.

"Grandma's going to make rouladen," without knowing if that was even a word, "and home-made buns." A strong aroma of vanilla came to me too, but I didn't think it was food-related.

We arrived to discover that indeed rouladen and home-made buns were to be served, something I had never seen her make, but perhaps my mom and uncles had.

My cousin Trevor sat down and began to draw a picture of a hand that later morphed into a spider, just as in my vision but that previously had made no sense.

His brother Steven shared a video of his band rehearsing, and the logo he'd designed for it.

They'd brought Trevor's new cat Mojo along to meet Grandma, who loved animals. It had a heart-shaped patch of fur on its back.

The icing on the cake: Auntie Tracy gave me a gift of vanilla-scented candles.

When Uncle Orbit arrived, we had a discussion in which he mentioned that he'd had a dream in which an eighteen-inch-long crocodile emerged from my heart. This was extremely fascinating. My totem animal emerging from my heart chakra seemed like a powerful sign.

Later, in conversation Grandpa told a story of how his front tire had gone flat, part of the car's suspension had broken as a result and the assembly had come loose. That resembled the vision of the square tire I had seen on his car, symbolic of his eccentric but interesting car modifications.

What a powerfully fascinating day! I allowed feelings of intrigue to linger as long as possible.

The last thing that happened during that week that showed precognition was that I had made a new contact in the art world. Her name was Monique. She had invited me to participate in a large exhibition with many other artists she was curating at Science World. I agreed immediately, as it was something I had seen coming.

All these events only seemed to increase the tension in the air. In particular, there were the most powerful visions still to unfold: the car accidents. If all other events had come to pass exactly as shown, then what did that mean for the ones still forming?

My dread of an impending severe injury in an auto accident was profound. I became paralyzed with fear – my thoughts repeatedly returned to that random bag of groceries I'd seen – surely that was something so obscure that it must mean my fate was sealed and imminent. I had spent some time placed physically in that experience, although there was no real way to know if that was in fact the timeline I was still on.

I decided the best possible safeguard was to avoid leaving the house entirely. I stayed indoors as long as humanly possible and only left when desperately low on food or if my body really required exercise when the pain of my current injury became more pronounced. Even though I had taken precautions to avoid such a serious incident, I realized that if it was something that was *supposed* to happen, there was no way to avoid the inevitable. Be that as it may, I was unable to surrender to the idea of sustaining another crippling injury and took every preventive measure imaginable.

For months I was terrified to leave the house or drive my car down the stretch of road to and from my boyfriend's house. One thing that was not accurate about the vision was that at the time I drove a black two-door coupe, not a silver four-door sedan. With difficulty I avoided that route, thinking I could avoid fate. As the weeks passed, it became increasing difficult to conceal my phobia. Necessity required that I leave the house to keep my basic affairs in order. Trying to maintain a certain degree of flexibility while still taking rather superstitious measures to ensure I wasn't walking into an unwanted fate, I limited driving to daytime, as I had seen the event occur at night. I was able to successfully maintain this methodology for a surprisingly long time. However, over months there came a need to also drive at night. As the months and years passed, the fear also subsided. I wanted to forget the experience, having no way to interpret the message for how to live my life.

30.

The Calm Before *the* Storm

EIGHT OR NINE days after the travels with my guide, in a conversation with my mother, I mentioned weather events as they happened.

She seemed completely unresponsive, as if to say, "*So what?*"

When I reminded her of our previous conversation about my predictions the same night as the experience, I found to my amazement it had never taken place, at least not according to her memory of that night. I felt sick. Was I losing my mind? How was that possible?

I recounted the two-hour talk with her, in which I went into great detail, but apparently that had never happened, despite a vivid memory of being so frustrated trying to communicate that I had grabbed her arm. Surely she would have remembered that! I had believed we were both completely awake but, when I thought it over, had to admit her arm had been very cold to the touch and extremely soft. It was strange that I now also remembered my own body had felt that way before, while sitting in the car with Mikey.

Another three weeks later, I discovered that the fight with Alexander that night had never taken place either. That information proved challenging to assimilate, as I had to set the stage with questions about a fight I had experienced but he had not, placing myself out on a limb. It seemed possible that none of the things I'd remembered had happened, at least not in this dimension's frequency range. And yet I had experienced those events. Their memories had the features any normal waking memory would, and in fact in some ways were more vivid than many ordinary ones. What was the difference between them, if any? Furthermore, in our interactions those people had not responded in ways I felt desirable. In fact they had done the opposite of what I wanted. If those conversations were something my mind had created, they would have been a lot more predictable, with responses I would have thought of. Also, it did not feel like I was interacting with my own consciousness as within a dream, when upon waking you can see how you created your own dream environment to process daily experience, perhaps to compensate for an unbalanced attitude. Maybe my wish to speak to no one as I entered the front door had been granted and I'd simply gone to bed. But that still didn't explain my bruises or the items lost from my purse and my car. Those things had happened. Those events were as real as the other memories sandwiched between. I needed to entertain all possibilities in order to hone in on the greatest truth, if only for peace of mind. I just didn't know – as more strangeness ensued.

So what was the message here? If I had experienced a non-ordinary state, beyond what society may consider "normal," in fact it *also* was reality, part of a greater whole. Furthermore, if an individual's personal reality is comprised of their interpretation of everything they experienced during the span of their life, then this experience belonged to mine. This was not an easy conclusion to grasp. While I so readily accepted this truth while OOB, the challenge came in assimilating it when back in my body, bumping up against the limiting beliefs of others, including my own. My ego flooded my mind daily with disparaging thoughts and feelings, such as: *If this really was such a rare experience, then what makes you so special? You don't really believe you could be that important. No one will ever believe you!* While I couldn't agree with that, in many ways it had a point. All I did know was that it had happened, whether anyone chose to believe me or not.

Before the Sanat experience, I had a lot of time on my hands to sit and reflect on life, given the state of my body. Many nights spent wondering what the meaning of life was, I knew I wasn't created to pursue a path that didn't have heart, to use Castaneda's term, and yet my true path remained elusive. Now, on the other side of the experience, in some ways I felt more lost than ever. There were nevertheless a few facts I knew to be true: (1) I had some greater purpose to fulfil (we all have one), but I did not know enough to determine what that was. (2) I had a divine plan that I was very behind on, so this experience was needed to bring me up to speed. (3) I was more than just my physical form, and life continues after so-called death. That last thought was the most reassuring of all. What a gift to be able to experience that truth in person! On the one hand, I felt overwhelmed by my plan. But on the other hand, I felt invincible and fearless, armed with the knowledge that nothing that bad could ever happen to me. My soul would continue to exist and I would retain consciousness no matter what.

What a gift I now possessed! I wished to be able to somehow give know-ledge of this truth to others. What a gift that would be! Yet I did not feel confident enough to try. I wondered, *What is the point of little ol' me being shown all these things?* Prior to this, I felt I'd had a very average and some-what boring life. I had always sensed a deeper energy within, but looking at my life now, the former life seems small, especially in contrast to what I had been shown. I struggled to feel worthy of such a gift from the Divine, wondering how it was possible. I was neither that socially influential nor an authority on anything, so what right had I to broadcast my story? Who would listen? I believed, given the right circumstances, what I had seen could potentially help many, the masses even, if it was communicated in the right way. I settled to allow more time to pass, continuing with passive inner reflection in the hope that time would yield direction.

Thinking it might help settle me back into my body, I decided to have a reiki session with a friend who is a master of the therapy. Many emotional upsets surfaced after that experience. I looked for anything to help ease the process. I felt I now had major decisions to make for my life, but was also being held mentally in jail by parts of myself in denial about what happened, creating further procrastination. Was I prepared to leave my love because of a "dream"? Was I prepared to write a book and out myself as a so-called back-from-the-dead spiritual person? Was I willing to try to verbalize something so seemingly beyond my conscious awareness? Was I willing to let go of all the friends who did not serve my best interests? And if I did all this, what would I be left with? The question I should have been asking was, what do I have to lose?

The reiki session did not seem to have many immediate effects, but may have influenced subsequent out-of-body journeys, especially their frequency, as I had stopped going OOB for some time – it was too traumatic and I was unprepared to digest more information. Sometimes the frayed thread of the memory of the Sanat experience seemed in danger of snapping. Said another way, it was like an ember, and I made sure to stoke the fire often to keep the impression alive.

Not long after the session, a desire arose to spend more time in singularity merged with the I AM, the most desirable state I had experienced that night. I began to seek it out often. Although there was no clear way to get there, I attempted conscious projections while tuning in to the frequency of the Infinite I AM. Sometimes I could "find" it, sometimes I could not. Having no proper background in meditation, at least in this life, I had a very small toolkit and just one tool: intuition. I wondered if perhaps it was set up this way intentionally so as not be inundated with instructions and human rules, which could hinder or even block my progress when trying to connect back to God. *And yet,* I thought, *some training really would have helped.*

After some time in singularity, I found myself in a lucid dream, crawling through a very dark tunnel. It ended in a large brick archway that opened onto a colourless scene. There was a ledge I had to cross that led to a brightly lit alley, which seemed to be indoors, ending in a big hall with many tables. A large number of the people gathered there were of Asian ethnicities. Some I guessed might be Mongolian. They were all sitting on the floor, apparently in anticipation of some impending event. I thought I was probably the only white person present.

I whispered to a man next to me, "What are we waiting for?"

He whispered back, "We are waiting for the master to speak."

As time went by, more and more people took their seats in a circle around me. Soon I was fielding questions, and after answering a few, realized that I was the one they were waiting to hear. *I was their so-called enlightened one, the master!* Alarmed, I protested as politely as I could, but they insisted that in fact I was the very person they had expected.

All of a sudden there was a massive earthquake. The floor rippled as the whole building shook violently. Everyone dashed for the exits. I realized that I was no longer female. I was a man! – a Mongolian man – who had no time to wonder about it.

Beside me were two young girls who looked so alike they must have been twins. They were terrified. I put a girl on each shoulder, escaping along the same route I'd taken to enter, along the ledge, towards the brick archway, and headed for the long cobbled tunnel. The ledge had hand grips that consisted of strange phallic growths that resembled tusks and male genitals at the same time. They were in fact plants, which became obvious as we got closer and they began to bloom. I clung to them as we made our great escape along the ledge, and with a great weight on my back. As we approached the archway, it lit up with a radiant red-gold vibrating glow. We were safe, and the OBE ended.

Upon hearing this, Uncle Orbit asked, "Was that dream a sign that you now had the power to save yourself from an unwanted fate, to switch channels, so to speak?"

"I think so, yes," I answered. "Or perhaps I visited students from a past life, possibly even still in embodiment. It could mean any number of things. I'd been told in a reading, which I'd begged my mom for when I was sixteen, that I had a very tall Mongolian guide. In retrospect, perhaps that was just a different aspect of myself that had shown up for the session to guide me. On the other hand, maybe the reader's intuition had tuned into that vivid dream experience in my future. Which came first, the Mongolian guide or the dream? Time is a very human thing.

"My next task, I decided, because I now understand that I've been creating all my experiences on every level, is to make my existence easier by learning how to perfect my powers of manifestation and use them to avoid any unwanted events, especially like the ones I saw in those timelines when I suffered brain damage.

"What I really want is to become a successful artist and live the most joyous life possible. That's the timeline I want to fulfil. Speaking of car accidents, maybe part of the answer to the question of why that extraordinary experience happened to me was because of being rear-ended in that car accident just previous to it. Remember? I'd been so unhappy in my career path in college, had just dropped out and was waitressing. The accident only added to my difficulties by giving me so much pain that I had to quit working. It forced a decision way sooner than I would ever have made without it. I'd felt so trapped in my body that it gradually built up a strong desire to be free, so strong that I actually left my physical body's manifestation behind and was granted that incredible experience with my guide."

He nodded and offered an opinion: "Your accident could be viewed as having served you by increasing your desire for freedom. In some of the mystical traditions it's said that without a desire for freedom as intense as a drowning person has for air liberation will be delayed indefinitely because the ego will co-opt the highest truths for its own ends, at best satisfied with the pleasures of the mind, but short of the goal. At worst it will feel entitled to cook up dogma out of it to enslave the ignorant. Some wonder if a desire to be free of desire can be liberating – desirelessness by definition is already free – but maybe you have to start somewhere, provided you have fire in your belly and the gumption, like at the end of *Tales of Power* when don Juan and don Genaro take Castaneda to the edge of a cliff. If he leaps into the abyss, he gets a gold star and a sorcerer's badge. This time he jumps. What do you think?"

"Knowing the truth is what sets us free," I responded. "I feel that I have been shown much but still have a long way to go with processing it. I consciously know many things, but it's hard to practise them daily and make them second nature. Like, I know we only enslave ourselves by identifying with temporary things – bodies, personalities, beauty, ugliness, success, failure, wealth, poverty, bloodlines, nationalities, religions, which are dualistic constructs – but to be able to negate all those things as identity takes a huge and consistent effort. I think it takes a lot of energy to implement what I know, energy I'm still gathering."

The truth of the matter was, all speculation aside, I still had no idea of the purpose of that fantastic experience. One thing was clear: while I thought I possessed an entry-level spiritual IQ, my soul, on the other hand, was very advanced. At some point I had *earned* that attainment. I came to this conclusion through the realization that it takes a soul with a high level of control and other qualifications to orchestrate something of such significance as part of their plan. Even just the permission to do so suggests the being must have accomplished a lot to have their plan authorized as worthwhile. If it wasn't, why would the Divine permit it? After all, the Divine is not permitted to burst our individual manifestation bubbles that preserve the game as what it is.

Yet there was no way I wanted another car accident, especially one that resulted in years of brain damage or even paralysis. I don't think anyone could blame me. I understood that my actions were highly motivated by fear. Even the desire to perfect my manifestation was just to avoid any unpleasant events. Fear was preventing the desire to understand the bigger picture. The better question would have been, why would events such as these be installed in someone's plan to begin with? What purpose could they serve?

In some ways, after the experience I had a false sense of advancement, in the sense that I was operating under the presumption that I had the power to avoid objectionable parts of my plan. It would remain only a presumption.

My uncle asked one last question: "Well, that's reassuring. So how exactly did you steer clear of all the equally difficult timelines you saw connected with the car accident in your vision of that rainy night driving back home from Alexander's place?"

31.

Aftermath

AFTER WHAT COULD be considered the most powerful and significant experience of my life, all returned to normal for quite some time, years in fact. After surviving the first week back and all the predictions that had followed, slowly life began to take on its normal shape. The clairvoyance faded over the next few months. It was interesting how something that once seemed like a curse now left me feeling vulnerable without it. Yet it was for the best, as I had proven that knowing what was going to happen did not equip me to know what to do about it.

As life returned to baseline, I found myself slowly relaxing into the surprise of daily life. I contemplated the enormity of my otherworldly adventure each day. It was something that had shaken me so deeply, to the core, that it was hard to ignore. I wondered what could possibly trigger the less desirable fates I had seen – for example, being homeless – and if there was anything I should be doing now to prevent it. After all, I had also seen my best possible future and my larger-than-life higher self. I thought about her often and decided that she was something more important to focus on, since you bring about what you think about. In fact I even dyed my hair dark like hers to bring more of her energy into my life.

Try as I might, my thoughts resumed trying to solve a problem that couldn't be solved as I rehashed the events of that night from beginning to end. It was peculiar that, although I had seen many alternative timelines, the one that never changed was the one with the car accident at the start of that night. No matter how much I thought about it, I was never able to determine an alternative memory with the "more reasonable explanation" I was searching for. It seemed fixed. If anything, I was only able to extract further details about the crash itself. I found this incredibly frustrating and hard to accept. It was perplexing. But then I became curious: If true, which I still hesitated to accept, then why was I saved and allowed to return to my life? Why had I died so that I could be shown future disasters? Whatever I was supposed to be doing now must be of great importance, but I hadn't the foggiest idea of what it was.

There was reassurance that I had made the right choice by dropping out of sports medicine studies. This was confirmed by the Elders, who had spoken directly of my plan as an artist. At least I got that part right. Be that as it may, I was still being met with great scepticism at home from my boyfriend, who banned the topic altogether. As confusing as it all was, I found myself repeatedly returning to deep gratitude for everything that had happened, even if I did not know the reason why.

I'd been warned after the fact by Sanat Kumara to know better than to look into my future, but still did not fully understand what that mistake had cost, other than I had become nervous about leaving the house, afraid of my own shadow. Perhaps observing them meant that new futures needed to be created to maintain a certain level of ambiguity. Or perhaps the danger lay in observing the negative ones. Maybe I was more likely to attract those due to fear. I simply did not know.

As the days became months, I began to wonder if I had seen those time-lines correctly. Perhaps I had already made the shift in consciousness and had mastered the lessons, thus not requiring some horrible accident as the occasion for learning. Really, I was just in the bartering stage of acceptance.

Upon examining my daily life honestly, I admitted this was a highly optimistic thought, as I could not claim to have implemented any changes in my life yet. Whatever lesson I was hoping to skip would presumably be quite minor, as I had not had any significant realizations worthy of averting devastating crashes or otherwise.

I was slow to break up with Alexander. I felt a sadness when in his company and remembered my guide's words that it would not serve me to stay, dragging out whatever bittersweet days we had left until one day I might have the courage to see what was waiting for me on the other side of change. Despite our differences, he was the love of my life. We never seemed to find a good enough reason to break up. Or to stay together, for that matter. He provided comfort and security. Without his friendship it was hard to imagine a happy life. Yet one's happiness should never rest solely on the shoulders of another. That is too great a load for anyone to bear. Only one's deepest essence can do that. I had yet to find my own inner source of joy. This fact revealed how much restructuring my life required.

As time went by, and I wondered what I was supposed to be doing with my life, something became overwhelmingly clear. Alexander could not accept my experience. I knew he questioned my sanity for believing it, although he would never admit it unless provoked in an argument. By extension, this inferred that he could not accept me either. I had looked into our future together and saw he would never fully accept me just as I am. The unedited yet playful, carefree version of myself, who did not try to say the right thing for the sake of him hearing what he wanted to hear, was like an actor who has grown tired of speaking her lines from a script. I imagined a relationship with someone with whom I could share my truths, as fantastic as they are, if that was even possible. If so, it seemed far distant, as I could not even visualize the type of partner I dared dream of.

One day, after months in silent reflection, I came to the realization that I was tired of wearing so many masks. Most of them were subtle, minor ways in which I had edited my persona to be more pleasing to him, ways in which I did not allow my true personality to shine. I was done with repression. I felt really good about this train of thought, so good that I was finally empowered to share it with Alexander, knowing what I would be met with. I told him that I wanted to be my authentic self, unapologetically uninhibited.

This did not sit well with him. He suggested that it was a bad idea, and what would I want to do that for?

I brought up countless comparisons with people we knew who lived their lives truly openly, including several recording artists he worked with daily, illustrating how well it was working for them, never mind the advice in countless self-help books he had given me over the years. Yet I was met with a firm no and could feel his will trying to push me back into the box he helped create over the previous six years. That was enough for me to finally take a leap of faith. I had unconsciously given him an ultimatum. If he could really contradict his own belief system by verbally telling me not to be myself, then he had made the choice for me. This was advice he never would give anyone. I could see his emotions were heavily clouded. He could feel us growing apart. His advice came from a place of fear, and I knew I would miss him. Still, I was liberated by finally giving myself permission to be me. Now it didn't matter what *anyone* else had to say. I had spent years in denial, the last thing I ever wanted to repeat.

It was hard to end six years of dating. The Sanat experience happened around year four. It took an additional two years for things to become final. We had a long, drawn-out separation that seemed to be ending amicably, until one evening when we decided to reconnect to see how each other was doing. This ended in a fight of such magnitude that we would never recover, resulting in my left collar bone being broken accidentally as he wrestled me to the ground while falling on top of me. As traumatic as it was, it felt like something orchestrated by the Divine, as otherwise it seemed we would keep returning to each other. It had to be something significant because there was a lot of comfort keeping us together, which was also blocking growth.

I did not take the break-up well. My physical health, already declining, became even worse. For four years I had been suffering with injuries from the first accident in which I was rear-ended, living off my credit card for the majority of that period to bridge the gap between art sales. The insurance claim resulted in some funds, which essentially only paid off the medical debt incurred during that time.

The final diagnosis was that I was born with hyperfleximobility. This allows joints to naturally move beyond the normal range of motion. The condition makes healing from injuries more difficult because the patient will consistently overextend but not notice, possibly resulting in the widespread muscle spasms and locks that I had become so accustomed to. In addition, I had sustained soft tissue damage to my neck from the impact. I also had been born with spina bifida occulta and scoliosis. Some specialists thought I also had fibromyalgia but, to be honest, no one in Western medicine really had the answer. Eventually they all gave up diagnosis and treatment when my symptoms failed to respond positively to their prognoses. Their recommendation over the years was increased dosages of medication. I was too young for that type of sentence, so did not find this a real answer. To surrender to acceptance of steadily decreasing mobility and to continue to increase medications did not translate to a feeling of progress towards healing. It felt more like capitulation.

During those years after the crash, I pursued every treatment possible, from natural and holistic (complementary and alternative) to allopathic (conventional) therapies. I also humoured the doctors, only because I knew my insurance claim depended on it. I tried every drug they prescribed, just to say I had done my best. I applied all the knowledge I had gathered during my years studying the body in college, yet failed to yield positive results. It seemed any medical advice I followed made the problem worse. The registered massage therapist treatments especially were far too aggressive and always resulted in several days of pain and bedrest, no matter the pressure applied in treatment. All the professional medical advice seemed to contradict my intuition, but deep down I was still looking for an external agent to heal me. This led me to feel lost and hopeless, very much a victim of circumstance, as I had given my power away to so many professionals and come up empty-handed. There came a point where I had reached a dead end with the medical profession. They informed me that I would never run again and would be lucky to walk long distances. As a long-distance runner when younger, I felt my freedom was slowly being taken away, permanently. I felt exhausted from trying for so long, researching alternative breakthroughs, even trying to further my understanding of how pain is interpreted in the body to start with. Yet given four years of trying, of efforts to eat well, of suffering through the therapies that often made me feel so much worse, of the weeks I would lie in bed debilitated by one or another area of my body spasming or searing nerve pain, which led to countless sleepless nights – often ending in tears and feeling trapped – I cracked. I could not take it anymore. Over those four years my will had slowly been broken. I had lost my relationship. Alexander had even accused me of faking my injuries, as I seemed to always be in pain. I felt I had nothing to show for trying my absolute best and started not to care anymore, since my actions were not leading to what I sought.

I reconnected with a girlfriend one evening whom I had known almost my whole life, who was also suffering from severe long-term pain from a broken collar bone that had never set right. She offered me a low dose of oxycodone, synthetic heroin. It was not a long-term solution by any standard, being a narcotic, but I only needed a brief respite, to remember the contrast of what it felt like to not be in pain, since I could not remember life without it. Many years previously, when I had broken my arm in three places, oxycodone had been prescribed for a short period. It had worked miracles. After having exhausted every alternative, I did not feel I had a lot to lose.

Quality of life had reached such a low that my entire day oscillated between rehabilitation exercises while in great pain or resting. Very little time was spent painting or away from home because bad experiences on days when I tried to do too much ended with flare-ups in public and difficulties getting home. It seemed easier to stay in my enclosed environment. If my back or upper body started spasming, then I could lie down or take my medication and ride it out. Sometimes a spasm would last for weeks, at its worst as long as two months.

So while a drug of oxycodone's calibre was not something I had consciously decided to seek out, it did one day find me. Patience and tolerance had diminished to zero. I just wanted to be my normal self again, to be able to walk in my neighbourhood or shop for groceries without having to take elaborate precautions. I felt I had been wronged. It wasn't fair, in my opinion. I felt trapped in a disabled person's body.

I hoped, rather too optimistically perhaps, that oxycodone could trigger a natural healing response. If one's body has been fighting inflammation and nerve pain for years, the damage from the stress may become irreparable. At first, it was the miracle I was looking for – one incredibly low dose made a new person of me for nearly two weeks – something no therapy, no amount of meditation and no prescription had ever been able to afford: deep sleep and freedom from pain. I woke up after a blissful ten hours feeling completely refreshed and without any indication of disability. It was as though every muscle that had been screaming for its life prior to this now had just arrived back from the spa, unaware there was ever a problem to begin with. The contrast was astounding. It no longer felt like my body was violently attacking itself. At first I felt grateful and wondered how long this deep-sleep repair would last. I thought to myself, *Well, perhaps this is something we take in case of a super emergency.* It was like pressing a hard reset. Yet there was sadness in knowing relief might not last, so I cherished the moments when I could talk to people and laugh, shower and blow-dry my hair – all in the same day. I had my life back, temporarily.

The price for blocking the pain would have to be paid. While I had stayed true to my promise, only succumbing to the help of the drug if I was in incredible pain, sadly it seemed only a temporary solution. Over two months the dosage and frequency increased dramatically, true to the nature of the substance, since it works by increasing the body's pain threshold.

I had underestimated how weak my will was to tolerate pain, and also the rate at which one adapts to such a drug, which is quite fast. While I was taking it I was able to work and enjoy more of the full, busy life I loved and was accustomed to. It all seemed so worthwhile. I remembered the state of my life before discovering this manufactured support. It filled me with fear, the idea of returning back to that lifestyle, if you could call it that. It was more like barely living at all. A couple of months of normalcy seemed worth the risk. At least the rest might provide a fighting chance to refill my reservoirs. But I assure you it did not.

While I experienced no craving mentally, there was no powerfully blissful euphoria as some have reported. It was more like having the entirety of my full mental capacity freed from the all-consuming thoughts of pain. With this freedom, or mental RAM available, I was able to think, do and create as I had before the accident. After just a short time it became apparent that while oxycodone was giving it was also taking. I began to feel polluted with a feeling of artificiality and the substance bringing me down.

I became exhausted if I didn't take it. Finally it began to obscure the pain only if an absurdly high dosage was taken, beyond comprehension by most medical standards. In a way, I had taken a speedy shortcut to the advice of the medical advisors, that is, increasing dosages of medications for the rest of my life. Still young, I was aware that this was no longer the solution.

I naively tried stopping using the drug, but with devastating results, my first incomplete attempt. Yet my will was strong and I knew there was no alternative, so began proper research to prepare to try again. This involved a radical shift in internal dialogue as well, as I knew very well what I would go back to: a world of pain. I was not sure how I was going to ever provide for myself after it was over or if I would ever be high-functioning again. The notion of enacting my "highest plan" seemed like a long-forgotten pipe dream. If that plan existed, it was elusive and all but unknowable.

I accepted the ramifications of my actions. After the better part of six months into the next year I was very close to being my normal self, not healed from my injuries, but no longer dealing with nightmarish side effects.

Though I did not know it at the time, this victory was but the first in a long series of battles I was about to endure, a phase I entered into next I like to refer to as the Dark Ages. While some Buddhist philosophers might say there is no right or wrong, no good or bad, that everything simply just "is" – and I agree in theory – in practice what I proceeded to enter into was nothing short of evil.

Not knowing what to believe about life and existence anymore, I tried to cope by seeking distractions in the external world. This attitude was reflected in my romantic relationships when I chose a long-term relationship that encouraged my rebellious side instead of pushing me towards self-growth.

We started off as friends, planning art shows together and creating inventions. Lucas presented himself as a philanthropist wanting to help save the world. He had a fascinating mind and many outrageously creative ambitions. I could listen to him for hours. He was also incredibly generous in trying to support and uplift the people around him. Then came a time when our relationship reached a pivotal juncture, where I would decide if we should remain friends or if it was something more. I decided to show him a draft of this book as a test. While he seemed forward-looking in many ways, the content of the book belonged to a genre that pushed beyond his limits of acceptability. I could tell he was holding back his true opinion when he laughed softly and told me it was "really something," furrowed brow included.

I received strong signals that he was not a person I should date, primarily because he openly admitted that spirituality was not what he sought. Yet unconsciously I maintained an unfounded optimism that I might persuade him to see the other side of life, given enough time, considering he was such an advanced technological genius in so many ways. I saw tremendous potential in him to help humanity in a radically meaningful way. Not knowing how to help myself, I subconsciously thought I might play a role in influencing the planet by helping shape his philosophy. Yet old lessons returned. Lucas too felt he was correct in the methodologies he had learned and adopted over the years, seemingly cancelling out my truth by default. Though it was nothing he really did or said outwardly, I was too weak-willed and eager to abandon my truth, as I allowed doubt to overshadow my beliefs. I had unconsciously broken my vow and entered into a relationship with someone who did not believe in my otherworldly experiences, overriding my intuition with the rebuttal that I wasn't sure that acceptance mattered.

Everything comes at a price. In many ways, this relationship was an improvement in the sense it gave the illusion of greater freedom. Lucas didn't downright disagree with me and get angry because our beliefs differed, yet I knew he silently believed I was an airy-fairy spiritual type. I was unaware that by choosing a relationship with someone so dominant, holding primarily atheistic beliefs, that he had the power to silence mine. Feeling greatly inferior with regard to intellectual IQ, his being significantly higher than mine, it proved hard to convince him of anything he didn't already believe.

It was now 2012. For the next two years I watched more and more of my spiritual self dissolve into the background, again for fear of ridicule. I failed to recognize that I was not being true to myself by repeating the lesson I had endured with Alexander: *to learn how to speak my own truths and not adopt the beliefs of others by osmosis.* This was a painful teaching to go through again as I attempted to alter my character in a way that would allow Lucas to love me unconditionally. It's important to assimilate a lesson before moving on to the next one, otherwise it will manifest in a repeated situation, often with increased severity. In hindsight, perhaps I was looking for someone to fix my broken heart in the same way I was looking for a doctor to cure my body.

I followed the advice received while OOB and had since let go of many longstanding friendships, as we had grown apart. This led me to a less than ideal scenario: I suddenly was surrounded by people who in some ways understood me well enough, but they all suffered from a significant life pain of some kind, the walking wounded. While maintaining the immense fortitude it took not to relapse, I began to experiment with less addictive drugs as I had when younger, yet this was all a distraction, serving to tie up my curious seeking mind in something to preoccupy it. None of these people really knew me. They all had their own best interests in mind. Still, at heart I was seeking more experiences with the Divine.

From my perspective, my guides had left me with just enough information to know I was on the wrong path, but not enough to understand my purpose in life nor my current trials. I felt angry and hurt that Sanat was not present to help me when I needed him the most, leaving me in the hands of fate. The truth was that I hoped I would die. Leaving my body behind and returning to those higher planes of pain-free weightlessness had an incredible appeal. I had experienced them first-hand and knew this was the desired state to return to, thinking in vain that if I were so lucky as to have my life end prematurely, I might be allowed to remain "up there" indefinitely, with Sanat.

Nevertheless, I did manage to discover one medical miracle: a psychiatrist who offered Botox injections specifically for spasticity, treating both nerve pain and the muscles themselves. While the price was significant, the results were too, affording me an eighty per cent reduction in pain from my conditions. It was a miracle. And although I needed injections fairly frequently, I absorbed the cost gladly as a small price to pay for physical freedom, especially since it was free of any addictive side effects. Things were looking up. After all, if I could stabilize my body, the rest would follow. In some ways, the injections gave my youth back. After dealing with chronic pain for so long, I had felt far more than twice my age.

The spiritual path forgotten, my life had become about survival, constantly waiting for the next shoe to drop, forgetting everything I had been taught while with Sanat, no longer wondering whether my life had some sort of divine purpose, which seemed only for those who have the luxury to dream.

Shortly after reforming my life by attempting to return to my normal, healthy, clean-cut self, I was sexually assaulted by a friend I was trying to help who was suffering from mental disorders. This event proved incredibly damaging to my well-being, something that I had never seen coming and was utterly unprepared for. I was so hurt it happened while I was trying to help save his life, only adding insult to injury. Also, I was deeply concerned the man I loved would end our relationship as a result.

This compounded the existing traumas of the final fight with Alexander and the resulting broken collar bone along with the years of physical pain. I felt vulnerable and didn't understand how I had created this situation. I had tried to follow the guidance I'd received years ago: I had continued painting, I had left Alexander, I had disassociated from the people shown. Yet here I was. I thought I had been following my intuition when I was called to help the friend who violated me. However, intuition could not possibly have led me here. I felt I had the infamous scarlet letter on my chest, and everyone knew.

By this time I had invested most of my savings in the companies I'd been developing over the previous four years, which so far had netted only a small return. With finances dwindling to my last $20,000, I felt an urgency to seek employment, even though I was not emotionally capable of much. I was so traumatized I could barely leave the house. Lucas talked me out of looking for work and urged me to invest the last of my money in my pursuits: if I had to fail, I must give my all first. He promised to catch me if I fell. All but a few steps away from catatonia, I felt his judgment was likely better than mine. I believed him.

Not long after the assault, our relationship began to deteriorate and ended. This coincided with my birthday as well as Mother's Day. I was asked to move out. All of the inventions we'd been developing over the previous two years were cancelled immediately. To make matters worse, I had followed his financial advice and now possessed less than a few hundred dollars. We had also discussed marriage. Taking the loss very hard, to me it felt like yet another titanic rejection.

Devastated to say the least, too upset to try to reflect, I felt barely alive. The simple act of breathing suddenly seemed laborious. I returned to my place in Coal Harbour, with enough money to last until the end of the month. I thought I must be blind. I had trusted my friend not to injure me. He violated my person. I had trusted my love to be there for me. He abandoned me, leaving me with nothing. In no way was I blameless, however. I was mature enough to understand that I had contributed to the events that led me here, and it seemed we initiated something within one another that caused us to not always respond in a way I would define as love.

In the midst of this great depression, a friend's photos were posted online. We had met in Vancouver. This friend had recently relocated to sunny Arizona, a place that seemed to hold so much light that all its residents were happy. I thought this was likely my soul just seeking asylum in a metaphor, wanting to escape the destruction I had associated with living in my city. That hunch proved to be unexpectedly fruitful, however. As I began taking the next steps ahead in my plan, I was powerfully guided to visit the Grand Canyon State.

The trip proved enlightening. It seemed a place where I could heal. The desert heat alone provided a diminishment of symptoms. I laughed that I was now akin to the northern Snowbirds who fly down south to ease their bones. On the flight back, I was unsure how I could move to that sunny land for a lengthier stay, but knew remaining in Vancouver was not part of the plan. The flight was very turbulent, as it was the stormy season. We flew through two sandstorms before nearly running out of fuel while circling Minneapolis airport waiting for a layover. A large thunderstorm raged over the airport. Our plane was running on fumes, fifth in the line waiting for a runway. I had a lot of time to think during that flight. Something my friend I'd been visiting had said stuck with me, that if it ever came to life being so bad that a person had nothing to live for, they should simply sell everything, leave their life behind and do everything in their power to find happiness. This seemed staggeringly providential advice, as this was exactly what I needed to hear.

What should have been a very quick flight extended to a very lengthy nail-biter, the perfect circumstance to send nearly the whole plane, including me, into a panic. Considering my friend's words more deeply, as I sincerely felt this could be one of my last moments, I remembered I could look upwards and ask for intervention. I prayed to the I AM, if He was indeed listening, that if the plane was allowed to land safely, I would drop everything, sell all my belongings and move to the desert. If the deal was life *or* death, I would find a way.

When I arrived home safely, I had no idea how I could manifest what I had promised, yet in that tenuous moment I had felt connected to the Greater. I meant every word I'd said. I pondered for days whether there was a way to stay in Vancouver and return to working. The answer was no. I had too much emotional turmoil from heartbreak, abuse, ill health and the prospect of poverty, not a state conducive to progress. If left alone I relived painful memories of the past repeatedly, torturing myself with mental conflict, wishing I had received the fairy-tale ending I had hoped for. I turned within and asked how to fulfil my promise, and was shown to contact my ex to ask for guidance.

In a miraculous twist, he offered to pay my expenses to live abroad for a year and heal. I gave up my apartment in Coal Harbour, unable to afford it, and instantly manifested a room-mate in Arizona, a girl I had met briefly while out for breakfast there. All signs seemed to point to this as the direction I should take. In hindsight, I was hanging together just well enough to make some highly constructive changes. I sold as much furniture and art as I could prior to departure, using the income to support the move. I left all my friends behind, not knowing what my new life would be like.

Before I left Vancouver, I had just begun aerial acrobatic painting for events through a local circus company. Quite enjoying the performances, I decided it was something I wanted to pursue in the desert. When that ceased to pan out the way I had hoped due to visa issues, it became apparent the sojourn was just for healing. Trying to move forward as much as possible, I started looking for a healer in Arizona. While not sure of exactly what I was looking for, I had the impression a shaman should be considered. It was a solution I hadn't tried.

Before I knew it, 2015 had arrived. I began to receive signals that my time living abroad was coming to a close. I landed a part in the Canadian national reality show *Crash Gallery,* painting in competition with other artists on television. I also received news from home that my grandmother had suffered a major stroke and was paralyzed. Ironically, again this news was delivered on Mother's Day, coinciding with my birthday. I wondered, *What is it about this time of year?* Although much had healed while living abroad, it was still incomplete. Deeper levels were just getting exposed. I felt coming home was premature. Nevertheless, it was clear I must return. Many things were asking for my attention.

I was greatly concerned about my grandmother. It did not sound like a good situation the people around her were dealing with. I felt the duty to help ease the burden on my family by helping look after her, now in a nursing home after being hospitalized for some time. It was clear that her paralysis was not making it easy to transition. She repeatedly tried to barter a return to the former home she loved so much, not accepting her new situation. She was not faring well under the complete care of others. As a caregiver herself, it was not in her nature.

In her final stages, she had been given a long time for contemplation while unable to move. As time passed, hidden anxieties began to crystallize into realizations. Part of her panic was due to regrets that surfaced about how she had lived her life. In this disempowered state, she could see the people who really cared for her and the ways that she had not let them in. She also began to doubt her religious beliefs and questioned why she hadn't done more self-examination earlier, quite fearful about what she was about to meet on the "other side." More than anything, she wanted more time to make things right.

I was not coping with the situation well either, empathically absorbing much of her pain. Pain and illness in my own physical body increased as a result, temporarily undoing much of the work I had done on myself while away, not understanding how to shield myself from the pain of someone I care so much for. I think I unconsciously almost felt it my obligation to feel what she was feeling. Or perhaps it just showed how sensitive I had become. But I felt everything, to the point of undergoing my own testing for lupus, which was perplexing to both to me and my doctors.

While helping my grandma acclimate to the care home, I accepted several dates with someone I had known since high school. He'd become a successful mortgage broker and seemed to have his act together. We had grown up together, as he was a part of my larger group of friends. While I did not feel that he was necessarily the one for me, it was a welcome break from the stressful transition back to Vancouver. He seemed rather taken aback that I'd agreed to go on a date with him and revealed that he had an enormous crush on me in high school. This was completely new information. I had always thought he was nice. However, as our few dates proceeded he did not seem to be dismantling the pedestal he'd placed me on. I suspected this might be an obstacle to further progress.

I awoke on July 21, 2015 with a terrible anxiety, which wasn't out of the ordinary, given that my life was not exactly placid, but it was overwhelming enough that I didn't think I was going to be able to attend our date that evening. I tried to cancel, not saying why. But he sounded like he was having a really hard day himself and needed the company. As a caretaker-type person myself, I felt I could not say no and picked up some gifts along the way, only to find him in a perfectly fine mood, with no signs of being downcast. In fact he shared he'd hit an all-time sales record that day and seemed positively elated. This felt very weird. Warning sirens started to sound inside me, raising a red flag. I quickly mentally replayed our phone call. There was no question: I felt misled and immediately wanted to return home.

The date proceeded nevertheless. We went for dinner at a local oyster bar. There was a strange anxious energy between us. Something shifted as dinner ended. We got into a fight in the street outside the establishment. I had noticed him glancing at my phone during dinner. My only conclusion was that there was something he thought he saw there that set him off.

While I never would have labelled him volatile, I had always known him as just a friend, not a close friend, however. In retrospect, I had seen an alpha male dominance displayed on several occasions, primarily over other males. It was easily dismissed, having taken place in the distant past. These memories had not been readily available at the forefront of my mind when I had considered dating or else perhaps I would have opted to stay home.

I was standing facing him as I tried to comprehend why he was so profoundly aggravated.

He was yelling at me loudly.

My whole body tensed.

Amidst the disparagement I distinctly remember hearing something to the effect of, "*Who do you think you are?!*"

This was unacceptable no matter what he was upset about. With both hands I lightly pushed his shoulders, making him take a step back. I turned and walked away, not sure where I was going. My car was at his place, but I felt the need to put some distance between us. We'd both had wine at dinner, so I did not intend to drive. I thought perhaps I needed to go to a friend's house instead. Then the unexpected happened.

He pushed me from behind.

Because I was in no way expecting to get shoved, I was completely relaxed and unable to brace myself as I went flying face first into a parked car.

The last thing I remember was seeing its bumper coming directly towards my face, then the strong impact as I lost consciousness. I blacked out momentarily. I came to, screaming in unbearable pain. I had no vision and was entirely unable to open my eyes. Ears ringing loudly, I heard the voice of my date still present, relieved to know he was close by. I could not tell what he was doing, but I could hear objects moving around me. He seemed very agitated by the sound of my wailing, something I was completely unable to control.

He said he was going to call for help.

I begged him to stay with me.

He refused. He then took my purse, but left my phone, placing it by my head. Why he did that, I am not sure. At the time I thought maybe he was concerned for my valuables.

Unable to see or stay alert without the sound of someone's voice, I went into the darkness and lay in the streets of Kitsilano unconscious for some time.

A stranger passed by, fortunately, saw my state and called an ambulance. He tried to wake me, with not much luck.

Only a few garbled words escaped. I remained unconscious for several hours and woke alarmed to find myself in the trauma ward of Vancouver General Hospital. I was in unspeakable pain originating primarily from above my left eye, with no memory of what had happened. I vaguely remembered being on a date, but upon being asked for anything more than that, my injuries began to throb with such force that I had to remain motionless.

It was interesting that my immediate reaction was to blame myself. I quite naturally assumed that I had done something to deserve this, although what that thoughtless action was I could not say.

At intervals the hospital staff continued to press further as to what happened.

I said that I'd been on a date, and my friend was the last person I had seen, so he must know what happened.

They permitted me to call him on my phone.

He arrived shortly thereafter and, mysteriously, with my bag.

The staff, unlike me in their right minds, thought it was highly suspicious that he had my purse and keys. They informed me that I'd suffered a significant blunt force trauma to the head, which had caused internal hemorrhaging and a fracture in my skull. I was going to need further MRIs to see the full extent of the damage and whether surgery was needed to put pins in.

I became instantly extremely panicked, grasping the severity of the situation. I begged to speak to my date, feeling he must have a reasonable explanation.

The hospital staff disallowed speaking to him directly, as they had their own set of questions they wanted to ask before they would allow him to speak to me. They interrogated him for his explanation as to how he got my bag and where he was when the injury happened. They argued that it is very unlike a woman to leave a date to go home without even her keys or purse.

He stuck to his story that he had no idea what had happened, that I had run away. He claimed to have looked for me, yet my phone showed he had never called even once, but returned to his home with my bag.

The hospital informed me that, from all the information they could gather, he had assaulted me and left me for dead, given the extent of my injuries. Had a passerby not found me, I could have bled internally and not survived. They offered to press charges, to which I immediately declined.

They then sent over a social worker, a female who attended to abuse cases such as this.

I found it all so unnecessary and felt they made a great error somehow. I couldn't believe what I was hearing. Clearly there had been some mistake. How could anyone do anything that violent to a stranger, never mind someone they'd known nearly forever?

They further informed me that I had suffered significant brain damage and had a serious concussion, one that would take considerable time to recover from. I was instructed to avoid any stress. My blood pressure must not rise for three months for fear of a blood clot or more hemorrhaging, in which case I could still suddenly die.

Not surprisingly I became incredibly stressed at hearing this information. This was, ironically, exactly the type of situation I should avoid. Hearing the news alone sent my blood pressure through the roof. If the first near-death experience with the semi wasn't enough, this most recent close call and being left for dead was.

For some time I felt the need to prove my assailant innocent. My heart was incapable of believing otherwise. Even though the hospital had forbidden me to speak to him, I decided the only way I could definitely put the situation to rest was to call him to hear his side of the story. Before doing so, I waited to see if he would reach out first. I had not seen or spoken to him since he came to the hospital. More than ten days passed, in which I was able to gain a more clear perspective. I found it odd that he had not reached out sooner, given the number of dates we had been on, never mind our long-standing friendship. If someone was completely innocent, wouldn't they be considerably concerned for their friend's well-being, considering they had just almost died while in their company?

I felt this phone call was a crucial moment. It was important that I be maximally lucid so that I might determine the truth of what had happened. I prepared myself mentally for each possibility so I would be available to see the truth when it presented itself. Potentially I had made some terrible error, spontaneously run away and launched myself into a parked car. This was a stretch. Possibility number two: I had spontaneously run away and happened to bump into a stranger I have no memory of, who then assaulted me and left me with my phone, while somehow giving my purse to my date. Or possibility three, the simplest but the hardest to swallow: it was him. He pushed me.

He said he'd been really busy at work, but was curious to know how I was doing. His words sounded dry and his speech slow.

I said I was not doing well, that in fact I was still in the borderline stages, fighting for my life in many ways, but I wanted a chance to hear his side of the story as to what had happened.

His account had changed since his hospital visit. This time he stated that I had left the washroom at the restaurant looking upset and never came back.

I asked why he had thought I'd done that, to which he had no reply. I told him I vividly remembered having a fight with him. He had become increasingly upset very quickly, had not known his own strength and accidentally pushed me into the bumper of a car, face first.

I was met with silence and a palpable pause.

My intuition, which had been steadily increasing since the start of the call, began to now scream at me of his guilt.

He gave a very unbelievable reply, just saying he wasn't sure what happened, but did not deny it.

I asked, if I had run out of the restaurant, why hadn't he found me, as my body had been found within sight of the establishment?

To that he had no reply other than to just keep on repeating what he clearly had rehearsed, that he had looked, circled a two-block radius and returned home, hoping I would be there.

I summoned the will to ask one final question: If he was looking all over for me concerned about where I was, then why hadn't he called?

To that he also had no response. After giving him a long time to answer, he finally said he didn't know.

My sense of flight-or-fight was now screaming for me to get off the call, which I promptly did. I have never spoken to him again. That call had taken me so unexpectedly. While I had prepared for all outcomes, I had been strong in my conviction that I was to blame, wanting to shoulder the weight of the responsibility. I felt sick and afraid for my life.

When I had originally consulted the emergency doctors, I asked them if there was any possible way these injuries could have been sustained by some thoughtless action of my own, to which they informed me that it was impossible due to the tremendously sturdy nature of the human skull. They repeated that the amount of force was greater than what I could produce. At the time I had wondered if it was possible that I had defied the laws of physics and proven them wrong. The resolution that came from the call, however, steered me to accept their original diagnosis. It was also the only theory that supported my memories.

By that very unsettling phone call and the number of errors in his explanations, I was able to determine he was absolutely lying. I had chills hearing his confused and conflicting explanations of his version of events. A month later I tried to press criminal charges based on the doctors' recommendations. The charges did not stick. It seemed something the police were not overly interested in pursuing. They did not have a video of the attack, so that was where their policing reached its limits.

Little did I know the first of the two brutal timelines had just been fulfilled: *the foreseen brain damage that would take the majority of a year to recover from.*

Life resumed as well as it could. About two weeks after the head trauma, I went to visit my grandma with my mom. I knew upon seeing her it was going to be the day she transitioned. She had developed a strange large growth on her stomach. It was suspected she had an undiagnosed stomach cancer. She now also displayed incredibly swollen lymph nodes and even under medication was in great pain.

Momentarily alone in her room with her, I then did something unusual. I felt guided to place my hand on her stomach. First I thought it best to form a bridge through me to the Divine and began to create a vortex, pulling her excessive pain away from her back to Source. Once the gate was opened, I asked it to continue to keep processing for her. Feeling into her stomach – it did not feel good; it was incredibly fiery and turbulent – I did sense a slowing of activity once the work had begun. Since I had never done anything like this before, I was not really sure what to do next, but hoped the Divine might perform some small miracle through me for her, based on my love and desire for her to be relieved. It seemed my call was heard as I continued to be guided, except now the message I was hearing was that I needed to connect to her soul.

I refocused and held her hand closest to mine, while placing my right hand over her heart. She was almost not even there, spirit and mind. It was so hard to see her this way, but I knew it was important for her passage and I sensed this could make a great difference, in what way I did not know. I called in her soul and was able to connect to a flicker of her that was still holding on, strongly being pushed away by the pain. I sent her a tremendous amount of love directly from my heart, not in words, but in feeling-energy. We were quiet for a long time. Then I told her she had all our permission to let go. My mother was not quite ready or prepared, hoping it could be a while longer, but I felt I had a far greater assessment of her state. I could see it would not be to her benefit. My grandma was reluctant to listen. I needed to state this truth repeatedly, while also assuring her that everything was going to be more than fine, that now she could be connected to Love, that our relationship would continue in a different way. Just then something quite peculiar happened. I saw a mysterious diamond of light forming in her solar plexus.

I turned to my mom and urged her to call the whole family to come to the nursing home to give their respects. She was reluctant at first, then acceded. We returned home later that evening. I remained flooded with tremendous anxiety and fear all evening. Grandma was close to falling into a coma, barely conscious when we last left. It was now past dinner time and we had not received news one way or the other. Unable to sleep, I stayed up restless, painting and weeping. A strange tension inside me wanted to release. Finally at 1:05 in the morning there was a prompt shift in my spirit. I suddenly felt elated, like I could breathe easy, *knowing* everything was going to be okay. Not knowing where the relief came from or why, I crawled into bed peacefully. Then I paused, holding my breath. I knew where my source of peace had come from. She had just passed. I rolled over on my back and shed a few tears of happiness for her. Tremendous relief washed over me. I was sure we would get a call in the morning.

Not even five minutes had passed when I heard a stirring upstairs that sounded like my mother talking on the phone, followed by loud footfalls down the stairs as she came to crawl in bed with me and told me the news I already knew: Grandma had passed.

The awareness arose that I had been experiencing all that she was feeling in the moments leading up to her death, processing with her empathically. It was a powerfully moving experience for me to be able to confirm, through the report given to my mom, that I had indeed felt her exact minute of passing, even though we were almost one hundred kilometres apart in different cities. It also served as validation that everything I had experienced in the hospice with her prior to that day had happened as I experienced it.

They say that, at the initial stages of a person's passing, often their spirit is still nearby. We were promptly greeted by my grandmother while my mom and I were up late sitting on the sofa talking. Her gentle but powerfully present spirit came and blanketed the entire house in purple and pink energy that I recognized immediately as hers. I was surprised I was sensitive enough to attune to this, my mother also, but less so. I wondered if Grandma had anything that she would like to say.

At first it was more just a feeling that I received from her, one that radiated total contentment, peace and harmony, underlaid with a gleeful tone of, "You were right." She exhibited such exuberant freedom and, judging by her size, truly was in an expanded state, covering the whole house with her presence. I then began to receive some specific messages from her, but having never relayed messages from spirit before, my medial gift was not yet articulate. At first they did not come through in formed words. For example, I did not hear her speaking directly into my ear. It started with a nudge, as if she were tapping me on my right shoulder, telling me to pay attention, as she had something she wanted to say. Now relaxed, she was able to send me the strong feeling of asking for forgiveness. This was directed towards my mom mostly, wishing that she had been more present for her during her life.

Nothing like this had ever happened to me before. I had never shown any such ability. While Grandma and I had not been that close during her life, we had become very close in the months preceding her death. That experience proved quite transformational for us both, creating a very strong psychic connection. It did dawn on me that there were many indications that greater gifts were waking up within me, yet these were spaced out months apart. So many life events were pressing at once that the upgrade was able to slip under the radar, almost entirely unnoticed. There was much I didn't know about handling these abilities, such as how to discriminate and shield myself from other people's emotions.

Her passing hit me hard. Some time later my grandfather, who had been consequently moved into the same care home, also passed. Yet I was not taken by surprise. It seemed like loss and death were a part of life I was intimately familiar with.

There was one small victory: I managed to win the reality show in honour of her right before my grandmother's passing. In order to perform, I had been unable to spend time with her and needed that to count for something. I was, however, able to return to spending time with her and share the news. For that I am forever grateful.

Yet I felt I had no time to process their passing. My emotions had to be put on hold, as numerous facets of life continued to destabilize due to seemingly external events beyond my control. To start with, my mom's and aunt's house sold immediately before I had been hospitalized with the head trauma. It had been set up with a short-term escrow. We needed to be out in less than two weeks. This put them in a frantic scramble to pack the entire house and ready themselves for each moving to separate residences. The stress on them had been so great that I believed I had no choice but to drive myself home from downtown still badly concussed. If I had called, it would have required both of them to leave work early, drive long distances and arrange some sort of Austin shuffle with cars in order to gather mine. This stress was not something I was willing to offload onto them. To make matters worse, I did not have a place to move to and had not foreseen being disabled, otherwise I may have been in more of a hurry to solidify plans. Worse still, I now had to begin the task of apartment-hunting sporting an alarmingly black eye, which may have seemed altogether suspect from a landlord's perspective, and overwhelming impossible from mine.

I did not know what to make of existence, both my past experience and the present circumstance I would not wish on anyone, even my worst enemy.

There was yet another surprise lurking behind the scenes to complicate things. I had left for Arizona in a hurry. The problem of storing my belongings proved to be challenging on my budget. A solution presented itself: I was able to store my artwork in my old basement suite temporarily. My furniture, books and various household items I could leave with a close friend, who had kept a storage locker for years with very few of his belongings in it.

At the time, it was the miracle I needed. There was no other clear alternative at hand. Now faced with collecting those items, I had the sinking feeling that I had made the wrong decision. After many attempts, I finally received a call telling me the storage company claimed my friend had missed a payment, even though there was a valid card on file. Despite any argument one might make, it did not erase the fact that the contents of the locker had been sold months before. With everything I owned gone – I was breathless.

On the upside, I had nothing to move. On the downside, I had neither bed nor destination. In the moments of lucidity while resting from the effects of the concussion, which were numerous, I managed to summon enough focus to find a place slightly outside the city limits, and within six days of the date set to vacate my mother's townhouse. By the grace of powers unknown, I managed to survive the next few months, complete the move and just be. I manifested the perfect place – clean, quiet and secluded, though very small.

For fear I may go on at length about what I've endured, I will condense as best I can. The most significant events have been recorded as they happened, in some cases written down to allow the book to not get too off-topic from matters of the Divine. There were many additional minor events, but for the sake of simplicity I have included only the most pertinent. Since the head trauma, I was shattered entirely. The blinding fear I experienced in any given moment is not something I would wish upon anyone. The entire world was now a foreign place. It felt like I was a disease it was trying to reject, rather unsuccessfully at that, since I was still alive. However, I did not feel alive.

The days were desperately long. I was relieved when each ended, not knowing why, because tomorrow I knew I would have to wake up and do it all over again. The brain damage was pronounced. I would get lost while driving or walking. Suddenly the most familiar neighbourhood was something I had never seen before. I would cry, was short of breath, experienced blinding headaches, nausea and endured lengthy panic attacks if I exerted myself in the least possible way, sometimes for no reason at all.

The strangest symptom was even months after the external signs of the attack had vanished: I still saw the large black bruise down the side of my face, which for some reason reminded me of Edgar Allan Poe's *The Tell-Tale Heart*.

I reflected: somehow over the past few years, due to external events, I had manifested several periods when I was forced into situations in which I could not work. First, the rear-ender, which barely left me with the ability to walk up a flight of stairs; the sexual assault, leading to that debilitating break-up, ending with me living abroad; then enduring the lasting effects of the head trauma and psychological repercussions from the concussion. Still, I finally had a space to just be alone, which at this point was all I wanted.

I still received some financial support, which allowed just falling short of paying bills each month, but did not include food. While I had been a nationally represented artist in Toronto, and I had been selling my art steadily internationally, long lapses due to life traumas prevented me from painting as consistently as is required to make a larger dent in the art world that would be more sustaining. My medical bills weren't helping the situation either. It is hard enough to make it as a full-time artist when things are going your way.

This whole phase of the previous five years seemed so uncharacteristic. The me I had known was reliable, punctual, had incredible foresight, was a hard worker – I used to work three jobs – I never would have put myself in a situation where I had only six days to move, never mind lost all my belongings. The me I knew was safety-conscious, practical and more responsible than most people I have known. Be that as it may, the common denominator was me. But what was the cause? Was each incident something that could be easily explained as a momentarily lapse in judgement? It was terrifying to think this trend could continue. Surely I would end up dead.

While I viewed myself as a very peaceful person, my whole life long friends have told me I was too nice, too open, too trusting. To that I would say this state of openness and trust was a large determining factor in earning an unspeakably beautiful journey through other planes of existence. Where has distrust got anyone? I could not argue with the fact that bad things seemed to happen the moment I left the house. I wanted to minimize the possibility of any further wildly crazy and injurious events.

I now had no friends, by choice, and no belongings, not by choice. I relied on the generosity of donations from family and acquaintances to jump-start rebuilding my life. The bittersweet passing of my beloved grandmother had allowed me to inherit some of her things, now serving as a daily reminder that she was no longer present.

Never once did I maintain any anger at the people who had wronged me. I did not feel that would improve my situation. I did not curse them or wish bad things would come their way. In retrospect, perhaps all those years spent in training at Sanat's school, going through the hallway doors, had taught me one skill I could carry forward into daily life: to forgive immediately.

Yet something inside had changed. I had no sense of security in the world. There were no soothing words my mother could say – or anyone else, for that matter – to ease the impact of what had happened. There was no reason for it, at least from my perspective. And yet I found it impossible to forge my pain and weld it into misanthropy. I knew not everyone went through experiences like mine as I watched many of my old friends get married and buy houses. In fact I knew there were people in the world who led beautifully calm, obliviously blissful lives. I wondered where I had gone wrong to not deserve that too. Was it because it was my last life? I *so* desired to be one of them, one who had a family or even a pet to come home to. Happiness was such a foreign concept, one that happened to others, but not to me, as I continually lowered my expectations of what I thought I deserved in life.

While I may have adopted one of the lessons learned in that training room with Sanat – forgiving immediately – I missed another: the ability to go through major life events without picking up undesirable habits. Partially due to the concussion and partially due to life in general, my uncontrolled stress levels needed to find relief. I was drawn to a strange habit I had picked up while travelling and did what I think a lot of people might have done in my situation: I started smoking cigarettes, unfortunately, a lot.

While formerly I'd found smoking absolutely repugnant, never say never. Perhaps it was a reflection of my inner state and desire to all but almost entirely give up. Normally I strove for increased health. Alas, that me did not exist right now, but Survival Me did. This was her request. Everyone in my circle knew it was something very out of character. That self seemed like she existed lifetimes ago. What I really needed now was a reason to get out of bed in the morning. Chain-smoking through the panic attacks outdoors did have an advantage in that I was now getting a lot more fresh air, something I hadn't had in a while.

I had made some positive changes over the previous two years, despite all the interfering events, in that I no longer took prescription medications for pain, anxiety or anything else. I hadn't even taken a Tylenol in years. This was small consolation, as I did not feel better for it. The concussion had dramatically increased my anxiety. To bridge the gap from the amount I was able to release daily naturally, I slowly adopted lesser vices. I started drinking wine a bit more often than preferred. In some ways, it often allowed at least a little relaxation to look forward to at the end of the day. I knew these two choices were not sustainable or healthy long-term. But there was no possibility I was going back on prescriptions. Frankly, no one knew how to assess my situation better than me. Despite what it may have looked like, I felt I was slowly getting a handle on things, given enough time.

I was not so closed off that I did not reach out for help. In fact when I was in an open enough state to share, I would tell someone my story. This audience included friends, family and sometimes health professionals. Time and time again this proved to be a mistake. Others became so upset and overcome with emotion they would often cry, feeling so bad for me, not knowing how I was still alive. I was not looking for pity. It seemed finding a person strong enough to *hear* my story proved challenging. For a time I attended weekly sessions with a therapist just so someone would listen. However, I was looking for constructive advice. It seemed I was in uncharted territory. No one seemed to know what to say.

I had one close friend, Amanda, whom I had met in the States. She stood by me, not that she had anything in particular to say – she had enough to deal with of her own – but listening to her problems was comforting. She had a very humorous way about her. I could just listen for hours. We kept in touch after I moved home to Canada, and it was comforting to have another soul to connect with, even just on the other end of the phone, even if we weren't saying anything important. She was strong enough to be a mirror.

Career-wise, art was the only thing that was working for me. I had received a large number of requests to participate in various shows around the city. Some were group shows, another was a solo exhibition. I had sold many commissions and had much online success, yet I was still not consistently thriving. After the Sanat experience, it seemed the only thing that really held my attention was painting the universe as a subject.

A fascination with the cosmos had been long-standing, before my experience was underway. I'd been taking a 100-gig online course called *Understanding the Universe* from The Teaching Company when it occurred. I had already completed my first universe painting entitled *Incomprehensible* and was hooked on the subject matter. Many of the artists of the world had explored the various styles and palettes of landscapes ad nauseam. I did not want to be an artist painting something I already understood. Where was the growth in that? What would I learn by painting a pear in still life? What could I teach others? Outer space was relatively uncharted territory.

After the experience, which seemed to engrave my course in stone, I embarked on a series that would allow my full creative expression to shine, one in which the universe is painted in as many shapes, forms, styles and media as are in existence, thus entitled the *Infinite Universe Series,* stretching my abilities as an artist to take on many different styles, from the "normal" representational way we view things, considered by many as "realism," to the highly abstract and interpretive.

The majority of the body of work consists of images I have created based on experiences I've had with the Divine. There are, however, a select few that were painted from photos of the universe taken by NASA of such inherent beauty and profound perfection that I felt I could not design a better constellation than the Divine had, some of which moved me so powerfully my heart would overflow with tears of gratitude and amazement as I painted for hours on end. The paintings differ from photographs in that they embody the energy of that region in space by creating a psychic cord to it, thus drawing out its potential guidance, protection, advice and knowledge. In that regard, they are alive.

After all, it is said in physics and spirituality that if you can think of something it is in existence somewhere, as humans are incapable of having an idea that doesn't already exist in higher planes. All ideas originate from Source, later transmitted down to us, filtered through the layers of awareness, creating the illusion of original thought.

Painting all the places I had seen OOB became the only activity that comforted my restless soul. I was infused with a feeling so sublime, as though some part of me were learning, gaining understanding, even if I did not know what it was yet. I also understood that what I was trying to express on canvas was something so arcane but efficacious that it was important to continue the task even if the true meaning of the work was lost on many, caring not if it sold.

This was a shift from a business perspective, as previously my commissions and original landscapes were selling exceedingly well, commanding a higher price than most artists' work I knew. Yet I withdrew into quiet acquiescence with my soul, understanding that being a landscape artist was no longer in my plan, nor the path with heart.

Over the years I had collected substantial information about the universe, which I felt eager to share with others, yet at my shows I was often met with silence, and very rarely a well-considered question, leading me to feel disappointed to be largely misunderstood by the public. It was clear I hadn't found my audience, nor my voice.

Though this period of deeper self-discovery through art was very satisfying emotionally, I wondered: If creating these paintings really was in my plan as I had been shown, then why was I not being supported financially by them?

To this people might say, "Well, why didn't you get a job?"

Believe me, I thought of that, considering at length that as a great solution to many of my problems. Yet every time I began the search and submitted applications for interviews, success was blocked in every possible way. Promising phone calls and emails connected with my art would roll in on cue, causing me to drop everything to meet their potential career breakthrough deadlines. All signs seemed to indicate that I was on the right path. Great success was to be had from just a few more paintings and a few more all-nighters to create them. These nudges from the universe continued until I had six shows planned, but no money to fund them, knowing if they were in my plan the universe would find a way. During this period of poverty, I really felt I was one wrong step from living on the streets. That motivated me to work even harder.

Monetarily I was supplied just enough monthly to pay for my very small apartment plus an even smaller art studio, most bills and "some" food. My credit card was maxed out, as every month I was bridging the gap since long before living abroad. Now at its limit, I was $20,000 in debt. I didn't exactly fancy myself a catch either, not that dating was a priority. As times became tighter, I ate less and spent many nights recalculating ways to save a few dollars. The only things I did not scrimp on were art supplies, for my primary potential source of income, and cigarettes, for joy.

I learned to make some very weird and mostly unappealing meals using random ingredients from my pantry. You might be surprised at how resourceful you can be when you have only a dollar a day for food after paying your monthly bills.

The injuries from the brain trauma began to fade. I showed signs of improvement. That, however, seemed to be at the cost of another body part, my jaw. A new injury appeared that seemed to be ancillary to the strong blow to my head. Additionally, after two years of Botox injections, I had built up antibodies and become resistant to the treatment. In vain I attempted one final injection as close to my jaw as possible, albeit on borrowed funds.

Blinding pain radiated towards my crown, causing my jaw to spasm and crack. After again trying one last pass through the traditional medical system, hope arose when my general practitioner referenced a surgery I might qualify for and referred me to the last specialist I would ever see, an orthopedic surgeon.

Meeting this particular doctor ironically brought my dream of becoming the very same specialized professional I was studying for full circle. Regrettably, I had precariously high hopes, based on nothing other than another's opinion, as he informed me that any surgery would only worsen my condition. His most sincere recommendation was that I resume painkillers and other medications suggested by my alternate practitioners for life, gradually increasing the dosage with the onset of age. I thought surely there was at least an alternative physiotherapy exercise he could recommend, to which he said no. His advice remained unchanged.

I left his office in a ludicrous mood, so angry at the world, insulted and infuriated by his advice, or lack thereof – offended even – rhetorically asking myself, *Did he not know everything I had just been through?* While driving home I cycled through the many doors that seemed to slam shut in front of me, not that they were my potential path. I had already resolved that I was not going down the tried and failed route of medications. Physical therapy was not an option either. Smoking, as I was trying to clear my thoughts despite the fear of remaining this way forever, I began to process complex emotions quickly.

The last chance for a cure had left me empty-handed. What did this mean for me now? The doctor actually had the audacity to suggest that I go back on medications. That was absolutely not an option. It was as though I had been backed into a corner. I could not see a way out.

There was, however, one thing I hadn't tried, something I had been seeking since my time in the desert but had not found: a healer. That was the word that kept repeating in my head. One could argue a doctor is a healer. However, they hadn't succeeded yet, so I sensed this was a healer of a different kind. I had intuited the message when I lived in Arizona, but attempts to find the right one hadn't proved fruitful. Even at the time it seemed premature. Perhaps I needed a shaman, someone who had a different type of understanding and ways of working with incurable ailments. The term "miracle worker" was perhaps more apt. Whatever it was I was seeking, it had to be dramatically different to what I had already tried. Given my time spent searching for a cure, I was open to almost anything.

There was something else that happened during that drive home. A part of me was finished with trying. By the time I arrived at my door, upset and out of options, I sat down and did something profoundly unusual. That is to say I gave up – or better, I surrendered – letting go of everything, even my health. Nothing was working out for me anyhow, at least the way I was doing things, no matter how hard I tried. "Surrender" was a word I'd heard mentioned several times over the years. Any time it had come to me in the form of advice I took it, thanked the person and secretly laughed, as if giving up was something I would ever do. Even though I had the true meaning explained to me several times, I was very young and it fell on deaf ears, not wanting to understand. It was probably better that I did not realize that surrendering was what I was doing now or perhaps I would have prevented it out of habit.

Never one to speak publicly about my hardships, I had chosen to remain private about my trials and preferred to only use social media as a platform to share my art. However, sitting in my apartment now and having exhausted every possible resource, the last door slammed shut, I thought I had nothing left to lose. I wrote a detailed and carefully crafted post to my followers explaining my conditions and what I was seeking, asking for referrals to any exceptional, non-traditional, shamanistic, naturopathic geniuses out there. I included my email address at the bottom, as I was so upset with the world that I was not sure I wanted to engage publicly online for some time.

I did not know it then, but I had attuned to something quite remarkable by surrendering to posting that message which would soon change the course of my life and lead me to fulfilling my greater destiny. I turned off my laptop entirely to allow the surrendering to continue, as now that I had started, it felt so good.

It was then that I began to get waves of a most powerful realization wash over me, something I had known secretly all along but had kept hidden from myself. It was the knowledge that I, and I alone, had the power to heal myself. I paused to consider this new truth – or was it old?

With bated breath I fumbled in the darkness of my mind, looking for more information connected to this thread. How could this be true, how could I heal myself when no one else could? Perhaps there was the answer right there: *I can* and *I will* heal myself because no one else can. But no, there was more than that. What was it? The answer was elusive. It felt so close, on the tip of my tongue. Then it would vanish. Then – there it was – I was never going to find someone who was going to heal me, because somehow I alone was responsible for my problems. I alone had to heal them.

I didn't know how I was going to accomplish this, but deep down when I examined this fact it came back to me as truth. It seemed like a large task, considering the extent of both physical and mental healing I sensed I required, but I knew I had the power, a thought that had never crossed my mind before.

I realized that so long as I kept going to medical practitioners looking for miracle cures I would remain a victim of a deteriorating circumstance. Doctors could only mask the symptoms at best, not find the cause. Typically they seek to "treat" a condition and don't have the available time to spend with each patient identifying the root cause, so if the issue appears again, they treat it wth the same process or try a different method based on their method of diagnosis. While I did believe there were great doctors out there, that was unfortunately not my experience falling through the system.

During my time spent in chronic pain and concussion clinics, I learned that doctors are highly afraid to take on patients who have complex conditions. In fact I ended up cycling through at least five general practitioners, and each eventually dropped me like a hot potato because of their limitations in investigating the illness. Being overextended, overworked and drained of compassion may have also played a role. Yet at the time I also felt frustration, as I had looked to them for the answers they simply did not have.

This singular realization, that I and I alone had the power to heal myself, easily became the most revolutionary thought I'd had in a long time as I continued to meditate while awaiting a response to my post.

I allowed my mind to wander down a meandering path that seemed to be ushering me into new and refreshing avenues of thought. I began to think about how we are as children or when we are first born. We start off so fresh, so free of flaws. Life has not had time to burden us with heartache, bruises or scars. We are intrinsically pure, uncorrupted and uncompromised, not yet having learned that the world is one particular way or another. For the sake of this realization, I am not speaking directly to such things as congenital birth defects or disease. That is another topic entirely. I am speaking more in generalities.

The realization crystallized further: we are born of perfection. Our bodies, our very soul and our DNA are structures of mathematical precision. However, some of us exhibit perfection better than others. All the brightest minds in the world have been trying to solve the unsolvable question as to what causes matter to arrange in perfect mathematical geometries that coincidentally give life. The human form is complex and sophisticated, with all its various systems operating sympathetically, the "user" barely noticing they're there. To those who might say this is chance, I say if so this is the most ingenious, pleasing, beautiful stroke of luck that has ever happened, not once, but again and again and again, as the universe created not only human life but the mountains, the rivers, the planets and stars, all coordinating silently so as to not to disturb one another.

If life came about by chance, and we are the most advanced accidental manifestation, then consider how every object and every living thing fits perfectly into Metatron's Cube and the Flower of Life, signifying an order and logic so grand that it's far beyond our present ability to fathom fully. Human existence coming about by accident is then highly improbable, as it would insinuate *everything* by sheer coincidence fell into place in precisely perfect working order, the odds of which, statistically speaking, would be greater than googol and googolplex numbers. To illustrate how big a number that is, the astronomer Carl Sagan estimated that writing the latter out would be impossible, as it would require more space than is available in the known universe.

Over the years we deteriorate, yet it doesn't need to be that way. For a moment, a brief second, I was able to drop my guard enough to feel my true power to heal all my misfortunes. I just didn't know how to access it consistently. The gap between my present state and a healed state was wide. Outwardly there wasn't one area of my life that was in working order – physically, financially, romantically – you name it. That didn't change the fact that somehow *I knew I could fix everything.*

My call for help was answered, maybe a little too well. I jumped online to see I had received much support, reviewing well over sixty suggestions to check out various doctors and clinics around the world, most of whom were traditional Western ones, not what I had specified. I was more than willing to fly to the Himalayas and sit in an ashram for ten years if that's what it took.

I was overwhelmed by all the highly recommended referrals. It could take weeks to research each one. In pain now, and not feeling I had time for that, I asked to be shown who was the one I was looking for. In my post, I had included my email address. Ninety per cent of the respondents chose to comment directly on Facebook. Only two people had opted to email. One name stood out in particular, Eric Fattah. I couldn't explain it, but his name seemed to glow blue on my screen. His was the one and only response I chose to consider. I opened the email, and there was a genuine, well-thought-out message that had two suggestions: one to see a woman who was a spiritual healer and worked with angels, the other to see a highly reputed naturopath.

Immediately I was drawn to the angel worker, even though it had been the better part of a decade since I had considered metaphysics. Logically, the naturopath made more sense for many reasons, but if the problem was with my mind, then what I most definitely needed was a reading. When I thought of the naturopath, I got cold feelings. The message was: *He is not going to be able to figure this out. Maybe see him at a later date when you have more money.*

I agreed to see her, not knowing how I was possibly going to pay for it. I asked the universe to provide. Mere hours later, Eric, unsolicited, generously agreed to donate one of his credits with her. He had no way of knowing I would have not been able to see her otherwise. That single posting for a healer became a crucial turning point in what would start the next chapter of my life.

Eric and I became close friends. Before meeting in person, we had been connecting through deep correspondence via email. It was ages since I had spoken with anyone sincerely spiritual. It was a welcome breath of fresh air. I had not bothered looking him up on Facebook, but was enjoying the connection anyway. We started as friends. But that soon changed.

Since the Sanat experience, I had adopted a rather funny trait. A part of me still sought an explanation for my otherworldly adventure and thought the best way to find it was to ask every person I met. Well, almost every person. Perhaps this was the same tactic as calling every phone number I saw in television ads, thinking perseverance was bound to lead to success. A friendship would reach a point where I could be more candid, then the trait would appear. I rehearsed our conversation in advance, preparing for the relationship to potentially end after the strange story I was about to tell. More often than not, it surpassed the listener's threshold of belief, and I would lose them.

Other more compassionate friends would humour me. We'd remain friends, but it was something never mentioned in conversation again. It would become somewhat of a no-go topic, thus putting a limit on how close we could get. The few brave souls awake enough to *really* listen would be absolutely fascinated and enthralled, yet unable to contribute anything to the greater meaning I was looking for. But Eric – he was different.

32.

Twin Flames

DECEMBER 7, 2015 was the long-sought day when I would finally receive the answers I had been looking for in the six years since the experience with Sanat. Eric and I had been emailing back and forth. His helpful correspondence was much appreciated, since I'd allowed so few other people into my life. During one of our conversations, I learned he was quite ill. I looked for some way to repay the favour of the credit with the healer and for his insights in general.

I had sold my new car when I left for Arizona. That money was long since gone. In the interim my mother generously allowed me the use of my grandmother's car, a 2010 Kia Rio, which I then inherited. The little silver sedan was in great shape and had amazingly low kilometres for its age. I should have been more grateful for her gesture. Although the make and model was not particularly my style, that was not the reason I didn't like the car. I felt a profound heaviness when driving it, just another daily reminder that my grandmother wasn't around anymore.

While I didn't know what Eric's health challenge was, and while it did cross my mind it might not be a physical illness, I decided to make a care package for him nevertheless. I sensed it would be well-received, and it was the least I could do. Given my financial situation, it also happened to be the most I could do. I gathered up some crackers, Tylenol Cold & Sinus, Emergen-C and a package of Lipton's chicken noodle soup.

On a whim, before leaving the house, I decided to do an internet search to see who the mysterious stranger I'd been talking to was. I had not dressed for the occasion of meeting someone new, in fact looked rather dishevelled, in gym attire, not having showered, prepared to work out after delivering my gift. Upon seeing his photo, I recognized him instantly, remembering that I had been up late one night almost a year earlier staring at his profile. There had been a resurgence of interest in my art at the time, with more than 4,000 strangers requesting to be added to my account in less than a month. Eric had been one of them. Out of all the people who had replied and commented on my post, his had been the only name I'd been inspired to acknowledge.

About a year earlier he had shared a post about an upcoming trip with friends to swim with sea lions. They had a chef to cook for them and planned to have a great time. In the midst of my depression, I had longingly desired to be the sort of person who had friends like that: reliable, generous, outdoorsy and who had their lives together. This was my intuition when looking at his photos. I sensed he and his friends were drama-free – something I was not. I actually posted some small remark like, "That looks fun," which was uncharacteristic, since I did not know him. I had been very drawn to his profile photo for no apparent reason, and was compelled to find out more. His eyes had such uncommon kindness – he looked like a very old soul, I thought.

To my surprise and embarrassment, he had replied instantly, inviting me along! He did not know the mess of emotional energy he would be exposed to. I decided I did not want to risk throwing the group off balance.

Time passed. We did not communicate again until I posted my call for help on Facebook. I entered his address into my maps app. To my surprise he lived only six minutes from my house. Not only that, but his home was in the building right beside my gym. On the drive to deliver my gift, I recalled the evening before. While driving back from the gym, I had been rerouted due to construction, which led to being stuck outside a high-rise with a glowing vertical blue neon stripe extending to the top. I'd spent the better part of five minutes gazing into the lobby, wondering what sort of person lived there. It seemed I was about to receive the answer.

I guessed he was about twelve years my elder, quite tall and in very good shape. He had a darker complexion, and I learned that he was half Egyptian, half Norwegian.

We quickly got caught up in philosophical conversation. I found myself mesmerized while listening to him speak in great detail on various topics of which he was an adept, as he was well-versed as a mathematician, a physicist and in all types of engineering.

He had recently quit his job, in fact that very day, working for a company he had originally built, then sold. The sale had come with the contingency that he was required to continue working to see through to completion the next product launch of dive computers, as they could not be engineered without him. I was fascinated to discover Eric also had held several world records for freediving.

His heart was with a much larger plan, however: to help deliver free energy to the world. Highly intrigued, I asked many questions. He shared intricate details about antigravity technology and its origins. When he talked, he gave the impression that he understood it first-hand, and recounted numerous related historic events. Usually reserved until I can determine how knowledgable a person really is, I accepted that of this subject at least he demonstrated a total mastery I'd not encountered before. It was unlike any first impression I'd ever had. I thought his mind was a brilliant and rare balance of practical intelligence and spiritual knowledge.

Unable to break from conversation, I cancelled my outing to the gym. We took our discussion to a nearby sushi restaurant. I continued to listen attentively as he spoke about his plan. I did not think he was the type of person to make false claims, considering the depth of descriptive detail in his explanations and reasoning for each of his beliefs. He had also studied at one of the world's top spiritual institutions, the Radiant Rose Academy.

"It is in all of our plans to eventually develop our gifts and powers," he stated rather matter-of-factly, much to my delight.

"So we're all supposed to become psychic?"

"Yes, of course. It's the plan for the seventh Golden Age that the ascended masters and angels have made. It's part of the global awakening of the planet. You know it's not normal for us *not* to have powers, right? It's natural to know everything in advance, and it's only in *this simulation* that we've grown so accustomed to getting by without."

Astounded, I insisted on more information. I loved hearing him talk about the experience of life in terms of a simulation, something I had intuited on my own. It seemed I was talking with an unbiased encyclopedia of metaphysical knowledge. Listening carefully while he spoke, I tuned in intuitively to compare his ideas with what I had been shown. I was very careful about where I got my spiritual information and knew there were many sources who claimed to know the way. Perhaps they really did. Others just wanted to deceive. Yet when I examined his words, I got an overwhelming impression of truth. That excited me. I could not contain my joy in finding the first person I could have an authentic conversation with in years.

"What is an *ascended master?*" I pressed for an answer.

"An ascended master is a being who's evolved beyond all the lessons of the physical plane. They've become a master of the self and have raised their body to the fifth and sixth dimensions. It's from those states that they help the people of Earth to reach the same level of freedom. Because in this state they are connected to their full joy and love through their own God Presence, they never tire and no burden is too great. They're among the overseers helping the divine plan for humanity push forward, and they work in unison with all the other beings, such as angels and archangels, to make sure we all stay on track and are evolving towards the light – and eventually our eternal freedom."

"Wow, I don't even know what to say to that. That is so beautiful, thank you." I paused, taking a moment to reflect on everything he'd said. "It's so unusual to meet a person like you, who's so trained in math and science and is also so spiritual." I laughed. "Did you know that?"

Seemingly unaware of how attractive he was, he laughed too. "Yes, I do. I have been on the path a long time, more than twenty years, and know most of the great minds of the world who have existed in the past have also acknowledged the existence of these higher powers. What's more likely – that we created all this?" He gestured, making a sweeping motion with his arms. "That there's no God, and that we're all alone as the only intelligent life in the universe? Really, we're not that smart. We can barely keep from killing each other and have no idea how most of the forces of the universe really work. There've been other great civilizations that thrived before us, far more advanced but failed, such was Atlantis. It's now the plan for this era that this time we succeed in removing the last remaining veils."

I was very impressed with the strength of conviction in his voice. He emanated the vibrations of a person who had done much soul-searching on a long quest for answers, but unlike me, it appeared he had actually found many.

I could tell this was increasingly becoming a very important conversation in my life. I did not know if I would ever see him again, if our paths would cross, but while I didn't know him that well, I felt I'd known him forever. My intuition seemed to have not served me well in the past. I was reluctant to trust it again. I felt the pressure to ask the ever-burning questions my heart had been seeking answers to for years. *For the first time ever,* I thought, *I might be sitting across from the very person who could give me some genuine insights into what happened to me and why.*

He'd proven that he believed in such things as otherworldly beings, like angels, in past lives, antigravity technology and that he had a divine plan. Although I would typically wait weeks or months before ever presenting my out-of-body time-travelling abduction story to anyone, I felt now was the time, although apprehensive at the thought of it. He had also demonstrated far greater knowledge of precisely the subjects I was seeking than anyone I had met. *It isn't going to get much closer than this,* I thought. We'd really only just met. I was having to rapidly come to terms with the possibility of cutting this new friendship off at the knees. It was a sacrifice I had to be willing to make, so I pushed my feelings to the side and summoned the nerve to start from the beginning.

"So – I've actually been looking for some answers related to an event that happened to me years ago. I keep looking to meet someone who has any idea of what I'm talking about. Most people end up thinking I'm crazy or maybe even making it up, but perhaps you are just that person.

"About six years ago or so, I had the most unbelievable experience of my life, one that has left me rather messed up and lost ever since. One night I went out to a restaurant, and while I was surrounded by tons of people, somehow my guide managed to take over the body of one of my friends and took me on a tour of the universe. He was like a god – I don't know what else to call him – anyway, he was God, though maybe not *the* God. I never got his name and have been looking for him ever since. I was gone for a very, very long time, like we're talking decades, only it felt much longer. After that, I was put back into my body and haven't really known what to do since."

He seemed extremely fascinated. It was my turn to command attention. I watched his reactions carefully as I always did after sharing my story.

"That's very interesting," he said, apparently deep in thought. "That would mean that you must have a very big plan."

"I know, I've felt very behind on it ever since," I agreed. "Truthfully, I've no idea what I'm supposed to be doing."

He said, "Well, you should know, for something like that to happen, it would take an enormous amount of authority for permission. Your guide, who sounds like an ascended master, would've had to receive permission from the Great Divine Director who oversees this solar system, and they would have to agree it would align with the divine plan for the planet."

I said, "I've looked everywhere and haven't been able to find any information on anything similar happening to anyone. I've read some accounts of out-of-body experiences, but this was different. I haven't read any account of someone who was taken by a god, died and was gone for years."

"Well, you wouldn't find it," he responded. "What happened to you is very rare. I've read lots of spiritual books over the years, and even I have never heard a story quite like yours. The only accounts that come to mind are the 'Green Books' of Saint Germain. They were written by this guy named Guy Ballard in the 1930s, about similar experiences with Saint Germain. The first book is called *Unveiled Mysteries*."

My heart swelled with emotion, overjoyed to hear there was another person with whom I could relate. We sat in silence for a moment, I absorbing everything he was saying while trying to keep up with the conversation.

"Describe your guide to me. What did he look like?" he asked.

"He was blue, meaning his skin was blue, and he was illuminated with this remarkable aura. He was Indian, but when pressed to recall his face, I can only seem to connect to the feelings he filled me with."

"He's from India?" he asked, as if that was something important.

"Well, yes, he seemed very Indian. Is there someone that fits that description? I've been trying to find him for years."

"It could be Sanat Kumara," he said. "He's the one with the blue ray of power. He's also from Venus."

"I'm from Venus!" I exclaimed – out of nowhere – not understanding where my outburst had come from. I'd had no intention of making such a claim, yet once I had said it I knew it was true. Wasn't there a planet that my guide had taken me to? Couldn't that have been Venus? Upon hearing his name, I was again flooded with powerful feelings of truth, tingling sensations running up and down my arms. I had stumbled upon the name Sanat Kumara during my research directly after my experience. Something in a discussion with Uncle Orbit about Yogananda had triggered it. Somehow it led me on a guided search to find Sanat Kumara's Wikipedia page. I had immediately rejected the suggestion, as he sounded far too ancient and important to be my spiritual father. The illustrations available online also looked nothing like the form he presented to me.

"You're from Venus?" he asked.

"Well, yes, I am. I'm not sure why I said that. I just know I am. My guide did take me to a planet, and I'm pretty certain it was Venus. He also said he was my father and that he owed me. I'm not really sure what to believe." Searching my mind for further evidence to support my claim, I continued, "I'd never really considered that I was from Earth – or that anyone was from Earth, for that matter – I thought all of us were from other places. This certainly has never felt like home. As a child, my mom always told me we were from Venus, or perhaps that's something I thought I'd heard her say, but I'd always believed it to be true, and I know we are both from Venus. Maybe it connects back to that old saying, men are from Mars, women are from Venus." I laughed at hearing myself speak that out loud. Had I gone too far?

"Well, I've always had a deep connection to Venus, and for years I've had great depression and nostalgia from wanting to live on Venus. My favourite book is channelled by a being who's from there. It's called *A Dweller on Two Planets,* and I've read it so many times I almost know it by heart."

It had been a long night. A considerable amount of information had been shared. That had been the most unexpected but welcome surprise. I was so grateful for the first time in my life to have met someone who could help me fill in a few of the pieces of the puzzle, perhaps even big pieces.

I went home that night the happiest I had ever been in my life, crying tears of joy that the universe had brought that generous, advanced soul into my life, and most of all, that my call for answers had finally been heard.

33.

Which Timeline Are You From?

OVER THE DAYS and weeks what had started as warm friendship blossomed into something more. He seemed very burnt out after leaving his company, Liquivision. I wondered if it was the right timing for us. Unable to resist, we proceeded anyway.

Our first kiss was something not of this world, a quality I alone seemed to have felt. I was filled with an overwhelming surge of energy. That was the sign I needed that we were on the right track. Through a series of dreams and flashbacks to the original experience with Sanat, I began to understand that Eric was the suitor that Sanat brought to me to meet and that Eric was my twin flame. He was hesitant to accept that we were twins. It was not something he had intuited and knew how very rare it would be for twin flames to ever successfully come together romantically in a lifetime. Most often they would repel each other because of their strong differences. But more importantly, they would only ever be connected in a long-term manner if they both had an important plan to bring to fruition as partners. The power of their plan could override their apparent differences and create a workable living situation.

Our first date had triggered a renewal of my quest for knowledge and optimism that now I might actually get answers. With Eric's help, for the first time in my life I truly stepped foot on a more concrete and directed spiritual path and began to blaze forward with unstoppable speed, one that held a vast amount of readily available written and spoken knowledge that I now had access to and could readily absorb. He exposed me to both his library of knowledge and the Radiant Rose Academy.

It was nothing like I'd expected. With discernment intact I tried to cross-reference the teachings with what I'd been shown in my own experiences. As expected, the academy checked out. Try as I might, I was unable to find any incongruencies.

In my first class, a being called mighty Victory came through the foundation's younger "messenger," as they prefer to be called. I had never seen anyone channel before. To my surprise my third eye opened during the class. I could actually see Victory standing "in" the messenger's form. Not only that, the scene opened up to show a whole choir and a host of angels flanking the exposed rafters of a large mediaeval cathedral-style building that seemed to be coextensive with the same space in which we were sitting at the academy.

I seemed to experience a different type of class than the other students and carried on a private conversation with Victory. He spoke of the plan for the planet, as well as a detailed description of the paths of ascension and resurrection. When I first heard the word "resurrection" I thought the messenger must be joking or at least not speaking literally. However, after examining the demeanour of the student body and listening further, it was evident they did take it literally. They spoke of Jesus and what his demonstration all those years ago meant for us now. For the first time I felt pieces of information I had learned since birth start to click into place.

Divine law stated the terms for this Golden Age requires one person to awaken to their abilities within the game, continuing the work that Jesus started, except this time it needed to be done in the modern era with its technological advancements. This being would help a handful of advanced individuals come into their gifts, allowing a more rapid transformation of the planet. These beings will then serve as guiding hands, showing the larger population how to heal and ascend.

Victory also stated that success for this Golden Age has been guaranteed, meaning this time the Light would win inevitably. Initially this flooded me with relief at hearing we would no longer be allowed to drift deeper into our slumber, but after looking into the attitudes of the student body, I saw that everyone seemed a little too relaxed about it. I sensed they thought there was no need to take any action themselves, because these otherworldly beings had everything under control. I did not believe that, however, and proceeded to receive very different messages of my own.

If everyone turns to the person beside them and asks them to take out the garbage, who in turn asks the next person, eventually no one will have completed the task and we are left with a very big problem.

Immediately my plan began to download into my mind. I was given the reason why I was so far behind and what to do next, although I shared this with no one, feeling it was too private a moment and unconfident enough in my newfound vision. While I ended up only ever attending two classes, it was enough to set me on a powerful trajectory in the right direction. While logically it may have made sense to stay with the academy longer, I knew they were not teaching their students the information I was now seeking.

I began to study in private, day in and day out, twelve hours a day, sometimes fifteen. Now that I had found my path, I was ready to proceed at full throttle with no hesitation. I opted to learn their curriculum online, listening to hours of discourses by the masters even when housecleaning. For the first time ever, I felt greatly empowered by a sense of clear direction. Synchronistically, the more I studied, the more my gifts matured, as if to validate the teachings. I had discovered with certainty the two paths that lead us out of here and there was nothing that could impede my progress once started. I first focused my newfound unbridled enthusiasm on the path of ascension, which seemed like the logical thing to do, since it was something that was explicitly required.

One early January day Eric and I agreed to meet for dinner, which then allowed further pieces of the puzzle to fall into place. There were several things that still did not make sense about the Sanat experience, no matter how hard I tried to understand. In spite of the knowledge acquired, I could still not find clarity regarding the large truck barrelling down on us at the intersection. Didn't I die? How was that possible?

After speaking for some time, something seemed to click into place in Eric's highly analytical mind. Somehow he connected two events, the Sanat experience and the head trauma. That was something I had never considered.

"Well, if you did die, that would certainly be something likely required to impel you on such a significant journey. Permission would've been highly increased, allowing them to show you in far greater detail how the game really works, if you were no longer in a living physical body in the game. Then, say after being shown and choosing your highest plan, that would have given permission to insert you back into a different timeline, a timeline when you've consciously acknowledged and accepted your highest plan and, importantly, a timeline when you didn't die." He paused, still solving the equation in his head. "This would have had to be done at such a high level of detail that no one living would've been allowed to be affected. Their memory streams would have to be left intact, by cosmic law, as these beings aren't allowed to interfere in our lives," he stated.

"But no, that's not quite it. Perhaps the real you was always supposed to die in that semi accident, and the Divine used that event to create the permission for the Sanat experience, since you were going to die anyway. After revealing your plan, and you choosing the highest one, they reinserted you into the closest possible timeline so the two Sarazens' lives matched as best as possible. Theoretically, both versions of you lived side by side up until the head trauma. It was in the plan for Sarazen Number Two, whose life you assumed, to die in the head trauma incident. This would explain your duplicate memories, both for the Sanat experience and for the head trauma. Perhaps the vision you had of you begging the stranger to injure you was really the event happening on higher planes, staged in such a way that you wouldn't die and could continue on, now with this embodiment all to yourself.

"But in all honestly, something of this complexity and magnitude would have to be organized with Saint Germain, Sanat Kumara and your higher self because even now as I am piecing things together I feel that the true details are simply beyond human comprehension."

This all resonated with me, the best explanation I had heard yet. It was fascinating, and yet disturbing in a way: that would make me a ghost, a visitor from another timeline. As if I needed to fit in even less! If that was true, what happened to the other version of me whose life I had assumed? Did she merge into me or just simply cease to exist?

"There's one thing that doesn't fit, however," he continued, "that is, if you'd jumped timelines successfully, you could also say that during the head trauma you also would've had several different sets of memories about what happened. Those would be the corresponding timelines."

I looked at him, thoroughly impressed with his deductive reasoning. I had a secret I'd never told anyone out of fear of embarrassment: I did have several sets of conflicting memories of that evening.

The first set was the primary set, or the main Active Memory that was the most predominant. This was the one in which a fight ended with my date forcefully shoving me into the bumper of a car, unintentionally injuring me, but then intentionally leaving me unconscious and close to death.

The second memory was of leaving the restaurant, and after some time, in more of a dreamlike state. It was dreamlike because there was no sense of touch. I had wandered to a nearby corner store, where I found two employees who looked Lebanese or perhaps Iranian. There was some banter between me and the one at the till as I bought something small. Leaving the store, to the right of the entrance was a fairly steep hill. I saw an Indian man passing by. I turned towards him and for no apparent reason asked him to push me forcibly to the ground. He recoiled at my suggestion and asked me to repeat what I had said, immediately backing away with his hands in the air, as if saying he wouldn't dare touch me. I told him it was very important that he do so and insisted on his heeding my request, yet the quality of this conversation was blurred and soft, like that of a dream or imagination. Reluctantly, the man considered it, then eventually agreed to do me the favour. He stood behind me and pushed my head very forcibly into the concrete, then left promptly.

This second memory did not make any sense for many reasons, not something I could fathom taking place in any reality. I had no idea what to make of it. I would never ask anyone – stranger or otherwise – to push my head into the pavement. Even if even I did, good luck finding anyone who would agree to incriminate themselves in that way, never mind the first person asked. It was relatively early at night when the event took place, approximately 10:00 pm. Surely there would have been many passers-by, even if the man had agreed. It also didn't really feel like something I'd experienced. My predominant memory retained all the tactile feelings of the impact. This lesser memory did not surface until some time after I was in recovery.

The fact of the matter was that I had gone through my memories of that night many times trying to find the truth, but every time the more dominant truth remained: my date had attacked me. I had privately speculated that perhaps the second memory was a dream I had while already unconscious, maybe something close to what someone in a coma experiences.

Eric's face was lit up as though he had just opened Pandora's Box. He exclaimed that he now had the firm evidence required to solve the mystery as to what happened in both scenarios. He went into details regarding the physics required. He determined that both events had been very carefully inserted into my plan and in fact I must have had a hand in it. He stated that in both cases I had "died," which allowed alterations to the plan and alternate timelines to become accessible.

In one version with Mikey, I really had died in a traffic accident. I was then placed in the closest timeline possible that included the events in which I lived and fulfilled my highest plan; likewise in the head trauma version. I had never considered the head trauma a "magical" experience – in fact most unmagical! – but Eric's conclusions helped me to see otherwise. His argument was that in one timeline my date had really committed that horrible act. But in another, the violence had taken place in another dimension or timeline, in which my guide had helped it along. If that was true, then it was possible that in the current timeline my date truly was innocent. To press charges would be to incriminate an innocent man. Although it may require some fine-tuning, this was the strongest theory I had to explain how I was still breathing.

We sat together feeling like we were at the start of uncovering a real life mystery, an enigma of such proportions that it required a very open mind to deconstruct.

✳

Since I had so many problems, I thought, *Well, everybody has to start somewhere,* so I began the undertaking of seeking out guides that could help me master my problems, and fast. I learned of a being called Lord Maitreya and felt a strong resonance with him. We began working together daily over the next months. His main job is that of a helper to move a person through the tough times of life as quickly as possible so they may get to the wonderful new things their God Presence wants for them. That all sounded great to me. However, I also learned that most of the student body was terrified to work with him because, in that process, he mercilessly strips away everything that is not working – people, possessions and careers, for example – often very abruptly. It can seem like a lot at once because he is considered the master disciplinarian, responding without hesitation to those with a burning desire to change their life.

I certainly belonged to that category. If there were more upsets slated in my future, then I most definitely wanted to move past them as quickly as he promised. This also felt like a more empowering, direct approach, facing hardships head-on rather than simply enduring them.

As I worked with him, he most certainly lived up to his job description. I understood then why people are so afraid of him, yet I was not. I started to hear him speaking to me, pushing me quite hard while challenging me in difficult ways to let go of the bad habits I had accumulated. I loved him dearly and knew that if I kept at it eventually I would get to the good stuff promised on the other side. If not, at the very least I would fulfil my plan for whatever service was required of me so I could finally get the hell out of this Earth plane.

I had also learned recently that astrologically I was experiencing my first Saturn Return, which went direct the day I met Eric. From what I understood, it sounded like it could be quite decimating for some if they had many things in their life that were not in alignment. I couldn't even speculate what mine might hold. Perhaps that would explain what I had been experiencing already. Although feeling supremely on my path, I thought maybe life would just continue to get better and better.

I followed the advice from the few spiritual classes I had attended to the letter. Victory had given us homework, stating we were to practise gratitude every day, five times a day, for five different things, never repeating the same item throughout the day.

I just started Victory's lessons when something very unexpected began to change within my body: electric currents coursed and rippled through it. It would happen without fail whenever I asked myself a question, especially yes/no questions. If the answer was in the affirmative, I would feel a cool rippling current run all over my skin, especially over my arms and upper body. If the answer was in the negative, there would be no reaction at all. I could test the effect with multiple questions back to back. The results were startling. It appeared the gratitude exercise had opened some sort of doorway to guidance from my higher self. How wonderful!

The next class I attended was with a different spiritual organization. Jesus was set to be the master teaching the class. I was incredibly nervous but also curious to see if it really could be him. Jesus came through and said he wanted us to give generously to the homeless, to pack up some useful items to protect themselves from the elements, but most of all he wanted us to initiate authentic conversations with them, to acknowledge their existence and show them love and compassion. So often they are neglected and brushed off as they beg in the streets. Even though I was so close to homelessness myself, I jumped at any opportunity the masters suggested and did all the exercises. The class had proven exceptionally moving. There was no doubt in my mind it was Jesus who spoke. My clothes were stained with sweat during that class due to the intensity of the experience and the heat that had steadily increased in the room.

Next was the task of carrying out Jesus' request. I had never heard Jesus speak through a messenger before, and any partial scepticism I had was absolutely blown out of the water once he began. Towards the end of the class, we each were permitted to stand up and hold his hands as he gave us a personal message. I was feeling quite shy and sweating profusely. I definitely didn't feel pure enough to stand before Jesus, now that I knew he was really present. I didn't know what to expect. Most of the messages that came through for others ahead of me seemed relatively generic. I was seated second to last. Not wanting to suffer the same plight as when meeting the Elders, I tried to clear my thoughts as much as possible.

He then said something quite remarkable as he gazed into my eyes: *"There is a blue man in your dreams. He is a great teacher who has shown you something very special. Some have referred to this teacher as The Ancient of Days. I will speak of him as beloved master teacher Sanat Kumara. I ask you to look into your heart and to call for his love to enfold you, and to remind you, in your own words might I just say, why the heck are you here? For you have asked this time and time and time and time and time and time and – you get it.*

"He is the one who will help you unravel this ancient mystery, for your journey has been long-standing. The wings of the angel Gabriel are with you. This is a guardian on this journey. And if you feel a closeness and a resonance in your heart with what I say, and you feel the love that is here, then you will feel an even greater love when you ask for his wings to enfold you, yes?

"Now, will you do me one favour? Will you not take yourself so seriously? Aren't you getting quite tired of that? Laugh a little more at all the little things. It is like defusing an inner bomb."

This was the most spellbinding information I had ever received, and directly from Jesus. I was entirely speechless, incredibly grateful but un-prepared for such an honour. Not only had I received one name, but two. And how did he know so much about me? How did he know I had asked myself what I am doing here so many times? That was something I hadn't even realized I'd been doing until it was so aptly pointed out. He also spoke directly of my out-of-body experiences with no prompting at all. It was the tangible miracle I needed to believe it was really him.

Therefore I did not hesitate when the request came to help the home-less, something I had already been doing on and off since I was fourteen. It was very cold outdoors. Soon it would be Christmas. I went home and over the next week sorted through all my belongings. I gathered old blankets, went through pantry items, old winter clothes, whatever I could find. I created individual care packages, two for men and four for women. I took old purses and filled them with helpful items, such as tampons, bandages, gloves, socks and crackers. I loaded them into my car, along with four hefty blankets, ready to head downtown.

At the same time, I was attempting to help save a girlfriend's life, another pattern that repeated over the years, seldom leading to being of any real help. At a very young age she'd had a child with Down's syndrome. She'd been in an abusive relationship that had just ended, and had begun to hang out with some gang members. One carried a gun and was stalking her. Sometimes she was very receptive to help and seemed as though she wanted change. Since leaving her boyfriend, she didn't really have anywhere to live and had left her child in her mother's care. I drove her to work from time to time, as it was quite a long trip by transit, well over an hour even by car. The extensive travel time had resulted in her almost being fired for arriving late on several occasions that month. I even offered to share my tiny apartment to help her get started, the one rule being no gangsters. I was willing to do whatever it took to help her, but had no interest in dipping my toe in any more casualty-causing lessons of my own.

I had committed to picking her up from work one evening. The car was loaded with all the care packages. I'd used all my money for gas, and had almost enough food for a week. I figured I would plan how to survive the rest of the month afterwards, still riding high on my message from Jesus. It would work out somehow. I thought I was meriting good karma in the process. I also wanted my friend to see me handing out the packages. I felt it could be a potential paradigm shift for her to see that there is more to life than just abusive men. One can actually be of service to others.

She watched as I handed out the donations and helped to give out a few herself. In the end, her mind was stuck in a rut. She chose to continue the cycle of abuse, the dangerous gamble with her life and her daughter's life. She declined my offer of help. We got into a huge argument. She left the spare key I had offered on my desk. I never saw her again.

It broke my heart to see her make that choice. I went to bed that night burdened with mixed feelings, defeated in my attempt to lift someone up but consoled to have tried. I had carried out the instructions of the ascended masters to the letter. For the first time in a very long time I felt contentment in my heart, convinced I really was on the right path. Everything was going to be okay.

34.

Divine Prophecy

I THOUGHT I could escape my fate – or destiny, you could call it. If the claim is true that the present affects the future, and the future in turns creates the past – retrocausality, as physicists call it – then I should have known there was no way to escape the things I had been shown all those years ago.

Late in the evening of January 22, 2016 I had been talking on the phone with Amanda while working on some projects at home. For no reason at all, a very anxious state began to form, in hindsight similar to the day I suffered the head trauma.

I had an early dinner, accompanied by two glasses of wine, as I worked on and off. The night wore on. I had no intention of leaving the house. I had everything needed right beside me. Amanda had even suggested I stay in. I agreed.

An unknown force began to nag me, strongly suggesting that I needed to leave the house. The time was approaching 1:30 in the morning. The reason was vague: Did I need to buy cigarettes or was it that I needed paint from my studio some distance away? Consciously, no part of me wanted to leave my apartment, but the compulsion was coming on so strongly that I was unsure it could be ignored. I've always had a strict rule to never drink and drive. A considerable amount of time had passed since drinking the wine, but it was an unbreakable rule nevertheless. Yet for some reason on this night I was unable to follow my own advice. I got dressed to go, leaving my windows open and the lights on, intending to be absent only briefly.

I was guided to a hill close to my house that I had never been to before. This is where the experience seemed to shift. I no longer was a consenting participant in the situation and viewed everything through my God Presence's eyes as a passive observer. This hilltop was an outstanding vantage point overlooking the beautiful city lights. I was filled with her feelings of melancholy as she exhaled and continued to set her plans into action. She reached into my pocket and threw away my phone. Apparently there was no need for it anymore. It started to rain. She guided my body into the car. I had no fear – her presence made me trust – only confusion as to why this

259

seemed important. She started to drive towards my studio, which was also on the way to a convenience store minutes from my home.

There were few cars on the road. But the rain made driving more difficult. As I approached a green flashing light, a car proceeded at high speed towards me from the opposite direction. However, people always drove relatively fast on this stretch, as the road previously was a highway. I watched with close attention as the oncoming car drifted slightly, crossing the centre line only metres ahead of my car. Left with very little time to react, I wasn't sure I could manage the manoeuvre required. Zeta released control of my body back to me. What good that would do me now, I wasn't sure. With only a second to spare, I cranked the steering wheel, pointlessly attempting to swerve out of the approaching vehicle's path.

With less than five feet left between us, I was then abruptly pushed out of the driver's seat and into the passenger's. I could not believe what I was seeing: Archangel Michael had taken my place and was driving! I felt very protected but highly confused, unable to intervene in my own fate as he steered the wheel. Time stopped. I had been here before, although I couldn't say how.

I was now back in the driver's seat, for a moment suspended in time, staring directly at the oncoming car. Powerless, I brimmed with anger and frustration. I had been trying so hard for so long. I had been striving to be a good person and to help others. I had survived so many challenges. Moreover, felt I had just found the meaning of life. I had only *just* met Eric, found the name of my guide and been directed to the spiritual information I had been seeking for my whole life. In fact I had never felt more on the right path, so how could this be? Surely it all had to count for *something*. It wasn't fair. *No!,* I exclaimed inwardly. I cried to the I AM Presence of the universe that I had only truly just discovered my plan. It was not right to pull me out now. I commanded that if he allowed me to live I would make absolutely sure I would fulfil my plan. I just needed a chance. I never thought I'd be put in a position where I'd be petitioning to keep my physical embodiment.

As if at a snap of the fingers, time resumed. The two worlds collided at high speed. My car spun around, completely totalled. Horrified, I jumped out. In complete shock, I wandered around the scene of the crash, gasping for air, not believing I had just survived such serious danger. My thoughts immediately went to the other vehicle. The other driver was not injured at all. Thank God. The entire block remained closed off for hours. After I disclosed that I'd had some wine earlier that evening, the police treated me like a criminal. They employed a very strange interrogation technique: threatening me, verbally assaulting me even though I was fully forthcoming. They pressured me to confess that I must be on drugs. I begged repeatedly for permission to call Eric. I was still in great shock. Having him by my side was all I wanted. Unable to find my phone, they offered to contact him. Still in shock, I wasn't sure of the proper spelling of his last name. They insulted me, saying, "*What kind of girlfriend are you who doesn't know your boyfriend's name?*" We had only been dating two months. I was confused. Did it had have one "t" or two? Given my level of shock, it was not the most unheard of response.

This was all over the top and not what I expected from officers of the law. While I expressed extreme remorse on the part I played, even for leaving the house, this was more like college hazing. After three inconclusive breathalyzer tests, they concluded they did not have enough evidence for an arrest. I was released and allowed to go to the hospital.

What followed in the next days and weeks were the events that forever showed me the true meaning of humility. If I had thought I'd lost everything before, I was wrong.

The insurance company found me at fault for the crash by default. It did not matter that the other driver had crossed the centre line. Any driver who has consumed any alcohol the same day of an accident is automatically considered at fault, regardless of circumstances, a new regulation I was unaware of, although I understood ignorance was no excuse. My clean driving record aside, it was irrelevant. The insurance company threatened me with a potential lawsuit costing millions and got my licence suspended for three months. That was funny because I could not afford to eat on a daily basis. There was no way I could afford such a sum. I would be forced to declare bankruptcy, something else I could not afford. The only consolation was that no one had died.

Eric was still going through his own healing process, undoing years of working too hard, unappreciated and undercompensated for the energy he had put into Liquivision. When my legal troubles came, it proved too much for our budding romance to take, and he was unable to provide the emotional support I needed to get through an event like the accident. So here I was, back to square one. Or square negative one, if I may.

In hindsight, there had been forewarning the event was coming, but I had disregarded it, filing it away somewhere out of mind. Less than a month earlier I'd had a dream in which Eric and I were together. The house we lived in was not built well, only a temporary shelter. Eric was not doing well emotionally and was wading through his own shit, quite literally.

I stepped outside the house, where I found a guide waiting for me in a car, a very old Cadillac that was idling roughly and backfiring. I had not seen this guide before and immediately became frightened. Like a character from a Stephen King novel, he looked and behaved like a hillbilly, very rough around the edges, one you could imagine chewing on a piece of straw. He gestured that I should get into the car. I jumped in. He continued to yell garbled obscenities. I understood none of it. We approached a low bridge that ran over top a small lake. He looked at me directly and yelled, "*You're gonna make me have to do this!*" I looked at him perplexed, not knowing what "this" was. I only knew I wasn't going to like it. Just then he grabbed the steering wheel and floored the accelerator. We catapulted over the side of the bridge as he deliberately plunged the car into the water.

I awoke directly on impact, hot tears steaming down my face. In shock after such a clear and forceful dream, I was left with the feeling that our guides wanted us apart and were taking action to forcibly separate us, based on Eric's much-needed recovery. Naturally I did not assume an etherial being was soon going to grab the wheel of my car in the waking state. Later dreams suggested it was too soon for a relationship. Yet there was never a strong enough feeling that we should stop dating, though we had considered taking a break.

Utterly broke and feeling very alone, I now had nothing but time to consider the events of my life as a whole, how my actions had led me to this point. To finally find true love and to have it taken away. To almost die so many times and yet live, seemingly with nothing to show for it. To finally find the answers to the meaning of life, or so I thought, then to be punished and have all my rights stripped away.

I wondered if any of this had been Maitreya's doing, as I commanded him ferociously to accelerate all my lessons. It seemed likely that would break Eric and me apart, at least temporarily. Perhaps the student body at the academy was justified in being afraid after all.

I began to look for clarity through the pain. It had been a very turbulent past few years. I wasn't sure if everything happened for a reason anymore. The persistently dramatic events made me wonder whether there was a message I was just not getting.

My body had begun to heal in the previous months while getting back on the path. Alas, the devastating blow of yet another disturbing incident was a big setback. The widespread physical pain returned with renewed vengeance. Yet I refused to fold my cards completely, and it did not return as badly as before, when I'd been unable to walk.

I sat in silence for days, not in meditation or anything quite so profound – I simply could not move. The blows had been so hard, the accident and Eric leaving me, that I replayed the sequence of events over and over to find the point at which I went wrong so that I could correct my mistakes. If I allowed my mind to travel back in time further, to the head trauma or anything prior to that, I would spiral hopelessly into an even deeper pit of confusion and despair.

This time I did not reach out for support. What I was going through was so much bigger than anyone could help with. Now it was me against the world. To invite anyone into that process would have been futile and only clouded my understanding with their opinion. There was nothing of value anyone else could contribute.

At first I believed this world held nothing for me anymore. I had no money, no car, massive debt, no friends, but most importantly, no love. I saw no prospects when looking into my future, nothing but a dense cloud of melancholy. I spent a long time contemplating taking my own life, but it didn't seem possible, given how many times I'd been brought back. How could I go from such an incredible degree of rock-bottom to a prosperous, happy life? I knew then that if I were ever able to accomplish such a feat, it really would be a true life story worth writing. But I would need to make it out alive first.

It took weeks before the explosion of heightened emotions was able to crystallize into something I could describe even to myself. My consequent dramatically enlarged feelings were blurred together in the expanding sphere of wreckage until I could sort them out.

I saw no one. I spoke to no one. It was as though there were a thick fog around me, splintered with shards from the crash and haunting whispers, words of love, memories of Eric. Yet I had no visceral connection to any of these things, partly due to remnants of unhealed brain damage.

After a month suspended in a state of shock, I now entered the stages of grief. After shock came denial. Then came the pain and guilt for all the actions that had led me to this dark place. I blamed myself for everything that had ever gone wrong and was merciless in my self-hatred.

Then the anger began to rise and transform into something new: bargaining. I tried to renegotiate the events of the past, trying in vain repeatedly to envision a reality that panned out differently, one in which I was able to sidestep the larger lessons, be more financially ahead and have a lasting relationship. When I failed to change my past by mere thought alone, I turned my attention towards my present circumstances, bleak as they were. I could not be angry at Eric, although the thought of him filled me with an enormous sadness. I could not be angry at the accident either. I then tried a new approach, begging the Creator to help facilitate the immediate fast-forwarding of this painful period of trials and testing.

When I summoned the will to look further back into my life, I thought of my date who had left me incapacitated and fighting for my life. If I'd taken a wrong turn, it wasn't because of karma in this lifetime. Perhaps I was paying the price for horrible things I had done so long ago there was no way of remembering them. When suicidal thoughts returned, I had to consider that essentially I had been brought back from the dead twice. What could stop a third return? An unusual sense of power began to grow. The knowledge of immortality, that it was impossible for me to die, angered me.

The obstacle before me was that I now had full understanding of the mechanisms that drove the universe, including the cycle of incarnation, which I had visually seen first-hand during my experience. Even if I did succeed in destroying my body, one thing was certain: if I thought things were bad now, they would certainly get a lot worse. Taking your own life is the worst act of ingratitude you could ever show the Creator. Descending to the nether realms of even worse incarnations was not something I was prepared for. Not only did I not want to reincarnate, I wanted my Individualized Consciousness to vanish from existence altogether or at least recycle back into Source, free of suffering. I was just done.

I summoned enough energy to return to my studies to see if there was any way I could accomplish such a task. After much time, I found one reference to a soul who was so hopelessly lost and had been given so many chances that he was recycled into blades of grass. Recycling is not the I AM's preference. Normally, a soul's failure to learn results in greatly extended lessons. Ultimately, I concluded, there is absolutely no easy escape from the simulation. I learned that the only way out is through, to heal, to become one with love and fulfil my divine plan, which, given my state of separation, was not the news I wanted to hear.

This would bring me to the next stages of grief: reflection, depression and loneliness. I reflected long on life, looking all the way back to the earliest memories. What was the meaning of it all? And just like Jesus had said, I found myself ironically back to the same ancient question: *Why am I here?* That was the question that would shape the rest of my life.

It is said that when you are existentially stuck, you merely haven't asked the right question. That rang true for me now. I began to entertain constructive thoughts. My self-evaluation process shifted from self-pity and despair to investigation. I began to feel quite impressed by the magnitude of the destruction I'd survived over the years instead of being defeated by it. It really was a formidable path I had walked. But what did it all mean?

The circular thought process began to take me back to the out-of-body experience with Sanat Kumara I had tried so hard to forget, not out of ingratitude, but out of not knowing what to make of it. For the majority of the last decade I had by and large forgotten about the presence of those helpful beings. In light of recent events, that amazing experience appeared to be the best thing that had ever happened to me. I looked back on that part of my journey with my guide with much affection and wanted to return to the disembodied state in which everything was effortless. Why had I been shown all that if I was not even capable of changing my circumstances? I began to strongly desire direct and clear conversations with my guides more than anything. There had to be answers to my questions. If so, their omniscience could provide them.

One night, while sitting in my apartment, I began to pray, not something I did often, but now was as good a time as any. On the off chance someone was actually listening, perhaps if I was genuine enough my request would merit a reply. With all my heart I prayed for clear interactions with my guides, if only there was a message or perhaps a second out-of-body experience as significant as the first, then I could come to a new level of understanding.

In that moment, my call for help was answered. Surprised, I heard a small voice within say, "You do have a letter from your guides, and it is written in your book."

Taken aback, I protested in defiance: *Anything but that!*

In all the years that had passed since the experience, I'd never been able to read my own account. Everything had seemed still too fresh. I didn't really think I would find anything worth knowing in it anyway, aside from ramblings about the strangest night of my life. In hindsight, perhaps I wasn't drawn to it sooner because I hadn't grown enough to understand what I had written.

I sat for hours considering what to do. Circling back to my original train of thought, if taking my own life was my final option, I may as well read the book first to see what was in the "letter."

For the first time in seven years I opened the manuscript and dived into the story of the mysterious night when my whole concept of reality was forever rearranged. To my astonishment, it was a most fascinating account, surpassing in its prophetic accuracy. In fact it was like being back "there" all over again. Reading the conversations with my guide brought tears to my eyes. It triggered the memories long suppressed. I had a love for him unlike any other. He had given me the gift of fully connecting with and feeling true, authentic Divine Love. Reading on, I was excited to extract bits and pieces of information that might be helpful or applicable, not really sure of what I was looking for. I went through the book with a critical eye, looking for holes in my story or segments that had been embellished. I found none.

I stayed up all night, committed to finish what I had started. Then the moment came, more than halfway through the manuscript, when I read the passages that directly stated that I would have brain damage and a car accident that was a head-on collision – in a silver sedan no less! How was that possible? At the time of the head-on collision I had been driving my grandma's car – the infamous silver sedan that had been seen all those years ago.

My stomach churned and nausea roiled as I tried to process the information before me. I had written the accounts of both events verbatim: an incident causing significant brain damage and a head-on collision. In a flash, memories of how scared I had been to leave my apartment returned. I'd long forgotten all about that. For weeks I had refused to leave the house, then that softened to just refusing to drive at night. Eventually so much time elapsed that it became necessary, and the fact remained that I had not owned a silver car at that time. The car I'd driven for years at the time of my clairvoyant vision was black. I thought I had foreseen wrongly, thus escaped my fate. How could I possibly be that accurate? It became impossible to dismiss both what I was going through now and the validity of the night that changed my life.

This account was something I had no way to explain. Reading the manuscript settled it: everything that had happened really did happen. There was no other "logical" explanation. I was humbled, in awe of the powers of the Divine. What grand forces had been acting on me all these years?

I began to cycle through many feelings, the first being shock and awe, amazed that they had kept true to their promise to level me. Then I became afraid: *Well, if all that could happen, then what's next?* After all, I had not foreseen anything further. Evidently, the book had predicted the following seven years of my life in detail, then ended. Where was my guidebook for what happens next?

I then experienced a deep relief, now equipped with the knowledge that the traumatic events I'd been involved in truly had been unavoidable all along. They were not a result of some careless action. They were also not due to my intuition being incorrect. This inferred I no longer needed to question my internal compass, as it had very effectively led me to my plan. Forgiveness of myself began to blossom like a rose in my heart, where previously all my self-hatred and remorse at lack of responsibility had been stored. For the first time I felt truly amazed that I had survived my own plan. What a spectacularly strange story.

There really was a reason behind all of the events, I just didn't know what. That reason was of little importance to me now, but I found relief in just knowing that the position I was in *was* the plan.

The more volatile feelings subsided, giving way to curiosity. Why would I be shown such things? Why had it been so important to know of these events in advance if in fact they were inevitable? Was it to create the faith to really *believe* in life after death? If that was the reason, the OBE alone would have sufficed. But more than that, was it to encourage faith in the life and divine plan of my living spirit in the present? Was there a way for me to contact those beings again? Would I ever see my guide again? What was the plan?

Every question I asked myself only created another series of questions. The one I kept returning to was: *Will I ever see my guide again?*

There was another peculiarity that I came across when revisiting my account: that I was not from Earth. I had always wondered if there were space aliens and laughed to think I was one. Surely I would have known something like that all along. This would also mean I was an alien to Earth or, more politely stated, a visitor. No wonder I felt I'd never belonged.

Perhaps my blurting out to Eric that I was from Venus was in fact an uncensored truth that had escaped during a moment of exceptional lucidity. This was a strong intuition that I needed to look deeper into before all parts of my being would accept it fully, and yet it resonated immediately. The higher parts of me were acknowledging it as true.

I am neither the first nor the only person to come from somewhere else on a mission to help Earth. After it had been stuck in a destructive spiral for millennia, Sanat Kumara was given the role of healer of the planet. He issued a call for help as he searched the universe to find beings who held enough light to survive the challenging environment. He gathered millions of souls as volunteers who would undergo training to ensure success. At present, only three million of them are still considered spiritually awake enough to remember they have come here as assistants or that their life has a plan.

One of those beings Sanat Kumara found was none other than Jesus the Christ, who at that time presided over a kingdom quite far away, his home in the Golden Shrine Galaxy. Sanat, only having a brief moment to convey the plight of the people, telepathically showed him the situation on Earth, or Tetlachordia, as it has been named by the ascended masters channelled through the academy. His vision must have been compelling because Emmanuel of the Golden Shrine Galaxy, Jesus Christ, agreed to help immediately, giving the first demonstration of our true, natural, divine heritage. Since then he has agreed to stay to the completion of the game, long overextending his initial agreement.

Jesus, before coming to this world, was already a king of kings. His spiritual stature served him every step of the way. The darkness encompassing the Earth was far greater than today. However, unlike now, there were no modern technological advancements to interfere and impede his plan. In some ways the two epochs balance each other. There is something to be said for the clever individual that can learn to use technology as an aid to freedom. Jesus was able to complete his plan in a single lifetime, an exceedingly rare achievement. He left behind the record of his example. This information is both accessible from within and above to remember our greatness.

I wondered how I factored into the grand plan.

Part II

36.

Life

IT IS SAID that those who have chosen to create for themselves the most difficult and challenging plans stand to have the greatest breakthroughs. In class, the Buddha once asked us students that if given the choice to take the slow easy path or the fast hard path, which would we choose? The answer came that each path contained the same number of lessons in overcoming adversity and hardship, meaning there is no easy path, yet the rate at which we progress dictates the duration. A life devoid of adversity is also devoid of growth and learning. If there is nothing to overcome, where is the challenge?

My realizations of late led to an interesting point on the path. *The Book of Job* came to mind. I laughed, imagining God making a deal with the Devil to torture me, little me looking upwards, exclaiming, "I still love you!" I decided that if it was my luck in life to live an existence filled with wildly unpredictable events, then I was going to *choose* to be happy. If the events *had* to take place, however painful, there was no law that stated I had to suffer as well.

This was the missing realization. My heart for the first time was freed from a future I'd felt previously chained to. The idea – that whatever was set to happen, I could remain happy for it – liberated me.

Looking into my future, even if it held wildly unpredictable events one after another, I saw happiness because it was what I choose to embody as of now.

Filled with a renewed desire to make progress, I refocused my attention on healing. I had shown proficiency in understanding the teachings, the skills required and the common sense to implement them.

It had also become clear, from the question posed by the Buddha, that my higher self had chosen the *fast hard path,* a journey that was so challenging it would almost break my will due to the high risk from a plethora of timelines in which I died from one cause or another.

Yet it was seen that, this being my last life, there was an incredible degree of attainment still required to achieve my highest plan, Zeta's calculated risks seemingly paying off thus far, as I am alive to tell the tale. While I am an old soul by Earth standards, I am a young soul by the universe's. Compared to beings like Sanat Kumara and Melchizedek, I am but a newborn.

In light of this old information becoming new again through revisiting my manuscript, I started the process of upgrading the many dark emotions that had plagued me since the crash and from many years prior to it.

I now had stored a great deal of practical spiritual information to apply to everyday life, such as the knowledge and names of a great many guides, along with various healing techniques. I began learning how to invoke my new higher-dimensional friends for help and change. I began to study all of the angels and ascended masters in greater detail, gaining insights into each of their gifts and abilities, as well as learn more of the specifics of permission and what was required of a person to elicit such help successfully.

I learned that, while there are guides everywhere who are essentially trying to help everyone all of the time, there are certain behaviours that both repel and attract more help to you. It is said that it's best to not simply ask for the ascended host to rid you of your problems, it is better to be the type of person who attracts their assistance through action. A person who is showing they are trying very hard to make constructive changes in their life is a lot more likely to receive angelic support when asked for. Or by not even asking at all, hence creating greater permission for the Divine to step in and help. The Divine is not permitted to remove obstacles from your path, but it can help the person who is using their own volition already.

I continued working with Maitreya through the chaos. He remained my best friend and closest guide, sometimes so close I could feel him standing directly beside me. I knew he had facilitated the speed at which these disasters had happened, but I had also commanded his assistance when I asked him to push me quickly through my lessons. I no longer cared and love him just the same.

He would come up beside me, especially when I was walking. Turning to me, he would ask cheerfully, "Would you like to go running?" I would fill with ecstasy immediately. Something about him was so sublime. This was his way of saying let's get off to the races. When I would start "running" with Maitreya, life had a tendency to gradually move very fast, so fast I almost could not keep up. Eventually I would need to "take a knee," as they say in American football.

After more than two months of invoking Maitreya many times daily for his "ascended master management services," on Good Friday, 2016 I went into a deep meditation. After a long time spent pausing all human thoughts, I received the message that I should do a standing meditation I had heard of but had never done before – White Fire.

I put on a recorded discourse that Eric had sent me before we broke up, featuring Sujata Kumara, an ascended master, who spoke of it directly. As I was standing, I began to command and visualize powerful white flames running through the entirety of my being while also filling my whole apartment. It seemed as powerful as I had heard. I had not been doing it more than five minutes when I began to sweat profusely. I felt faint. However, I soon was forced to stop and open my eyes – as the ground started shaking below me – naturally assuming my meditation had unfortunately coincided with a small earthquake, with perhaps aftershocks to follow.

I stood pleasantly corrected. Feelings of the deepest gratitude washed over me, as directly in my line of sight Maitreya was now standing before me in tangible physical form.

This was the day that the first half of my life would close and the second half of my life open. I remain forever changed by the conversation that followed.

Epilogue

I HAVE WRITTEN this book, not as a declaration of belief or advice on to how go about the business of living – while I am rich in experience, I feel I lack the wisdom or divine perspective to instruct others – but to encapsulate and preserve my experiences as completely as possible. However strange they have been, this has become the story of my life. I am very much still a student of the Divine. In many ways, the further I have advanced in my quest for knowledge of what we really are the more humbled I have become. I look back on the person I was ten years ago and can really see how experience has taught me how little I know now compared to the understanding of the self and life that she believed she possessed then.

It has taken me considerable time to process my initial NDE and to be able to condense it into words that have any power to portray the impact of it on my life. During those years, I wandered lost, not having the guidance needed to help solidify new beliefs that had formed as a result of the experience. One could say it was my plan to wander the Earth for ten years, but I like to think that could have been expedited, given the right information and support. Perhaps my sharing this account of life on the "other side" and my journeys out-of-body will encourage others to do the same.

It is my hope for this book to potentially provide relief for others who too have had their cage rattled by the Divine. It seems this is the way it's set up for most spiritual people, that it's common to walk the path alone for a predestined period of time, especially at first, to allow the formation and integration of personal beliefs free of the influence of others who could potentially hinder or even halt one's progress. If this book helps to provide solace or clarity to one person, then it has served its purpose by giving light to others that I wished I could have given myself.

Much time has passed, yet to this day I have not shared this experience in its entirety with even my own mother, though this is not due to lack of desire. On the contrary, although I had wanted to share it deeply with her and many other people in my life, the thought of sharing it prematurely did not feel right. So many of the important details get lost in casual conversation, never mind that human attention is hard to sustain. They have proven very difficult to form into words even after ten years of patient scribbling. Inevitably it felt better to present the events as a whole and in the order they happened, and as sequentially as possible, given the branching nature of the experience itself. I strongly felt this was the only way that the messages communicated to me by the Divine could begin to be decoded and understood.

Another phenomenon that appeared when writing this book was the ability to write. As mentioned, English was my weakest subject in school, although I excelled in others. When it came to the task of sharing my experience with the world, I was overwhelmed to say the least. Miraculously, seemingly overnight, a block was lifted from my mind around November and December of 2017. When previously I'd felt daunted and at a loss for words, lacking confidence in my ability to clearly articulate myself using so meticulous a platform, suddenly I was filled with confidence and an inner knowing that I possessed everything needed to see this through to completion. Whether this was divine intervention, past-life attainment as a writer coming to the rescue or finally having accumulated enough life experience to put matters into words remains a mystery to me and to some of my closest friends and family, often to their astonishment. When my mother heard a detailed account of the very first part of my journey out-of-body and the theory that I'd died and am originally from another timeline, to my surprise she was in full agreement. It made perfect sense to her, as for years our individual interpretations of past events had seldom lined up. She had always puzzled over that, but was now pleased to find an explanation.

The greatest obstacle to writing this book was a deep fear that I could potentially influence people in a detrimental way by sharing my account. Releasing that fear has made putting it in written form possible. This is why I say to the reader that it is a wise student who does not accept every piece of information at face value. The best students are highly inquisitive and enjoy questioning what they discover. Intuition serves as guide on the journey of discovering truth, and perhaps what is only accepted as partial truth now can, in time, be confirmed via experience.

This account has been my best attempt at narration of the events in my life as they occurred, to the best of my writing ability, which is still in the blossoming stage. What started off as a task to write this for my own learning and to better understand the purpose of my life has transformed into something much larger. I now feel perhaps there is something in this worth sharing with others. For the already awake individual, this book stands to open a door fully that was already partially ajar, to validate and provide information to build on prior life experience and knowledge.

When I think of the difficult task I was given, to try to put something so beautiful, so esoteric and so spectacular into words, I am reminded that the truth does not need to shout, nor does it need to be concerned with the agreement or acknowledgment of others. This has not been my aim. Truth is not limiting in any way. It is illuminating, uplifting and liberating, although painful at times when it sheds light on outworn ideologies.

Truth just is. Knowledge of the truth will set you free.

Appendix

Earth *as a* Simulation

THERE IS A cloaking mechanism that prevents us from seeing life present in the universe all around us: our lowered vibration. If it were obvious, then it wouldn't be much of a challenge, would it? The experience had to be designed so well, down to the smallest details, that even under great scrutiny only the determined mind could begin to figure it out. It is quite a challenging task to describe the nature of the simulation verbally, but I will try to the best of my ability to share what I have discovered in my search for answers. If we are to keep an open mind, to understand that life is not everything that it seems to be, then we are less likely to shoot down the idea that perhaps we are right when we say we are all participating in the "game of life," as it's often called.

The game does glitch occasionally. There are interesting examples throughout history as evidence we can easily research. But first I would like to pose a question: What is the definition of a simulation when applied to the nature of reality? To begin with, in a simulation you would be able to rewind events and start over if it wasn't going to plan, similar to a video game when you click "restart." That is because the foundation for the gaming environment isn't physical, yet there is a platform the system runs on that houses all the software and rulesets that govern it.

If life is not a simulation, then it should behave "normally" and consistently. There should be no anomalies that dramatically challenge that idea, if everything is really as it seems. If the term "simulation" bothers you, which comes from computer technology and serves as an understandable metaphor in our technological era, "closed learning system" is what it really is.

EXAMPLE A – NDEs AND OBEs

Many people have had near-death experiences and OBEs. They have brought back numerous accounts of life on "the other side." These people come from different backgrounds and a variety of faiths. All of these independent accounts share many similarities. For example, they reconnect with family and loved ones, travel to other planets or are shown things there is no possible way they could have known otherwise. Perhaps if there were only one account it could be easily dismissed, but when the evidence is examined as a whole, it becomes clear there is something much larger at play that is more mysterious and amazing than most of us could ever imagine.

Consider Eben Alexander, the famous neurosurgeon, who after a near-death experience of his own penned the book *Proof of Heaven: A Neurosurgeon's Journey into the Afterlife.* His tale is equally as far out as mine and provides further supporting evidence that there is much going on in these "invisible realms" that we cannot see with the naked eye nor interact with.

EXAMPLE B – ADMIRAL RICHARD BYRD AND THE HOLLOW EARTH

Admiral Richard Byrd in 1926 was the most famous man in the world for having flown over the North Pole at a time when aircraft was new technology. As a public figure, he was a decorated military man and an adventurer. His fame only grew after further explorations of both polar regions. There are few people who could be considered more reliable. He explored Antarctica several times, and made a return trip to the North Pole in 1947, where it is said he claimed this time to have flown into the Earth, where he claimed to have met benevolent beings who wanted to share a message to further peace, as they were opposed to repeating patterns of war.

Not many believed his claim. Mankind greatly wanted to delete his account from the records, as it doesn't fit into our limited view of the way life is structured. Whether this account is true or not remains to be seen. It has come under great scrutiny. However, there are many accounts of people who have claimed to witness similar encounters in the far north. I say there cannot be so much smoke without some fire.

Many have tried to find this location by using the old flight paths, but with no luck in finding a semi-tropical region of land or an unknown benevolent race. If there was such an opening, indeed it would appear it was only meant for him.

EXAMPLE C – TIME TRAVEL

The Philadelphia Experiment, which took place in 1943 with the *USS Eldridge,* with recruit Edward Cameron (aka Al Bielek) aboard, along with his brother Duncan, was a high-energy cloaking experiment. As a side effect, Bielek claimed the two of them time-travelled to the year 2137, then he alone to the year 2749 for two years, after which he went back to pick up his brother, then on to the year 1983. Many died when the ship successfully disappeared from view in 1943, and he was thought to have been among them. We he returned some years later many thought he was crazy. He told a tall tale of what the future held and claimed to have lived there. Yet as time passed and events developed as described, people realized he had been telling the truth all along. This was largely due to the Montauk Experiment, which was a continuation of Nikola Tesla's work, in 1983, which in effect created the second "wormhole" for him to travel through. This means we effectively and accidentally tore a hole in the fabric of time, and while many died in that experience, one time-travelled.

EXAMPLE D – THE COMPUTER SIMULATION HYPOTHESIS

In many ways science has started to catch up to the idea that we are living in a simulation, notably espoused by the highly regarded business magnate and engineer Elon Musk. Simply stated, the fact that we as a whole have shown the desire to build our own simulations and create virtual realities demonstrates that the odds are billions to one that we are not already living in a simulation now. The credit for this argument goes to Nick Bostrom, professor of philosophy at Oxford University.

Billions of dollars are now invested to learn whether we are already living in a simulation. While it may be slightly off the mark by trying to solve such a complex idea using human categories, it is a reasonable hypothesis worth testing. Examples of such research have been published in *Scientific American,* in an article entitled "Are We Living in a Computer Simulation?" Here is a quote from that piece: "'If the simulation hypothesis is valid then we open the door to eternal life and resurrection and things that formally have been discussed in the realm of religion,' Gates suggested." James Gates is a theoretical physicist at the University of Maryland.

In an article published by *Express.co.uk,* entitled "We Will Prove We're in a Simulation," there are claims that science is getting close. The piece reads: "Many people in Silicon Valley have become obsessed with the simulation hypothesis, the argument that what we experience as reality is in fact fabricated in a computer, two tech billionaires have gone so far as to secretly engage scientists to work on breaking us out of the simulation."

As always, there is truth in fiction, as no original idea comes to us that hasn't already been conceived in the Divine Mind. The movie *The Matrix* is an excellent example. There is a scene in which the protagonist Neo is watching a child bend a spoon with his mind only, similar to how Uri Geller famously did. The boy tells Neo, "Do not try and bend the spoon, that's impossible. Instead, only try to realize the truth… There is no spoon… Then you'll see it is not the spoon that bends, it is only yourself." The same can be said of our reality. We exist, our soul is real, yet everything in the phenomenal world around us is an illusion of the 3D-matrix we live in. And while we are not trapped in a computer simulation – that is a very human way of thinking, as a computer is the best analogy most humans can think of – it is a convenient model.

When we take into consideration that there are also people who claim to be from different "timelines" – myself included – that is not something that should be possible if there is only one consistent linear version of reality. The fact that we all experience our own slightly different version of reality – due to the nature of perception and how the senses, the brain and the mind interact – is supporting evidence as well.

We create our own simulations here. The Earth is our testing ground. The rest of the universe is going on with other activities and experiments while we are here collectively trying to wake up from our collective dream.

EXAMPLE E – THE WISDOM OF THE AGES

What mystics, scholars, philosophers, yogis and spiritual teachers have shown us is that through their long and persistent quest for true knowledge, powers were achieved, as well as the revelation of our divine origins. Once the illusion – or simulation – is understood, it no longer has the power to hold us here, thus these wise beings were able to return to the baseline universe that exists outside our experiment and report what they discovered.

Let's consider why the majority of the planet believes in one religion or another. Many believe that Jesus, or God-Powerful beings like Jesus, walked the Earth and demonstrated their gifts at some time. Teachings from both the East and West point us towards the truth that God is within us. The Buddha has left a record of much of his teachings that show us the truth of the impermanence of the phenomenal world. He also taught us that once a being is able to drop all that is false and adopt the five powers – faith, energy, mindfulness, concentration and wisdom – they are able to liberate themselves, achieving great freedom from the suffering inherent in duality. Jesus' demonstration showed exactly what the Buddha had described, what can happen when all that is false has been renounced. It was so powerful a demonstration that it is the reason for our annual calendar having started at year zero. It has to be a pretty big event for the planet to base its start on it. Jesus himself stated that his apostles would do even greater things than he did. Something like this will happen again in our lifetimes when our collective consciousness is ready for it.

THE CONCLUSION

These five pieces of evidence when considered all together begin to paint an incredibly interesting picture of the true nature of our reality. The ability to travel through time, the testimony of countless people who have left the game and seen the "other side," credible people who have put their reputations on the line to stand firm in their testimonials, combined with numerous accounts throughout history of those who regained their powers and freedom by cutting through the illusion that is "the game" are part of the undeniable evidence that life is not what it appears to be, especially when we demonstrate our ability to affect it ourselves through intention.

These accounts, along with information about the Illuminati and the privatized banking system I mentioned earlier, are not easily discovered. It has taken the better part of my life to examine them thoroughly. A lot of the information I've unearthed has attempted to lead me astray, as much of what is presented on the internet is riddled with partial truths.

I caution the reader: do your own research, impartially and painstakingly, as mainstream media consistently wants to preserve the experiment intact. One could say it is actually the collective will of those people who do not want to wake up that keeps the simulation going.

Glossary

Active Now: The most prominent and clearest version of events that one is operating in, most often with reference to alternate timelines.

Active Memory Stream: A memory series that is different from ordinary memory in that what the senses report in the most complete detail is experienced in the present as reality, but which is the replay of a recording of the past. An Active Memory is not subject to influence by the witness.

Ascension: The expansion of awareness to include vibratory dimensions beyond the three-dimensional material plane, releasing and healing all that is not the self in the return to original wholeness, and the realization of never having been separate from it. The biography of the Tibetan yogi Milarepa is an example.

Ascended being (ascended master): A being who has lived a lifetime on Earth and completed the process of ascension. From this fully empowered state these beings often act as guides to those still in embodiment, helping them master their lives in the same manner to discover their ultimate freedom.

Ascended master realms: The higher-dimensional planes, typically the fifth and sixth dimensions, but not limited to them.

Akashic records, *akasha* (Sanskrit: space, sky): The universal perfect and flawless record-keeping system containing every experience, every feeling, word and thought, preserved in pristine condition not bound by space and time. They include all lives a being has ever had on Earth, and the lives of all beings in this universe. These records are accessible to beings still in embodiment and can be accessed in meditation to facilitate healing or greater understanding of the self.

Avatar: A manifestation of a deity in bodily form; an incarnate divine teacher; an icon or figure representing a particular player or person in a video game, internet forum, etc.

Gaming has borrowed the Sanskrit word *avatar* (*ava,* down; *tara,* to cross) to effectively represent the action figure humans generally take themselves to be, but it's really a collection of apparently moving pixels subject to a ruleset within the larger ruleset of a particular game. If the player gets so involved as to identify with the avatar, suffering is inevitable. There's nothing to win or lose in the apparent dimension of existence, only to enjoy, but only if ignorance has been negated by self-knowledge.

Causal body: Literally, the cause of the phenomenal world; the unconscious (psychology); God, the Creator (religion); *maya,* the power that makes non-duality appear as duality, the root of words such as magic, matter, matrix and mother; what makes the impossible possible (yoga).

Clairaudience: The faculty of hearing the inaudible. The gift of hearing in which the perceiver hears their guides the same way anyone not deaf hears another's speech.

Clairvoyance: The faculty of sight of things or future events beyond normal sensory perception, associated with the third eye of yoga philosophy, where the *ajna chakra* is located, accessed through meditation in order to know and communicate with non-ordinary realms, angels, etc.

Consciousness: Awareness, being, existence, limitlessness, the self. Without attributes, it is all-pervasive, unlimited and formless; to use a linguistic term, it is the subject, not the object, hence it is the awareness of any given state, not the state itself. It is the Light in which light is known in all three states of mind: waking, dreaming and deep sleep.

In short, it is you, although not the personal you, but the immortal you, the "unborn," hence undying, the supreme identity, the substrate of experience.

Cosmic law: The body of moral, psychological, physical and spiritual laws that order the universe; *dharma* (Sanskrit: the way, the eternal law of the cosmos inherent in the very nature of things, expressed as right action).

281

Divine companion: The person who is most perfectly suited to you at any given time, and that changes as you each progress.

Divinity: Holiness, sanctity, godliness, divine nature; as "the Divinity": God.

DreamTime Training (DTT): A dream scenario or environment designed to move one's soul towards growth, facilitating healing of fears or wounds incurred during incarnations on the Earth plane. DTT dreams differ from ordinary dreams, which often have little meaning, in that they take place in higher planes and are constructed by the higher self and one's guides, especially when through free will the choice is made to advance on the path to ascension/resurrection to reconnect with the Divine.

Earth-time: The measurement of distance between two events on the Earth plane. Time operates differently in different dimensions, depending on the state an individual is experiencing.

Enlightenment: A strange idea really, because all that exists is the Light of lights, pure awareness. It has some value for the ignorant whose suffering becomes so intense that a burning desire for liberation makes them seekers. With any luck, they become finders. What they find is themselves, a cosmic joke that invokes hilarity in some, a sign of relief.

"What we are looking for is the one who is looking." ~ *Saint Francis of Assisi*

Enoch: An advanced being who lived one lifetime on Earth long ago. Enoch was mentioned in the Old Testament and also delivered his own text, *The Book of Enoch*. His book contains a set of "keys" for the Earth to receive, along with his sacred geometries.

Enoch completed his ascension with support from the great Archangel Sandalphon. It is also noted that Enoch is Metatron, also known as Metatron's Cube in mathematics – containing within it every shape in the universe. He is the first creation of the universe and his Flower of Life blueprint is encoded within everything as a result.

God-presence, individualized God-presence: The individualized expression of Source itself that connects the personality to everything that is; the energy that animates the physical body; one's higher self.

Great Central Sun: The tangible structure that exists within Source itself, the main hub of focused action/creation, where important decisions are formulated and executed by numerous committees of beings to carry out a multitude of activities to maintain the universe's balance. It is also the collective home of individualized God Presences.

Gross body: The physical, material body most people identify with as self; the "food sheath" of yogic tradition, or "meat suit." It is born and dies.

Guide: A being who oversees an individual's life with a vested interest in moving them forward on the path to ascension. For the purposes of this book, the term is most often used when referring to disembodied beings who provide their help from higher planes.

Higher Dimensional Communication (HDC): A form of advanced communication that is experienced when one is in the higher planes of existence. An individual is able to experience this through OBE or a near-death experience (NDE). This is also the natural state of communication for beings who are not in embodiment.

HDC is an all-encompassing way of communicating that is similar to telepathy, but more broad to also include many other sensory perceptions present in the physical body and additional sensations that are not present in "normal waking reality."

This form of communication style is very clear and a direct way for learning, as it leaves no room for error, vagueness or miscommunication.

Higher realms: Planes of existence of a higher vibrational rate than the physical, hence are subject to fewer limitations. For example, when in higher realms one can experience easy and instant manifestation. Interplanetary travel is so quick that it seems by mere thought alone because the mechanisms are seamless and effortless.

Higher self: God-presence, the Divinity, etc. which acts as a guide, responsible for intuition; also the sole reason for a being's existence.

I AM THAT I AM: In *The Book of Ezekiel* in the Old Testament, the name of God when Moses asks what he should say to the Israelites when they ask which god sent him; also, Yahweh, Jehovah, or I Am.

Infinite I AM: See above.

Karma: Sanskrit for "action." Implied are the results of action, either good or bad, whether slated for a particular incarnation, already evident or fructifying.

Melchizedek: In the Old Testament, a priest-king of Salem (Jerusalem). In the New Testament, Jesus is identified as a priest-king of the order of Melchizidek. He is one of the most ancient beings we know of still overseeing this universe.

His twin flame, the Queen of Light, was granted her wish to see everything in the universe after her ascension, and Melchizidek was allowed to journey with her. After seeing everything, they concluded that the Earth system was where they desired to serve until the simulation completes.

Metatron: According to Jewish apocrypha, the name Enoch received after his transformation into an angel.

In the tradition of the Kabbalah, he is the highest of the angels and serves as the celestial scribe or "recording angel," the one who communicated God's revelation to Moses.

Nirvana: A Sanskrit compound word meaning "blown out" as in an extinguished flame.

Non-duality: The fact of a single principle of existence, although appearing as duality within its scope, i.e. light and dark, up and down, masculine and feminine, yin and yang, and so on, each pole defining its counterpart.

Oneness: In the *Upanishads,* ancient Indian scriptures, non-duality is described as "one without a second" to distinguish it from "the One," which implies "two."

Out-of-body (OOB): Existence outside of the physical body, a term coined by Robert Monroe, author of *Journeys Out of the Body.* The experiencer in that state has another body, lighter and freer than before.

Out-of-body experience (OBE): An event corresponding to being out-of-body characterized by a feeling of liberation and expansion into non-ordinary domains, including adventures sometimes accidental, sometimes chosen, sometimes guided. OBE does not include the ability to interact with the physical plane, although exploration of it is freely available.

Person, personality: From Latin *per* (through) and *sonus* (sound); the persona was the mask an actor wore to amplify their voice and represent their fictional character in the drama, often a deity in ancient Greek theatre, where it was considered sacred and *catharsis* (purgation, release, purification) of its audience its goal. If an actor comes to believe they are the role, trouble ensues when they can't get "out of character."

After the Norman Conquest of England in 1066 AD, a human being (the Viking Normans adopted French:"*la personne*"). "Parson," a member of the clergy, is from the same root.

Planes of Bliss: A plane that exists within the upper rings of the Earth plane that is not as dense as life on Earth. Beings are able to go there between incarnations in order go process their experience, positive or negative, and to have a break between the hardships of living in the 3D environment.

Ramtha the Enlightened One: A 35,000-year-old discarnate being channelled by J.Z. Knight.

Real, reality: That which never changes, that which always is; truth. Western philosophy says that "it is a thing in itself, not as it can be described or distinguished," a vague and circular definition. Reality cannot be a thing, an object separate from the whole, but wholeness, completeness that lacks nothing, hence tradition calls it "holy."

Real-life event: An event that occurs in what most people classify as the normal waking state or normal waking reality in the Earth plane. Not a dream. Incidents that one witnesses, experiences and can influence.

Resurrected being: A being who is not only immortal but has transformed the physical body from one state (death) to rebirth in a higher-dimensional form, the original state; a being who has displaced the false human persona with the true self, now empowered to influence the human realm in seemingly miraculous ways in violation of the known laws of physics, but for the good of all.

Resurrection: Transformation of the human form back to its original divine form, a process that takes much time, dedication, fortitude, patience and practise to facilitate increasing connection to the greater portion of the soul that is eternal, omnipresent and omniscient. By purifying the body and mind of the individual, the stripping away of all that is false, the divine self can occupy the physical form.

A resurrected being appears godlike and can perform supernatural miracles because they have full understanding of all laws that operate in this system, and thus are able to bend them to their will.

Note that the resurrection is the pathway out of the game for all of its players. Individuals that choose the path of resurrection will stay until the very last person accomplishes their own freedom, similar to the *bodhisattva* ideal of Buddhism.

"Until we are all free, none of us is free." ~ *Emma Lazarus*

Sacred Fire: An alchemical spiritual flame that is visible in higher dimensions. This flame can be invoked by anyone in order to help move towards desired states of perfection.

Self: The essence of identity shared by all (Self); the personality (self) that distinguishes a person or individual from others.

Seventh Golden Age: The present spiritual age that we are living in. Previous Golden Ages have risen in throughout history. However, this one dates far further back than any of our records permit.

Between many of these Golden Ages there have been partial or total resets of the simulation when it was seen there was no outcome that would lead to the liberation of the planet. In those instances the people were taken up into higher planes while the divine set the stage for the next iteration.

It has been said that the present Golden Age will be the last for this learning simulation, as we have overextended our time in learning here by several million years. We are not permitted to fail this time, thus we have a great amount of divine support to help us ride the wave of our own evolution.

Shambhala: In ancient Hindu and Tibetan Buddhist traditions, a fabulous kingdom surrounded by snow mountains whose reality is visionary or spiritual as much as physical or geographic.

Simulation: A digital model, especially for the purposes of study.

Singularity: Borrowed from physics and mathematics, the point at which a function takes on infinite value; in this book, a state of being in which the merger of the individual self with the Whole leaves no trace momentarily or indefinitely (Sanskrit: *nirvana,* "blown out," as in a flame, the extinction of individuality); oneness with God and the omniscience of God.

Sinister Force: The collection of every evil manifestation that has ever been created by us on Earth since the start of our simulation, when the I AM race first cut their cords. It operates as a collective entity with its own volition. Because humanity as a whole has not perfected their manifestations to date, it is a collection of darkness that is being added to daily. Due to the law of karma, this force manifests as plagues, diseases, famines, devastating storms and other natural disasters, economic collapses, refugee crises, etc.

At the personal level, this force is a distraction that interferes with spiritual growth, discrediting intuition and spiritual teachings. Like the human ego, although fictional it nevertheless seems to have a life of its own and defends it at all costs.

If humanity as a whole were to evolve, it would no longer exist, because it is all that is untrue of the nature of reality, which is truth. Jesus called it a liar and the father of lies, the adversary, the ruler of this world.

Soul family: Just as we have a birth family on Earth, we each also have spiritual family that we are bonded with and connected to since before we entered into this experience. In many ways the bond with soul family can be even greater than familial ones here, as they have been our parents and family members for millennia, not just a single Earthly embodiment.

Many of us have our spiritual family here in the game with us, and all chose to experience the same lessons at the same time. Sometimes we have reincarnated with them over and over again, as soul family members tend to seek each other out. Just like in real life, we also can meet people who become our soul family because we share such resonance with them.

Source, or Source of Creation: God; Universal Mind; the Creator.

Space-time: That which is in a constant state of change. It is projected very convincingly by the mind as space. It is the "apparent," that which appears and disappears, like a movie's images. Time is the mental construct that measures apparent differences. Made of consciousness (the real), it is in itself neither real nor unreal, just as a ring is made of gold but is wholly gold, and the ring is only "name and form." It is called *maya*, the root of words such as magic, matter, matrix and mother, usually translated as "illusion," but "magic show" is better. Maya is a power in unlimited consciousness that makes it appear limited, otherwise it wouldn't be unlimited, thus making experience possible.

Subtle body: The triad of intellect (discrimination), mind (emotion) and ego (self-image); when out of balance, it is *viyoga*; the "mental sheath." Until *yoga* (yoke, union) clarifies it such that serenity reveals the reflection of the real in its calm surface, it is only able to project its subjective interpretation of objects in the twilight of clouded thoughts and the emotions they provoke. It is the body that (apparently) transmigrates between lifetimes. In the West, the closest concept is the soul.

Tetragrammaton: The Hebrew name of God transliterated in four letters as YHWH or JHVH and articulated as Yahweh or Jehovah.

The Divine: God.

The Happy Buddha, or the Laughing Buddha: Not the famous Gautama Buddha, or Shakyamuni Buddha, but a figure who emerged from Chinese folktales of the tenth century, based on a Ch'an monk named Ch'i-t'zu, or Qieci, from Fenghua, in what is now the province of Zhejiang. Ch'i-t'zu was an eccentric but much-loved character who worked small wonders, such as predicting the weather. He is depicted as fat because he is full, complete, lacking nothing, thus happy. Similarly, the Hindu elephant god Ganesh, the remover of obstacles, is fat for the same reason.

The Mother: The divine feminine, also known as Mother Akasha, the mother to us all. After the I AM created Metatron (the first creation), he then desired our universe to have polarity, and thus he created a male and female aspect. The female identifies with Mother Akasha; the male, Father Asun. These beings are tremendously powerful and together they have created everything in this universe. Mother Akasha has the final touch in creating new souls, breathing her breath of life into them.

288

The now: This is not among traditional terms, because time has always been considered a convenient fiction. Its popular use since Ram Dass's book *Be Here Now* was published in the sixties, then Eckhart Tolle's *The Power of Now* in the nineties, suggests that with effort the seeker could abide in the present as opposed to living in the past (attachment, sorrow) or the future (desire, fear).

This teaching may have some value for those who believe that time has power over them, but upon enquiry it proves to be impossible to practise. Maybe that's why Sanat Kumara objected to my use of the phrase "split-second." The word "presence" of course refers to the now as well, thus implying the past and the future in the same way, but suggests "absence" by contrast. God, reality, the self, is never not present, although to the clouded mind the sun of awareness is apparently dim or even lost in the twilight of ignorance, especially when in the "dark night of the soul" written of by Saint John of the Cross.

The world/universe: The ever-changing whirlpool of experience conceived of as a single object, formed of ideas arising from the causal body, i.e. the mind of God, so to speak. It is called *samsara chakra,* the wheel of existence, the "jaws of the crocodile." It is unreal, because it changes, but does exist (from Latin: stand out) because it can be experienced. Physicists nowadays are increasingly adopting the virtual reality model to represent it, a useful analogy.

Twin flame: A type of soul structure that is common in this universe, comprised of two portions. One half is predominantly feminine (70% female and 30% male), the other is predominantly masculine (70% male and 30% female). Twin flames are not often paired during incarnations, as there is often a strong aversion to each other due to their opposite polarities.

Upanishads: A series of ancient Hindu scriptures expounding the *Vedas* in predominately mystical and monistic terms.

Universal Intelligence: The inherent intelligence of God, which expresses itself impersonally in nature.

Vedas: The four collections of the earliest body of Indian scripture, the *Rig Veda, Sama Veda, Yajur Veda* and *Atharva Veda,* codifying the concepts and practices of Vedic religion, a complete lifestyle manual, the basis of classical Hinduism.

Vedanta: From Sanskrit *veda* (knowledge) and *anta* (end), literally the "end of knowledge" in two senses: (1) the appendices at the end of each *Upanishad* and (2) the final knowledge of reality, i.e. non-duality, neither a philosophy nor a religion, but a methodology for Self-realization and Self-actualization.

The Whole: The totality of existence, the universe, God.

Made in the USA
San Bernardino, CA
14 November 2018